Effeminism

Effeminism
The Economy of
Colonial Desire

Revathi Krishnaswamy

ANN ARBOR

THE UNIVERSITY OF MICHIGAN PRESS

Copyright © by the University of Michigan 1998
All rights reserved
Published in the United States of America by
The University of Michigan Press
Manufactured in the United States of America
⊗ Printed on acid-free paper

2001   2000   1999   1998   4   3   2   1

A CIP catalog record for this book is available from the British Library.

Library of Congress Cataloging-in-Publication Data

Krishnaswamy, Revathi, 1960–
    Effeminism : the economy of colonial desire / Revathi
Krishnaswamy.
        p.   cm.
    Includes bibliographical references and index.
    ISBN 0-472-10975-8 (cloth : alk. paper) np
    1. India—History—British occupation, 1765–1947. 2.
India—Politics and government—1765–1947. 3. English
literature—19th century—History and criticism. 4. English
literature—20th century—History and criticism. I. Title.
DS479 .K75 1998
954.03—ddc21   98-25517
                                                              CIP

Acknowledgments

It gives me great pleasure to thank the many friends, colleagues, mentors, and institutions whose critical acumen and generosity have sustained this project through many transmutations. Although it is clearly impossible to give a complete genealogy of this book, it undoubtedly bears the imprint of many heated discussions and debates I've had with various members of the Theory Group at the University of Alabama, Tuscaloosa. In particular, I'd like to thank Paul Herman, Rich Rand, David Miller, and Claudia Johnson for their intellectual support and encouragement.

I'm also grateful to Carla Frenccero at the University of California, Santa Cruz, for giving me the opportunity to participate as a Research Fellow in the Feminist Studies FRA program she directed at a time when I badly needed such institutionalized discipline. This program not only enabled me to exchange ideas with students and researchers working on related topics, it brought about one very memorable conversation with James Clifford, who generously took time out of his hectic schedule as director of the Center for Cultural Studies to make a few choice comments on my work.

I also want to especially thank Rajeswari Sunder Rajan and Meenakshi Mukherjee. Their intellectual support and personal friendship have meant a great deal more than they could possibly know.

This book continues to bear the traces of its inception as a doctoral dissertation at Kent State University. Professor Robert Bamberg's uncanny ability to ask the difficult questions, not to mention his profound entanglements with Freud, pushed me to look beyond the obvious. The critical rigor that professors Diana Culbertson and Louis Paskoff demanded of me proved invaluable during the early stages of this project. Indrani Mitra and Susan George supplied both friendship and intellectual input.

I am grateful to a California State University summer fund, granted to me by San Jose State University in 1998, that enabled me to complete work on the manuscript. The support of colleagues and students at the Department of English at San Jose State has been crucial in the final stages of this project.

I wish to thank the anonymous readers of the University of Michigan Press for their meticulous, constructive, and sympathetic evaluation of the project. I am deeply indebted to my editor, LeAnn Fields, for her abiding faith in the value of my work. This book would not have come to fruition without her encouragement and patience. I am also grateful to Melissa Holcombe and Alja Kooistra for their patient and scrupulous editing.

I cannot, of course, adequately thank Kamal Seth on whose friendship I've relied so heavily to retain my sanity and my humor.

Finally, this book is dedicated to all the members of my family whose untiring faith and unqualified love have sustained me. To Amma and Appa, for inspiring me as much with their imaginative practice of everyday life as with their intellectual endeavors; their assistance (material and immaterial) form the sinews of this book. To Kumar, for sharing with me the seismic stress occasioned in our lives by our two babies and two books; his spirit has transformed my emotional and mental landscapes. To Chandrika and Anand, for coming into my life and teaching me the importance of small things; their unrelenting demands have rescued me from the danger of taking my scholarly work too seriously.

Contents

1

Reading Colonial Erotics

India may truly be said to rank with Italy as a woman-
country, "loved of male lands" and exercising the same irre-
sistible magnetism, the same dominion over the hearts of men
. . . India, even to her intimates, seems still a veiled mystery,
aloof, yet alluring, like one of her own *purdah* princesses.
—Maud Diver, *Desmond's Daughter*

The production of the Orient as a figure of seduction, duplicity, and, more darkly, rape represents one of the most opaque and enduring practices in colonial discourse. From literature and history to anthropology and ethnography, the discursive generation of Otherness is fraught with tropologies of gender and metaphors of sexuality. The figure of woman, already available as an indeterminate predicate within Western phallocentric traditions, is replaced with the figure of the "native." Slipping quite unproblematically from biology to gender, and from gender to race, religion, culture, and geography, the terminology of sex in colonial discourse naturalizes and essentializes a diverse array of differences. Whether the Orient is emblematized as a perilous prehistoric blankness upon which the "civilized" cultures of the West imprint their moral codes or as a luscious landscape inviting ravishment and possession, the "femininity" of colonized territory has provided Orientalist narrative with its most abiding metaphor for the exoticism of the East, and rape has served as the most enduring paradigmatic trope for colonial relations. What does such an excessive reliance on the semantics of sexuality signify, and how should we, as readers-in-decolonization, understand the imbrications of gender in the rhetoric of the Raj?

Edward Said's *Orientalism*, perhaps the most powerful point of departure for postcolonial criticism, suggested that the sexual subjection of Oriental women to Western men "fairly stands for the pattern of relative strength between East and West and the discourse about the

Orient that it enabled."[1] Since Said's work does not examine gender as a category constitutive of colonialism,[2] sexuality appears almost as if it were just a metaphor for other, more important dynamics that are exclusively male. Said thus sees the sexualization of the Orient mainly as a symptom of empire's hermeneutical difficulties:

> Standing before a distant, barely intelligible civilization or cultural monument, the Orientalist scholar reduces the obscurity by translating, sympathetically portraying, inwardly grasping the hard-to-reach object. Yet the Orientalist remained outside the Orient, which, however much it was made to appear intelligible, remained beyond the Occident. This cultural, temporal, and geographical distance was expressed in metaphors of depth, secrecy, and sexual promise: phrases like "the veils of an Eastern bride" or the "inscrutable Orient" passed into the common language.[3]

While this explanation usefully emphasizes the complicity of European representation in Western colonialism, it has some important shortcomings.

First of all, Said's emphasis on the metaphor of gender tends to dehistoricize the semantics of sexuality, disconnecting it from the varied yet specific contexts in which Orientalism developed and deployed a whole array of sexual stereotypes. Feminization of Otherness therefore emerges in Said's reading as a monolithic, univalent, unchanging rhetorical phenomenon that seems integral, even natural or inevitable, to the masculine imperial interpretive (ad)venture. The homology between sexual and political dominance, undoubtedly operative in many diverse situations of oppression, is, however, neither a natural nor an essential condition of imperial discourse. In fact, during the early years of British rule in India, when the rulers came primarily from a feudal rather than a middle-class background, the notion of colonial rule as a "manly" or "husbandly" prerogative was not very central (although present) in colonial culture.[4] Colonialism had not yet been given the moral underpinnings of a civilizing mission. And the East India Company was not so much interested in governing India as in making money. Indeed, it was not until the early decades of the nineteenth century, when the middle-class evangelical spirit took hold, that British rulers began to draw, with reformist fervor, an equation between sexual, political, and moral hegemony.

The effects of such a sexualization of race, politics, and culture were often irregular and contradictory. Thus, for instance, the identification of racial and cultural superiority with white masculinity rendered the white woman in the colony anomalous, since she represented a concurrence of racial domination and sexual subordination. Similarly, the feminization of colonized culture constituted indigenous men as sites of contradiction: superior sex but inferior race. Said's theoretical model, based as it is on an unchanging binary opposition between colonizer and colonized, aggressor and victim, white and black, masculine and feminine, cannot register such anomalies of race and gender in colonial society. Yet it is precisely in these anomalous figures that the faultlines of colonial ideology become visible.

In fact, the most hegemonic narratives of late-nineteenth-century British imperialism frequently fail to reproduce Said's monolithic, omnipotent image of imperial masculinity. Instead, as my readings of Rudyard Kipling will demonstrate, the white man emerges as a deeply divided figure whose authority is constantly being undermined by an enormous sense of failure or futility. Produced during a time of deepening crisis in India, Kipling's tales of transgressions and breakdowns display the colonial body revolting against increasingly rigid imperial technologies of discipline and surveillance through freakish behavioral excess such as unmanly hysteria and unacceptable sexuality. The resistant and unassimilable modes of desire sedimented in Kipling's narratives, I shall argue, implicitly deconstruct the colonial opposition between English manliness and Indian effeminacy.

Said's interpretation of colonial erotics further assumes that feminization of colonized territory establishes male ownership over a female body. Ravishment, however, is often more about emasculating a male than about possessing a female. The ultimate goal of authorizing a European claim to ownership through a feminization of India(n) was to establish the dominance of white men not over brown women but over brown men, who were seen as the legitimate owners of brown women and as the real objects of colonial rule. In other words, I am suggesting that the real goal of feminization is effeminization—a process in which colonizing men use women/womanhood to delegitimize, discredit, and disempower colonized men.

Finally, Said's view of Orientalism as a unified omnipotent discourse ignores the critical role of the East as both accomplice and opponent in the history of colonialism. The discursive forms and ideological configurations of colonialism were not produced monolithically but inevitably in the mesh of collusion and contradiction between the colonizers and the colonized. It is important to recognize this in order to see not only differences and oppositions but also affiliations and overlaps between colonial perceptions and indigenous interests, as these have a significant bearing on subsequent history and sociocultural formation. The distorted and contradictory effect of colonialism on Indian women, for instance, cannot be charted without coming to grips with the extremely complex and enormously consequential ways in which elite Indian men adapted and elaborated the colonial homology between the sexual and the political to fit the evolving needs of Indian nationalism (a process that continues to mold postcolonial India). While many of the social reforms undertaken by nineteenth-century nationalists aimed at ostensibly improving the lives of Indian women, their real goal was to reclaim the lost manhood of Indian men, their material effect to recontain women within a reconstituted patriarchy. Indeed, the intensification of Indian patriarchy under British rule undercuts the force of salvationist narratives—be they colonial or nationalist—that claim to have liberated subaltern women.

The theoretical problem with many contemporary approaches to colonial discourse that use a Foucauldian-Saidian model is that they deal with colonialism as a predominantly discursive phenomenon and tend to treat the realm of discourse as autonomous and detached from material realities.[5] Moreover, following Said's practice, these studies largely ignore the calibrations and conflicts within Orientalist discourses, choosing instead to "stand outside the family quarrels of the Western philosophical tradition."[6] As a result, they not only represent Orientalism as a monolith, but cut themselves off from the possibility of appropriating its anti-colonial impulses for the politics of decolonization. In the end, they render colonized peoples and their cultures without history by granting total hegemony to colonial systems of representation and by failing to see that these representations are inextricably intermeshed with colonialism's constant negotiation with (precolonial/precapitalist) indigenous economic, social, and cultural practices.

Studies that seek to understand colonialism from a psychological perspective also pose certain problems.[7] These usually read colonial history and literature allegorically in terms of a supposedly universal psychosexual drama of repression, sublimation, and projection. Moreover, they typically take a hydraulic view of desire, making sexual repression appear completely amenable to political service. Recent scholarship, inspired primarily by Homi Bhabha's subtle theory of colonial subject constitution,[8] has indeed moved away from the Prospero-Caliban paradigm toward more nuanced analyses of the contradictions in colonial identity and the ambivalences in race relations. Although these studies have usefully complicated a reductive understanding of colonialism as an adversary, perpetually locked in a "Manichean" relationship of domination and resistance with an eternal Other,[9] they still do not take into account the various historical developments that affected race relations or the varied material contexts that produced specific arenas of operation for the colonizers as well as for certain elite groups among the colonized.

Historical/materialist scholarship on colonialism, especially the Gramscian-Marxist variety, has served both as a critique and as a corrective to these ahistorical approaches. By embedding the Orientalist enterprise within concrete contexts, historical/materialist scholarship, such as *Subaltern Studies,* has helped us understand the specific and particular ways in which colonial power operated. But, unfortunately, certain forms of historical/materialist criticism seem to empty history and literature of all libidinal investment, producing microanalyses in which colonialism emerges as a coherent set of public events, policies, and practices whose social, political, and cultural meanings are self-evident. By ignoring the play of desire and fantasy, such critiques tend to minimize the dissensions and divisions within colonialism.

My own reading of colonial erotics clearly obeys the imperative to historicize. Throughout this book I work on the assumption that desire is intensely political, that it is historically constituted and materially determined. At the same time, I insist on the dangerously explosive revolutionary potential that makes desire often intractable, at times even unproductive, in the larger economic, political, and cultural arena. My goal is to restore not only the political in the unconscious but also the unconscious in the political.[10] Following the resistant and unassimilable modes of desire inscribed in colonial narratives, my study aims to approach colonialism through historical failure, ideological inadequacy, and political contention.

Because literature's inscription of desire was a complex and contested phenomenon during the late nineteenth and early twentieth centuries, I attempt to enter the economy of colonial desire through the fictions of the British Raj. Fredric Jameson's definition of narrative as a "socially symbolic act" makes literature a dramatic expression of the complex interweave between the political and the psychological, between the outer and the inner, between reality and dream: "the aesthetic act is itself ideological, and the production of aesthetic or narrative form is to be seen as an ideological act in its own right, with the function of inventing imaginary or formal 'solutions' to unresolvable

social contradictions."[11] The multiple referentiality of literary signification allows us to explore the psychopolitical field of colonialism beyond
the discursive limits of historiography.

At the most general level, then, this book attempts to chart the
flows of colonial desire by examining the complex encodings of fears,
fascinations, and anxieties in Raj fiction. It therefore treats gender (along
with race, class, caste, etc.) as a constitutive category of colonialism.
More particularly, the book is an examination of the literary inscription
of colonial masculinity and masculine desire. As an important foundational notion of modernity, masculinity represents a critical site for colonialism, anti-colonialism, and nationalism. Yet, until recently, masculinity remained a largely transparent, inadequately theorized construct.
This study proposes to put masculinity at the center of British colonialism in India.

At the core of my investigation of colonial masculinity is the concept of effeminacy, which I consider to be an important "ideologeme"[12]
in a colonial discourse of race, class, caste, gender, and moral legitimacy.
I use the term *effeminism* to refer to a racialized pathologization of "femininity-in-masculinity." Tracing this racialization of sexuality/sexual-
ization of race in various nineteenth-century discourses, I contend that
Indian effeminacy is not so much a wrong or false colonial stereotype as
a distorted and misvalued recognition of an alternative ideal of masculinity. Detailing the erosion of androgyny as a Hindu ideal under
colonial rule and examining its subsequent resurrection through Gandhian nationalism, I reflect on the complex, contradictory, and changing
alliances between the categories of race, gender, sexuality, class, and
caste in colonial India.

The bulk of this book, however, is concerned with the effects of
colonial misrecognition. Working on the assumption that the distortion
and misvaluation of androgyny did not affect only the colonized but
also impacted the colonizers in unexpected ways, I attempt to demonstrate how effeminism simultaneously enabled and estranged British
rule in India. My study draws primarily on the works of three canonical
colonial writers whose works give symbolic shapes to the deepening
political crisis in India: Flora Annie Steel (1847–1929), Rudyard Kipling
(1865–1936), and E. M. Forster (1879–1970). Through close readings of
their works, I aim to demonstrate how each writer's ideological project
of negotiating his/her own complicated status within colonial society—
Steel as woman, Kipling as cultural hybrid, Forster as homosexual—is
simultaneously facilitated and frustrated by the ideologeme of effemi-

nacy. The fundamental argument implicit throughout my discussion is that the stereotype of Indian effeminacy should be regarded not as the product of a totally achieved colonial hegemony but as a process that reflects a continuous and contentious struggle to assert hegemony in the face of resistance.[13] To assert this is not to suggest that the stereotype is any less effective but, rather, to say that its very effectiveness is contingent upon breakdown and malfunctioning.

The readings offered in this book are, however, not intended to be comprehensive or conclusive interpretations of individual authors or texts, for the patterns I trace are neither the only ones that characterize colonial sexual ideology nor are they to be found exclusively in the texts or authors discussed here. Clearly, gender and sexuality have diverse and complex histories that neither originate nor culminate in but, rather, intersect at the crossroads of empire, where they are strategically elaborated and inextricably interwoven with discourses of race, class, nation, and culture. So, instead of invoking a transhistorical understanding of colonial desire, I make the argument that it is contingent upon being articulated in relation to the race, gender, class, and national anxieties of the time. My readings therefore emphasize the ways in which the language of sexuality in Anglo-Indian fiction is deeply implicated in the politics of colonial rule and anticolonial resistance.

In taking such an approach, I aim to move away from the practice of reading one mode of oppression in terms of another. For instance, many Western feminist readings, in what may be characterized as a neo-Orientalist maneuver, install the white woman as the privileged Other whose marginality within Western patriarchal society serves as the paradigm for understanding all other marginalities. Thus, the defense of *Jane Eyre* against Gayatri Spivak's charge that Jane's feminism is deeply implicated in the racial politics of colonialism, often expresses an anxiety to establish an identity between the European and the subaltern woman.[14] Similarly, some readings of *A Passage to India* view Adela's inferior gender status in British society as a metaphor for Aziz's inferior racial status in colonial society.[15] Because they erase the historical differences between colonial racial exploitation and patriarchal sexual oppression, such attempts to conflate the issues of race and gender perpetuate "the common language of imperialism . . . through what seeks to be an opposing methodology, suggesting that the continued equation between a colonized landscape and the female body represents an alteristist fallacy that causes considerable theoretical damage to both contemporary feminist and post-colonial discourses."[16] Therefore, throughout this book I have sought to emphasize the ways in which gender is linked to race and class through difference and dislocation rather than through similarity or identity.[17] I have approached masculinity as an overdetermined tropological site on which many uneven and contradictory axes of domination and subordination in colonial society are simultaneously constituted and contested.

As an investigation of the relationship between masculinity and empire, this study contributes to the growing scholarship on British masculinity, Indian masculinity, and colonialism. Until the 1970s scholarship on nineteenth-century British masculinity remained largely limited by an exclusively metropolitan frame of reference,[18] while scholarship on colonialism rarely applied gender as an analytical category to men and masculinity.[19] Only in the 1980s did scholars begin to focus on the link between masculinity and imperialism. Ashis Nandy's *The Intimate Enemy* (1983), an important pioneering work on the psychology of colonialism and masculinity, focused on the impact of modern Western notions of masculinity on the reordering of traditional conceptions of masculinity in India. A number of works specifically addressing British masculinity as an aspect of race, class, sexual, and imperial politics have also appeared.[20] But these generally give the colony only a limited role because they fail to recognize the full extent to which British masculinity is constituted by colonialism. The colony is treated either as an empty stage on which the national politics of gender or class get extended and played out or as an exotic backdrop against which British masculinity attains full maturity.

Drawing attention to this limitation in her recent study of colonial masculinity, Mrinalini Sinha forcefully demonstrates the constitutive impact of colonialism.[21] Sinha's nuanced historical account not only exposes the mutual implication of British and Indian masculinities in imperial politics, it shows how the gendered stereotypes of the "manly Englishman" and the "effeminate Bengali" were overdetermined by various intersecting ideologies of race, ethnicity, class, religion, and sexuality. While my own study is deeply indebted to Sinha's historical insights, there are significant differences between our positions. First and foremost, my contention is that the colonial stereotype of Indian effeminacy is not simply a false construct but rather a misvalued recognition of a real alternative ideal of masculinity (i.e., androgyny) in Hindu society. Second, I see effeminacy not just as the site of a limited challenge to specific colonial policies but the source of a potentially radical interrogation of colonial ideology. I argue that when defined as an embodiment of cultural hybridity, effeminacy may be seen as an "every-day form of resistance"[22] and as an important ideological weapon in the Gandhian arsenal. Finally, it is my view that the production of a colonial stereotype is a continuous ongoing process that inevitably involves slip-page, contradiction, and failure—a process in which every successful assertion of dominance simultaneously reveals an inability to attain total hegemony.

Chapter 2, "The Economy of Colonial Desire," lays out the theoret-ical grounds for this study by defining terms and setting parameters. Identifying the British Raj as a "homosocial" arena, the chapter traces the production of effeminacy in various nineteenth-century discourses. I use the term *effeminism* to designate the racialized construction of "femininity-in-masculinity" as a pathological condition. Tracing this construction in various nineteenth-century discourses (anthropological, ethnographic, historiographic, medical, psychological, psychoanalyti-cal, linguistic, and literary), I highlight the contradictions that fracture the stereotype of Indian effeminacy and the tensions that bracket impe-rial hegemony.

By pointing to the presence of androgyny as a credible and viable performance of masculinity in Hindu culture, I draw on Homi Bhabha's theory of colonial mimicry to theorize cultural hybridity as a form of androgyny that functions as an everyday form of resistance in colonial India. By examining how the ideals of androgyny and hybridity eroded during the second half of the nineteenth century with the rise of militant Hindu revivalist nationalism, I consider the ways in which Gandhian nationalism finally gave effeminacy a different scripting that wrested it away from the colonial paradigm.

The chapter closes with a brief discussion of the role of women—white as well as brown—in homosocial colonialism. Through such a survey of the psychopolitical terrain of the British Raj, I try to elicit "sahib," "memsahib," "Indian," and "Indian woman" as signifiers and subjects in colonial discourse.

Chapter 3, "Manufacturing Masculinity," traces the historical pro-duction of a chivalric model of masculinity as the preeminent emblem of nineteenth-century British imperialism. I present the Sepoy Mutiny of 1857 as a critical moment in which the British sought to crystallize this model. Examining popular colonial histories produced in the aftermath of the mutiny, I attempt to discern how race, gender, and sexuality are deployed as ideological counters in a homosocial game of colonial rule and anticolonial resistance. My discussion repeatedly draws attention to the slippages, contradictions, and failures that attend the manufacture of colonial stereotypes. The chapter concludes with an assessment of how well the policies and practices adopted by the colonial government in the years following the mutiny succeeded in consolidating Indian effeminacy as the real Other of English manliness.

Chapter 4, "Imperial Feminism in an Age of Homosocial Colonialism," focuses on the role of Anglo-Indian women as pawns and players in the machinations of empire. The Illbert Bill controversy of 1883–84 is a particularly significant historical moment that reveals English women in India at once resisting and reproducing their objectified status as homosocial exchange objects. Produced in the aftermath of the Illbert Bill controversy, Flora Annie Steel's *On the Face of the Waters* returns to the historical period of the mutiny to interrogate the gender role of Anglo-Indian women and to find a place for white female agency in colonial history. Steel's feminist project to constitute the Anglo-Indian woman as companionate colonialist is founded and founders upon a gendered interracial contest between the English woman and her Indian counterpart. She presents the Hindu patriarchal ideal of the "good wife," embodied in the sati, not only as the Other of liberated English womanhood but also as a model the English woman must emulate and excel.

My reading of Steel's novel thus places the relationship between English and Indian women in a somewhat different light. While supporting the widely accepted view that English women constituted Indian women as the Other in order to improve their own gender status within British and Anglo-Indian societies, I propose to show that the investment of male homosocial desire in the Indian woman, especially the sati and the domestic ideal she represented, was so deep and so strong that imperial feminism could not completely counter its force. The "good wife contest" in Steel's novel shows that the companionate colonialist, in contrast to the Hindu sati, may have the free will to reject the excesses of female self-immolation (i.e., she does not have to literally burn herself), but she still cannot reject the ideal of self-sacrifice as the ultimate standard of female virtue. The ideological role of the interracial good wife contest and the strategic function of sati in that contest, I argue, mark the limits of imperial feminism in an age of homosocial colonialism. By reinforcing racist and sexist ideologies, Steel's feminist enterprise enters into the very processes by which colonialism renews or extends itself.

Chapter 5, "Cartographies of Homosocial Terror," questions monolithic constructions of imperial authority by drawing attention to the "unmanly" hysteria that pervades Kipling's fictions. His tales of trans-gressions and breakdowns, of boundary slippage in the categories of gender, race, and identity, display the colonial body revolting against imperial technologies of discipline and surveillance through impermis-sible, freakish, behavioral excess such as unmanly hysteria and unac-ceptable sexuality. In fact, Kipling's Imperial Gothic makes available a startling thematic of male rape darkly figured through disguised and displaced images of supernatural invasion and occult possession. Thus, the English man in Kipling's stories emerges not as an omnipotent embodiment of imperial authority but, rather, as a deeply divided, cul-turally androgynous figure, torn between "going native" and "being sahib." Kipling's historic(al) "failure" to accept cultural hybridity makes his representations of Self and Other deeply disruptive, burdening the colonialist with a gloomy sense of fragility and futility about the civiliz-ing mission.

The culmination of this problematic of cultural androgyny in Kipling's fiction is, of course, *Kim*. My reading of this novel departs from previous readings in some important ways: first, I have refused to bracket the question of history from *Kim*, even if only to decry Kipling for deliberately and willfully writing a wish-fulfilling imperi-alistic tale; second, my insistence on the historical and the political, while broadly concurring with those who see Kipling's fiction of the 1890s as symbolic resolutions to the problems diagnosed in the fiction of the 1880s, recontextualizes *Kim* within a very specific historical debate that ensued in the mid-1880s—the native volunteer movement. Reading *Kim* as a symbolic resolution to the question of native volun-teering, I argue that, if Kipling's ingenious presentation of the colonial secret service as a suitable volunteer corps for the effeminate Indian complicates standard contemporary Anglo-Indian (and elite Indian) notions of effeminacy, his anxiety to recruit the effeminate Indian into the colonial secret service contains a repressed recognition of the terri-fying subversive potential of colonial androgyny. Furthermore, by placing the Westernized Huree Babu alongside the Indianized Kim, Kipling's text inadvertently turns effeminacy into a mirror that forces a recognition of the savage similarities binding these two cultural hybrids to the wheel of empire.

Chapter 6, "A Grammar of Colonial Desire," focuses on E. M. Forster's exploration of colonial relations. I present *A Passage to India* as a text that offers an entire grammar of colonial desire, a narrative that cod-ifies an entire spectrum of intra- and interracial male relations, from the most outrageously homosocial to the most subtly homoerotic. Forster's novel not only ridicules the racialized opposition between English manliness and Indian effeminacy in strident terms but also surreptitiously draws the homosocial into the orbit of the erotic, allowing us to posit a potential continuity between the homosocial and the homoerotic, between the sanctioned and the tabooed, between the speakable and the unspeakable in colonial culture. Following the disruptive trajectory of homoerotic desire in Forster's narrative, my reading locates in two marginal figures—an anonymous untouchable and an androgynous English man—the horizons and the boundaries of colonial intimacy.

Although, throughout the book, I have taken into account the role of Indians as both victims and participants in colonial history, I have nevertheless stayed with what may be considered canonical colonial texts, because my aim has been to focus on the ways in which the English colonial text is at once authorized and undermined by the mechanisms of masculine desire.

Yet the archival, critical, and interventionist mode I've adopted in reading these canonical colonial texts may be best understood in Pierre Macherey's terms: "What is important in a work is what it does not say. This is not the same as the careless notation 'what it refuses to say,' although that would be itself interesting: a method might be built on it, with the task of *measuring silences,* whether acknowledged or unacknowledged. But rather this, what the work *cannot* say is important, because there the elaboration of the utterance is carried out, in a sort of journey to silence."[23] I have, however, taken up Macherey's suggestion rather against the grain and have tried to measure not only what the text cannot say but also what it refuses to say.

All ventures into interpretation are perhaps ultimately autobiographical. Much of the personal investment in this study derives from my awareness of being situated on the complicitous margins of contemporary cultural studies. If the aim of critical exploration is to know oneself as a product of historical processes that have deposited an infinity of traces in oneself, this study is my attempt to recover the traces sedimented in myself. My focus on India may therefore be seen as a nostalgic search for "origins." The dangers involved in such a search are obvious, and they imply some new responsibilities. Many critiques of imperialism are often anticolonial in ways specified and promoted as properly empowering. Their sophisticated means of acculturation remain echoes of the master's voice even in dissent. I am uneasily aware of the inevitably ironic position of my own work within this implacable arena. In order to begin, however, I must ignore that my starting point is shaky, that my end will be inconclusive, and that the margins I necessarily marginalize will haunt my beginnings and my endings. As I chart my way across this perilous terrain, I would like to believe that, if on the one hand my work is complicitous with the discourses of empire, on the other hand it manages to interrogate some of the assumptions underlying those discourses. Perhaps only the ghosts that guard my margins can judge best.

2

The Economy of Colonial Desire

The Masks of Masculinity

"The East is East and the West is West and never the twain shall meet,"
claimed Rudyard Kipling in "The Ballad of East and West," and then
went on to imagine the ground on which this impossible meeting may
become possible: "when two strong men stand face to face, though they
come from the ends of the earth."[1] Kipling's vision of colonial intimacy
intriguingly predicates cultural and racial difference on a metaphoric
distinction between male strength and male weakness rather than on
the more conventional demarcation between masculinity and femininity. Masculinity is not only a foundational notion of modernity, but it is
also the cornerstone in the ideology of moral imperialism that prevailed
in British India from the late nineteenth century onward. The cult of
masculinity rationalized imperial rule by equating an aggressive, muscular, chivalric model of manliness with racial, national, cultural, and
moral superiority.

Modern masculinity was elaborated not only through an increasingly stricter demarcation between the sexes but also through a system-
atic "unmanning" of minorities within and foreigners without Europe.
According to this model, the ideal appearance of the English male (the
tall, strong, clean-cut English man) specifically excluded those who
were stunted, narrow-chested, excitable, easily wearied, or inefficient—
qualities associated with women, the lower classes, Jews, Papists,
Spaniards, the French, and colored peoples. Eschewing the "feminine"
virtues of early Christianity—meekness, mildness, and martyrdom—

the ideal of manliness emerging in eighteenth-century Europe combined a Greek aesthetics of the body with Roman militarism and
medieval chivalry. Johann Joachim Winckelmann (1717–68), archaeolo-
gist and art historian, was most influential in manufacturing an aesthetics of male beauty derived from descriptions of Greek sculpture. He represented the ideal male body as one that is harmonious in proportions
and projected strength as well as restraint. Anthropologists then used
this aesthetic criteria to identify differences between whites and nonwhites ("primitives"). Through cranial measurements and facial comparisons they exalted physical beauty as an attribute of superior European species. In the 1790s Winckelmann's ideal of beauty was used as a
standard by Peter Camper to classify races. The equation between
manly beauty and virtue that emerged through these comparisons and
classifications became an important aspect of modern masculinity. Such
a link between body and soul, outer and inner, physical and moral, was
more firmly cemented in the new eighteenth-century sciences of physiognomy, anthropology, and modern medicine. Thus, Johann Kaspar
Lavatar, founding practitioner of the science of physiognomy, adopted
Winckelmann's aesthetics to identify explicitly beauty with virtue and
ugliness with vice. For Lavatan beauty was a product of cleanliness,
love of work, and moderation. A similar sentiment is evident in the educational tract *Emile* (1762), in which Rousseau declares that wisdom and
understanding would inevitably follow from physical robustness and
good health.[2]

If masculine beauty was an expression of white European racial,
moral and cultural superiority, ugliness was evidence of nonwhite, non-
European inferiority. The disorderly appearance attributed to diverse
groups of foreigners and social misfits referred not only to physical
deformity, but it also implied lack of mental discipline and emotional
moderation. Modern medicine and psychology played a powerful role
in solidifying the link between body and soul through the very process
of designating and defining as diseased those who did not fit in. Among
the most common "diseases" attributed to the Other in the eighteenth
and nineteenth centuries was nervousness. Nervousness, linked to the
body, had been considered a sickness even during the seventeenth century, as evident in the views expressed by the famous English physician
Thomas Sydenham, who believed that women, because of their delicate
constitution, were more prone to nervousness and mental diseases than
men.[3] But in the following two centuries, encouraged by the eighteenth-
century cult of sensibility and by Romanticism, there was an enormous

fascination with nervous disorder throughout Europe. As more physi-
cians began to study the nervous system, illnesses that has earlier been
attributed to foul vapors or bad humors were now attributed to weak
nerves. In fact, shattered nerves were blamed for the predicaments of
modernity, for cultural and political decay, for rapid economic and
social change. Although seen as a mental illness, nervousness nevertheless affected the entire body through muscular contortions. In addition
to maintaining good physical health through exercise and sports, nervous disorders could be warded off by reining in one's imagination,
passions, and fantasies. A fanciful imagination, it was believed, could
drive a man to excesses, especially sexual excesses in the form of mas-
turbation, frequent intercourse, or homosexuality, all of which would
inevitably distort both body and mind.

Thus, toward the end of the nineteenth century a paranoid British
culture pictured itself under siege by immigrant hoards of physically
undesirable, morally degenerate aliens. It was feared that the mongrelization of the white race would lead to the disintegration of the
empire itself. To counter these fears Victorian myths of manhood and of
the empire as a vast paternalistic enterprise were manufactured, feeding
the notion that character was key to maintaining racial and cultural
superiority. Accordingly, the definition of manliness in British public
schools shifted first from Thomas Arnold's notion of "godliness and
goodlearning," in the 1830s, to the vigorous "muscular Christianity" of
the mid-Victorian period, associated with men such as Charles Kingsley
and Thomas Hughes, and, finally, to the "athleticism" of the 1870s,
which, popularized by writers like Samuel Smiles and Lord Baden-Powell (a close friend of Kipling), fed the recruiting campaigns for imperial
projects in the late nineteenth century.[4] Baden-Powell may be considered the architect of the idea that English character was a defense
against external threat. The Boy Scouts he founded became what
Michael Rosenthal terms the "character factory," an institutionalized
site for the production of "boy nature"—a class construct designed for
the lower classes in order to refashion them to conform to middle-class
interests. The Boy Scout code of character aimed at instant denial of
individualism, thought, and emotion, in favor of corporate loyalty and
group identity. The Boy Scout emphasis on pluck and determination
translated skills on the cricket field to the battlefields of empire.[5]

The trope of chivalry also constituted a privileged locus of colonial
self-image—one whose ideological origins may be traced back to the
aristocracy of medieval and Renaissance Europe. The ideology of

knighthood was instrumental in making and maintaining structures of power based on class (ruler and vassal in feudal society), gender (lady and knight in courtly love tradition), and religion (the Christians against the Islamic infidels as in the Crusades). The code of chivalry mediated these relations of power and dependence by setting up reciprocal bonds of duty and obligation. But, while chivalry reproduced and reinforced the knight's class and gender status, it also acted as a safety valve, providing young males of aspiring lower social strata with opportunities for upward mobility. Such a concept of chivalry, as Rajeswari Sunder Rajan points out, proved to be eminently adaptable to the context of colonization: "large numbers of young British men—administrators, soldiers, traders, educationalists, missionaries—found themselves unexpectedly authorized in the exercise of power over masses of Indians. But they also discovered that they had to undergo rites of initiation into the exercise of this power. The colonizer's racial superiority, however flagrant skin color or the trappings of power may have rendered it, had also to be demonstrated by acts of valor and authority."[6] This expectation, Sunder Rajan goes on to suggest, provided the legitimating narrative for colonial legislation on behalf of Indian women, who were cast as the hapless victims of a barbaric Indian patriarchy. The deficiency of Indian males in adequately embodying the chivalric ideal of manhood, the British argued, not only stunted interracial bonds but actually made India unfit for self-rule. The British believed that their exposure to a bracing, self-strengthening physical and moral climate at "home" (and in the frontier regions of India) made them natural leaders, while Indian men, lacking such exposure, remained weak and ineffectual. In fact, the distinction between male strength and weakness inscribed in Kipling's "Ballad of East and West" raises a larger question that increasingly haunts Anglo-India: (how) is it possible for (manly) English and (effeminate) Indian men to be friends?

Read against the grain, Kipling's infamous observation about strong men from the ends of the earth allows us to identify the British Raj as a "homosocial" space constituted by contending male fears, frustrations, and fascinations.[7] The entire structure of colonial homosociality, however, rests on the ideologeme of effeminacy. Effeminacy represents a critical and contentious idiom through which the racial and sexual ideologies of empire are mediated. Ashis Nandy describes the critical change in consciousness that colonialism produced in India as follows:

The polarity defined by the antonymous *purusatva* (the essence of masculinity), and *naritva* (the essence of femininity) was gradually supplanted, in the colonial culture of politics, by the antonyms of *purusatva* and *klibatva* (the essence of hermaphroditism). Femininity-in-masculinity was perceived as the final negation of a man's political identity, a pathology more dangerous than femininity itself.[8]

I shall use the term *effeminism* to refer to the racialized construction of "femininity-in-masculinity" as a pathological condition. While tracing the production of effeminacy in various nineteenth-century discourses, it will be my contention that Indian effeminacy should not be regarded simply as a false construct, an untrue stereotype, or an inverted projection, but should be seen, rather, as a misvalued and distorted recognition of something real in Indian culture. In other words, I am suggesting that there was indeed some basis for viewing Hindu society as effeminate, for not only did dominant strands of Hinduism reverse the Western equation of passivity with femininity and activity with masculinity, but androgyny, inspired by the medieval Bhakti movement, remained a forceful spiritual ideal for Hindu men at least until the first half of the nineteenth century. Let me hasten to add that neither of these views necessarily implies a pro-woman or feminist stance, because Hinduism generally devalued female activity to male stasis, while androgyny was held out as a liberating ideal primarily for men rather than for women. By the second half of the nineteenth century, however, a dramatic shift had occurred in the culture of colonial India: androgyny had been largely discredited as a positive spiritual ideal, and few Hindu men were able to escape the negative self-image of effeminacy.[9] It was Gandhian nationalism that finally revived, reformed, and elaborated androgyny as an alternative to colonial masculinity, thereby providing Indians with a powerful political plank from which to fight colonialism.

My second argument, and one that constitutes the core of this book, is based on the assumption that we need to study the ways in which a stereotype frames and limits the stereotyped as well as the stereotyper. Otherwise, we run the risk of reifying the omnipotent image of colonialism by granting it total hegemony over representation. In this respect it will be my contention that effeminism not only enabled British colonialism in India, but it also estranged colonial authority and bracketed colonial hegemony in certain important respects. My readings of Flora Annie Steel, Rudyard Kipling, and E. M. Forster, accordingly, emphasize how each writer's attempts to legitimize her or his own anomalous status in colonial society—as woman, as cultural hybrid, as homosexual respectively—are at once facilitated and circumscribed by the ideologeme of effeminacy.

As the following pages will make clear, I will be using the term *effeminacy* in three distinct yet related contexts. My first and most obvious application of the term relates to its historical use in colonial India as a derogatory label applied specifically to the elite, Hindu, Bengali male—and gradually, by extension, to all Indian men—to suggest that they are physically, intellectually, and morally, soft, frail, weak or cowardly, in short, "like a woman." My second use of the term *effeminacy* emphasizes a corollary of the first: the implied devaluation and disempowerment of women and femininity. As such, this book is concerned not only with the dynamics of colonial masculine desire but also with its differential effects on white and brown women. Finally, I use the term in a rather restricted, perhaps radical sense to denote the experience of biculturality or cultural androgyny that colonialism inevitably involved for both colonizer and colonized. Used in this sense, *effeminacy* becomes a kind of "mimicry," a production of "hybridity" that carries with it an explosive potential for resistance or subversion.[10] I shall elaborate each of these contexts by briefly tracing the historical production of effeminism.

Effeminism

There is considerable evidence to show that from the early years of colonial rule Europeans viewed Orientals in general and Indians in particular as a passive and indolent people. Thus, Robert Orme, the eighteenth-century British historian, declares: "breathing in the softest climates, having so few wants and receiving even the luxuries of other nations with little labour from their own soil, the Indian must have become the most effeminate inhabitant of the globe."[11] Many colonial texts use the word *effeminate* to describe the inhabitants of the Indian subcontinent. The word, George Mosse tells us, came into general usage in England during the eighteenth century, indicating an unmanly softness and delicacy.[12] Ketaki Dyson points out that the delicate physical features, dresses, and personal decorations of Oriental men were commented on in great detail by Anglo-Indians.[13] Descriptions of first landings on Indian shores attest to the dramatic way in which the dark male body must have impinged on the colonizing imagination. William Hodges, a professional artist under the patronage of Warren Hastings, records his first impression of "delicately framed" men with feminine hands and "mild, tranquil, and sedulously attentive" manners. Some of the men, Hodges observes, are "wholly naked," while others wear "long muslin dresses," their "black faces adorned with large gold ear-rings and white turbans." The "rustling of fine linen, and the general hum of unusual conversation" suggests to Hodges "an assembly of females."[14] This "spectacular" Oriental body is a product of what Christine Bolt has called the "hardening of race thinking" through various ideological practices that consolidated race as the most visible category in colonial society.[15] For Flora Annie Steel, who went out to India with her husband in 1867, the racial male body becomes an extension of the exoticism of the Indian landscape: "My first entry into India was in a masulah boat through the surf at Madras. It was exhilarating. Something quite new; something that held all possibilities. A boat that had not a nail in it; dark skinned boatmen with no clothes on, who did not look naked, a surf such as I had never seen before, thundering on the yellow sands."[16] E. M. Forster's entry into India focuses quite explicitly on the ambiguous beauty of the racial male body: "The last horrid meal on the horrid ship ended as we reached Bombay, and we went ashore in style in a native boat, an ugly crew but beautiful skins."[17] This hidden homoerotic look returns to complicate the ideological and aesthetic configurations of *A Passage to India,* generating some of the most arresting icons of male nudity in Anglo-Indian literature.

Over time *effeminacy* evolved from a vague adjective used to describe physical appearance or lifestyle into a powerful ideologeme deployed in many different discourses and in many varied contexts. Thus, for instance, William Jones, the Orientalist scholar and translator responsible for the most influential introduction of a textualized India to Europe in the late eighteenth century, relies heavily upon a vocabulary of effeminacy to describe and codify Eastern languages and literatures. In an essay on Oriental poetry Jones describes the Persians as characterized by "that softness, and love of pleasure, that indolence, and effeminacy, which have made them an easy prey to all the western and northern swarms."[18] Persian poetry is said to be greatly influenced by the Indians, who are "soft and voluptuous, but artful and insincere."[19] This particular strand of Orientalist scholarship provided indirect support for Anglicist belief in the moral superiority of English by implicitly defining European languages and literatures, especially English, as hard, energetic, rational, and masculine. Thus, contrary to common assumption, Orientalism and Anglicism were not just competing discourses but also complementary discourses in the larger project of colonialism.

Macaulay's "Minute" of 1835, which institutionalized compulsory English education in India, represents only the most infamous and influential expression of Anglicism, an ideology that generated a great deal of expansionist rhetoric in England. Observing the spread of English in 1838, one English man suggested that English

> is rapidly becoming the great medium of civilization, the language of law and literature to the Hindoo, of commerce to the African, of religion to the scattered islands of the Pacific. The range of its influence, even at the present day, is greater than ever was that of the Greek, the Latin, or the Arabic; and the circle widens yearly. Though it were not our living tongue, it would still, of all living languages, be the one most worthy of our study and our cultivation, as bearing most directly on the happiness of mankind.[20]

By the end of the century such views had become so pervasive that Rev. George, a clergyman deeply concerned with Britain's civilizing mission, could confidently declare that "other languages will remain, but will remain only as the obscure Patois of the world, while English will become the grand medium for all the business of government, for commerce, for law, for science, for literature, for philosophy, and divinity. Thus it will really be a universal language for the great material and spiritual interests of mankind."[21] Anglicist belief in the superiority of English rested on a racialized and gendered equation between language and nation. The Rev. George thus argued that "as the mind grows, the language grows, and adapts itself to the thinking of the people. Hence, a highly civilized race, will ever have, a highly accomplished language. The English tongue, is in all senses a very noble one."[22]

The enormously consequential ways in which such Anglicist assumptions entered into the formation of the "science" of modern linguistics in the late nineteenth and early twentieth centuries is a subject that is yet to be adequately addressed. For the purposes of the present discussion, however, I will only note that the gendered rhetoric used by both Orientalists as well as Anglicists continued to inform important strands of linguistics in the early decades of the twentieth century. For example, the influential grammarian and linguist Otto Jespersen argues that English is a "masculine" language since English consonants are "clearly and precisely pronounced."[23] After analyzing the first ten stanzas of Tennyson's *Locksley Hall*, he concludes that "the English language is a methodical, energetic, business-like and sober language, that does not care much for finery and elegance, but does care for logical consistency and is opposed to any attempt to narrow-in life by police regulations and strict rules either of grammar or of lexicon. As the language is, so also is the nation."[24] By contrast, Jespersen pointed to lexical diversity in "primitive languages" and argued that the presence of many words for "cow" in Zulu or for "grey" in Lithuanian, for instance, illustrates the fact that "primitive man did not see the wood from the trees."[25]

Effeminacy could serve both as cause and effect in colonial discourse. Thomas Babington Macaulay, law member for India in the 1830s and author of the infamous "Minute on Indian Education," is perhaps the most cited source on Indian effeminacy. In his essay on Robert Clive, the conqueror of Bengal, Macaulay described the Bengalis as follows:

> The race by whom this rich tract was peopled, enervated by a soft climate and accustomed to peaceful employments, bear the same relation to other Asiatics which the Asiatics generally bear to the bold and energetic children of Europe. The Castilians have a proverb, that in Valentia the earth is water and the men women, and the description is at least equally applicable to the vast plain of the lower Ganges. Whatever the Bengali does he does languidly. His favourite pursuits are sedentary. He shrinks from bodily exertion, and though voluble in dispute, and singularly pertinacious in the war of chicane he seldom engages in personal conflict, and scarcely ever enlists as a soldier. There never perhaps existed a people so thoroughly fitted for a foreign yoke.[26]

Macaulay offers effeminacy as both an explanation and a justification for India's loss of independence to Britain. Elaborating and enriching the notion of effeminacy in another essay, Macaulay made further observations about the inhabitants of Bengal:

> The physical organization of the Bengalee is feeble even to effeminacy. He lives in a constant vapour bath. His pursuits are sedentary, his limbs delicate, his movements languid. During many ages he has been trampled upon by men of bolder and more hardy breeds. Courage, independence, veracity, are qualities to which his constitution and his situation are equally unfavourable. His mind bears a singular analogy to his body. It is weak even to helplessness for purposes of manly resistance; but its suppleness and its tact move the children of sterner climates to admiration, not unmingled with contempt. All those arts which are the natural defense of the weak are more familiar to this subtle race than to the Ionian of the time of Juvenal, or to the Jew of the dark ages. What the horns are to the

buffalo, what the paw is to the tiger, what the sting is to the bee, what beauty, according to the old Greek song, is to woman, deceit is to the Bengalee. Large promises, smooth excuses, elaborate tissues of circumstantial falsehood, chicanery, perjury, forgery, are the weapons, offensive and defensive, of the people of the Lower Ganges. All these millions do not furnish one sepoy to the armies of the Company. But as usurers, as money changers, as sharp legal practitioners, no class of human beings can bear comparison with them. With all his softness, the Bengalee is by no means placable in his enmities, or prone to pity. The pertinacity with which he adheres to his purpose yields only to the immediate pressure of fear. Nor does he lack a certain kind of courage which is often wanting in his masters. To inevitable evils he is sometimes found to oppose a passive fortitude such as the Stoics attributed to their ideal sage.[27]

Through a phantasmatic proliferation of analogies Macaulay's passage reduces a jumble of geographic, physiological, ethnographic, and anthropological observations into the single overarching category of effeminacy that, nevertheless, remains an idiosyncratic and contradictory construct: feeble but delicate, weak yet resilient, cowardly but courageous, contemptuous yet admirable, the effeminate Indian unsettles the binary categories of colonial epistemology. The mildness and softness of the Indian are seen in shifting terms as an index of cultural sophistication and/or as a mark of racial inferiority—a textual conflict that is also written into James Mill's authoritative *History of British India*. Arguing that the beginnings of civilization are compatible with "great violence" as well as with "great gentleness,"[28] Mill concludes that "the Hindu, like the eunuch, excels in the qualities of a slave."[29]

Macaulay's eloquent observations about the effeminate inhabitants of Bengal, widely shared by subsequent generations of Anglo-Indians, took on a very specific significance in the stereotype of the "effeminate Bengali babu." During the nineteenth century, and especially in the years following the Sepoy Mutiny of 1857, the urban centers of Bengal emerged as sites of anticolonial resistance. The increasingly articulate, politically self-conscious, Western-educated, middle-class Hindu Bengali society demanded a greater role in the colonial administration. The figure of effeminacy consequently takes on certain marked characteristics that reflect the politics of post-Mutiny Raj. From a loosely defined attribute associated with the entire population of Bengal, and by extension to all of India, at times even to all of Asia, effeminacy evolves into an attribute associated very specifically with Western-educated Indians, a large majority of whom were Bengali Hindus. As Mrinalini Sinha points out, the notion of Bengali effeminacy was, on the one hand, restricted quite specifically to the Bengali "babus," while, on the other hand, it was elaborated to include the politically discontented middle class all over India. Indeed, the very word *babu*, Sinha notes, underwent a change in usage that reflects the rearticulation of colonial racial politics in changed material conditions: from being a term used as a title of respect (much like *Mr.* or *Esq.*) in the first half of the century, *babu* began to connote a social-climbing, money-grubbing mentality, until by the late nineteenth century it came to signify "the grandiose pretensions and the economic impotence of the potentially disloyal Anglicized or English-educated Indian."[30] Sinha quotes *The Hobson-Jobson*, a glossary of words and phrases used by the British in India compiled in the 1880s, to show that in the popular imagination the word *babu* had come to designate a "native clerk who writes in English" and that the word was used with "a slight savour of disparagement, as characterizing a superficially cultivated but too often effeminate Bengali."[31]

The stereotypical babu was thus an urban, English-educated, alienated "intellectual." English education, it was widely believed, compounded the Bengali's inherent cowardliness to produce personal malice and political sedition. In September 1888 an editorial in Lahore's *Civil and Military Gazette*—in which Kipling worked as a reporter—declared that "nowhere in any corner of his character has the Bengali a spark of the spirit which has guided Englishmen in taking and ruling India; and upon occasions of legislative difficulty, it is impossible that he could offer, of his own motion, any reasonable advice toward the maintenance of that rule. He is a shrewd judge of all matters regarding his own comfort."[32] This image of the effeminate babu reflects the political challenge newly posed by the Indian middle class to certain exclusive rights and privileges the British enjoyed in India. It also signals a shift in colonial attitudes toward Western-educated Indians, who are no longer seen in Macaulayean terms as mediators between the colonial administration and the rest of the Indian population but, rather, as an unrepresentative and artificial minority capable of expressing nothing but the anomalies of their own situation.

The figure of the Bengali babu in late-nineteenth-century India can be usefully understood in terms of the concept of "ressentiment." This notion was powerfully theorized by Friedrich Nietzsche to explain ethics in general and the Judeo-Christian tradition in particular as a revenge of the slaves upon the masters whereby, through an ideological ruse, the slaves infect the masters with a slave mentality, expressed in

the ethos of charity, and rob the masters of their natural vitality and aristocratic insolence. In *The Genealogy of Morals* Nietzsche describes the
operation of ressentiment as follows: "The slave uprising in ethics
begins when ressentiment becomes creative and brings forth its own
values: the ressentiment of those to whom the only authentic way of
reaction—that of deeds—is unavailable, and who preserve themselves
from harm through the exercise of imaginary vengeance."[33] Although in
Nietzsche's explanation *ressentiment* is proposed as a psychological
mechanism in the service of a critique of Victorian moralism and
hypocrisy, its secondary adaptations, as Fredric Jameson points out,
show that the concept has a more fundamentally political function:

> First, in a kind of exoteric and vulgar sense, the ideologeme of ressenti-
> ment can seem to account in a "psychological" and nonmaterialistic sense
> for the destructive envy the have-nots feel for the haves, and thus account
> for the otherwise inexplicable fact of a popular mass uprising against a
> hierarchical system of which the historian is concerned to demonstrate the
> essential wholesomeness and organic or communitarian virtue. Mean-
> while, in a secondary and more esoteric, "overdetermined" use, ressenti-
> ment can also explain the conduct of those who incited an otherwise
> essentially satisfied popular mass to such "unnatural" disorders: the ide-
> ologeme thus designates Nietzsche's "ascetic priests," the intellectuals par
> excellence—unsuccessful writers and poets, bad philosophers, bilious
> journalists, and failures of all kinds—whose private dissatisfactions lead
> them to their vocations as political and revolutionary militants.[34]

Such a formulation of ressentiment is useful for conceptualizing the
Bengali babu's role in nineteenth-century colonial politics and for
understanding the Bengali elite's struggle for hegemony under conditions of colonial rule. From being openly supportive of imperial authority during the mutiny the Bengali elite moved toward muted criticism of
specific colonial policies in the 1870s and 1880s, until finally by the turn
of the century it emerged as an aggressive and articulate inciter of public opinion against the British Raj. As its traditional property privileges
were gradually destroyed in the second half of the nineteenth century,
the Bengali elite scrambled to take advantage of the employment opportunities and other benefits of English education. If this move brought on
the ignominy and humiliation of petty bureaucratic or clerical work, it
nevertheless proved pivotal to specific Bengali/Indian groups, first in
articulating nationalist aspirations and subsequently in establishing
class hegemony in an emerging nation-state.

By the end of the nineteenth century, however, effeminacy had become the most powerful signifier of India's cultural decline, and the effeminate babu had become the quintessential embodiment of this degeneracy. Effeminacy came to be seen as one facet of a general pattern of moral shortcoming, a reflection of the diffuse sensuality and debilitating femininity in Indian society. Various pseudoscientific theories were put forth as explanations for India's loss of that virility the ancient Aryans had supposedly shared with their European counterparts. In addition to ecological or environmental factors, biological, economic, social, and religious factors were frequently identified as causes of cultural decline. Bengali effeminacy, for example, was variously attributed to the warm climate, enfeebling diet, mixed Aryan-Dravidian descent, premature maternity, the Hindu caste system, insecure property relations in Hindu society, and matrifocal Hinduism.

An important ingredient of Indian effeminacy was the open-ended, unorganized, polytheistic, matrifocal nature of Hinduism. In contrast to Judeo-Christian monotheism, which seemed robust, reasonable, ordered, and properly male, Hinduism, with its erotic, ecstatic cults, seemed improper, irrational, and feminine. During the early years of the nineteenth century the rise of evangelical influence hardened Anglo-Indian attitudes toward Hinduism into prejudice. Even British Orientalists like William Jones, who idealized the textualized Brahmanical Vedic past, bemoaned the contemporary state of Hindu beliefs. The mythology, iconography, and practice of popular Hinduism, which included promiscuous and androgynous gods like Krishna and Siva, aggressive embodiments of female sexuality such as the goddesses Kali, and the institution of temple dancers, contravened Judeo-Christian conceptions of gender and divinity. By the middle of the nineteenth century, when the evangelical fervor of earlier decades had been replaced by a more pragmatic, muscular Christianity, the colonial government redirected its old religious zeal toward education and social reform. And, since both the colonial government as well as the Indians invoked religious sanction for social practices such as sati and child marriage, it became easy to target Hinduism as a degenerate belief system underlying a morally bankrupt society.

Sigmund Freud, of course, located matriarchal polytheism in the prehistory of mankind: "The matriarchal structure of society was replaced by a patriarchal one . . . This turning from the mother to the father, however, signifies above all a victory of spirituality over the senses—that is to say, a step forward in culture, since maternity is proved by the senses whereas paternity is a surmise based on a deduction and a premise. This declaration in favour of the thought-process, thereby raising it above sense perception, has proved to be a step charged with serious consequences."[35] From this perspective the polytheist could only be an anthropological object; it would take monotheism to make him a subject of history. The Mosaic prohibitions against image making becomes, for Freud, an illustration of the subordination of sense perception/maternity to an abstract idea/paternity. Accordingly, he posits "instinctual renunciation," synonymous with patriarchy and monotheism, as the prerequisite for the establishment of civilization, which is characterized by the predominance of secondary rather than primary processes. Freud's repudiation of the oceanic is a corollary of his devaluation of the maternal, which he closely associated with polytheism. He actually attributes fascism to polytheism, or primitive instincts: "all the people who now excel in the practice of anti-Semitism became Christians only in relatively recent times . . . One might say they all are 'badly christened'; under the thin veneer of Christianity they have remained what their ancestors were, barbarically polytheistic."[36] In a striking passage that brings the sexual and political themes together, the link between Freud's own normative theories of culture, gender, sexuality, and the civilizing mission of English imperialism becomes clearly visible:

> It may encourage us to enquire whether the religion of Moses brought the people nothing else besides an enhancement of their self-esteem owing to their consciousness of having been chosen. And indeed another factor can be found. That religion also brought the Jews a far grander conception of God. Anyone who believed in this God had some kind of share in his greatness, might feel exalted himself. For an unbeliever this is not entirely self-evident; but we may perhaps make it easier to understand if we point to the sense of superiority felt by a Briton in a foreign country which has been made insecure owing to an insurrection—a feeling that is completely absent in a citizen of any small continental state. For the Briton counts on the fact that his Government will send along a warship if a hair of his head is hurt, and that the rebels understand that very well—whereas the small state possesses no warship at all. Thus, pride in the greatness of the British Empire has a root as well in the consciousness of the greater security—the protection—enjoyed by the individual Briton. This may resemble the conception of a grand God.[37]

In a wry comment on this remarkable passage Gayatri Spivak observes, "Transcendental imperialism by this Freudian account is a Jewish game accidentally practiced by the British."[38] The strange analogy Freud uses shows how closely his valuation of renunciation and sublimation as the

supremely male virtues is linked to his sanction of colonialism's civilizing mission.

From its inception psychoanalysis (wedded to anthropology in the
form of ethnopsychology) is imbricated in the ideologies of empire.
Highlighting the role of psychoanalysis as an instrument of British colo-
nialism in India, Christiane Hartnack shows how British members of the
International Psychoanalytical Association, especially Owen Berkeley-
Hill and Claud Dangar Daly, used psychoanalysis to pathologize the
Indian male as infantile and effeminate in order to justify colonial rule.
She also finds Freud's correspondence with various Indians indicative
of an indifference, even aversion, toward India.[39] Whatever feelings
Freud may have entertained toward India, his theories of culture cer-
tainly pathologize non-Western societies in ways that justified European
domination.[40]

In *Totem and Taboo* (1913) Freud compares the "primitive"—defined
as one who has not renounced libidinal strivings—to the neurotic, the
child, and the female.[41] The primitive mind is characterized by the dominance of primary processes, where the pleasure principle rules and
action substitutes for thought. It does not have access to the secondary
processes of thought and cogitation. The primitive, therefore, does not
possess the strong ego defenses necessary for reality testing. The prerequisite of civilization—the reality principle producing instinctual
renunciation of pleasures for deferred gratification—is allocated exclusively to the European man. In *Group Psychology and the Analysis of the
Ego* (1921) Freud equates the group mind of modern peoples with the
mental state of the primitive man, arguing that both are impulsive, incapable of deferring action by thought, are ruled by the unconscious, have
a sense of omnipotence, think in images, lack logic, and so tolerate contradiction.[42] Although this fragmented state is supposedly inherent in
all humans regardless of the level of culture, it is inferred that civilized
men are to be distinguished by the progressive drive toward a unifica-
tion of mental life. Failure of identity thus becomes essentialized as a
racial characteristic, and colonized cultures get pathologized as symptomatic of early mental processes. In Freud's equations between primitive
tribe and modern child/neurotic, the cultural Other, the colonized,
remains a collectivity that is never individualized. To the extent that
neurotics and children are atavistic, to the extent that primitives (or cultural and racial Others) are infantile and associated with the feminine,
the only civilized person is the European male.

This somewhat simplified sketch of Freud the imperialist obviously ignores his own precarious position as a Jew in a homogeneously Christian, anti-Semitic society.[43] Drawing attention to Freud's anomalous identity as both colonizer and colonized, Daniel Boyarin has argued that Freud did not so much possess the European Aryan phallus as desire it desperately: "Jews are not white / not quite in Homi Bhabha's felicitous formulation for other colonial subjects. Freud was at once the Other [neurotic, primitive, female] and the metropolitan, the 'Semite' among 'Aryans' and also the Jew desperately constructing his own whiteness through an othering of the colonized blacks."[44] Boyarin grounds his argument in the historical marginalization of Jews in fin-de-siècle Europe— a marginalization that, interestingly enough, rested on a stereotype of Jewish effeminacy.

Freud's theorizations of culture, gender, and sexuality, Boyarin suggests, represent a massive attempt to refute the charge of Jewish effeminacy (closely linked to homosexuality) by asserting a Jewish version of Protestant-Aryan masculinity (articulated as heterosexuality). Boyarin contends that Freud's rejection of his earlier seduction theory (dominated by the trope of hysteria and revolving mainly around women) in favor of the later theory with the Oedipus-castration complex (dominated by the neurosis and revolving exclusively around men) is not just a stereotypical case of patriarchal misogyny directed toward women alone but also a profound denial of womanly men as well. Freud's hysteria theory is thus not only about women but also about certain racially marked men (i.e., Jews). What Freud symbolically denied in the seduction theory and then returns symptomatically in the oedipal theory is the devastating knowledge that a boy/man might experience sexual desire in the manner of a girl/woman (read "passive," "desiring to be penetrated") or that a woman/mother might exhibit sexual aggression toward a boy/son. The oedipal theory represses these two figures—the passively desiring male and the actively desiring female—first, by positing a law of heterosexuality and, second, by having the boy actively spin erotic fantasies about the passive mother. Thus, Freud's desire to erase his own Jewish difference, which was coded as effeminate, drives him to normatize aggressive heterosexual white European masculinity and to effeminize and emasculate the colonized Others.[45] Boyarin's account of Freud allows us to raise further questions about the ideological scope of effeminism. If Freud's theorizations of culture, gender, and sexuality fed colonial conceptions of Asiatic effeminacy, did notions of effeminacy elaborated in Oriental theaters of colonialism nourish fin-de-siècle European perceptions of Jewish effeminacy? After all, the Sanskrit distinction between *Arya* and *un-Arya* found its way to Europe through Orientalists scholarship and played a role in the consolidation of the Jews as a Semitic "race" (in Freud's own lifetime).[46]

The metropolitan production of heterosexuality/homosexuality in nineteenth-century psychological/psychoanalytic, medical, and anthropological discourses interestingly intersects with the colonial elaboration of Indian effeminacy. The first British writer to explicitly identify the East as a homosexual terrain was Sir Richard Burton. Bringing together the conclusions of decades of travel and reading in the celebrated "Terminal Essay" of *Thousand Nights and a Night* (1885–88), Burton posited the existence of a "Sotadic Zone" running through the tropics and semitropics, representing those regions of the world where "pederasty" is as common as heterosexuality.[47] The word *pederasty* is also used by Freud in a 1897 letter: "It is to be supposed that the element essentially responsible for repression is always what is feminine . . . What men essentially repress is the pederastic element."[48] If normative heterosexual masculinity could be achieved only through a repression of the feminine "pederastic element," Burton's Sotadic Zone is a place populated by failed men.

Throughout the Judeo-Christian tradition sexuality between men had been infamous among those who knew about it at all precisely for having no name. The "unspeakable," "unmentionable," "not to be named among Christian men," are among the terms recorded by Louis Crompton.[49] Clearly, what allows Burton to speak the unspeakable, then, is the historical opportunity made available to him by empire.[50] In other words, homosexuality could be named more safely in an anthropological discourse about the colonized Other. Incidentally, Burton's career came to a sudden end when an elaborate private report he had written on the "eunuch brothels of Karachi" erroneously arrived before the Bombay government. An important aspect of Burton's "theory" of Oriental homosexuality is its emphasis on ecology. Burton insists that the influence of the Sotadic Zone on "the Vice" is "geographical and climatic, not racial."[51] "This insistence," Eve Sedgwick points out, "reflects an important element of the racism that accompanied British imperialism—an element that distinguishes it from American racism: its genetic basis, where asserted, is much less rigidly conceived. Americans are black or white from birth; colonials, on the other hand, can 'go' native for out there is a taint of climate, of moral ethos that, while most readily described in racial terms, is actually seen as contagious."[52]

The influence of Burton's ideas is evident in *The Underworld of India*

(1932), a lurid account of the seamy side of Indian life authored by Sir George MacMunn, a veteran of the Indian Army and a prolific writer on matters Indian, who even produced two appreciative commentaries on Kipling's work, *Rudyard Kipling: Craftsman* and *Kipling's Women*. In *The Underworld of India* MacMunn explicitly identifies homosexuality as the hidden hurdle to colonial friendships. In a passage that, read against the grain, could well serve as a gloss to the aborted eroticism between Fielding and Aziz in *A Passage to India*, MacMunn writes:

> While in the West homosexuality or pederasty is the sign of the degenerate or mentally unstable, and accompanies the disappearance of manliness and self-respect, in Asia, it is often the vice of the most resolute characters . . . Unfortunately, the most in other respects reputable of Eastern friends and conferencers may be so inclined, and it is the one hidden cause which stood in the past athwart friendship between Eastern and Western men, till all chance of the failing is ruled out.[53]

In Europe the cluster of associations around homosexuality almost always included effeminacy.[54] But India apparently presented a paradox, for homosexual practices were most commonly attributed not so much to the derided effeminate Bengali but, rather, to the more admired virile and manly "martial" races. What intrigues MacMunn most is that homosexual practices could exist among "the most resolute characters," among those very Indians who symbolized to him "the last words in daring and reckless courage."[55] Homosexual yet manly, heterosexual yet effeminate, Indian masculinity injects a fearful indeterminacy into the economy of colonial desire.

Both Burton and MacMunn are obsessively drawn to the Indian male courtesan, who, rather than the female prostitute, emerges as the most threatening source of cultural contagion. The female prostitute, whose threat to white purity was controlled through the importation of English women to the colony, actually becomes a more predictable (even reassuring) embodiment of India's Otherness. By contrast, the sexualized racial male body functioning as a viable medium of erotic/economic exchange not only remains unassimilated into the gendered configurations of empire but provides a deeply disturbed allegory for the disguised, disembodied homoeroticism in Anglo-Indian narrative.

The ascribed homosexuality of the Orient presents the colonizing male imagination with strange possibilities and unknown dangers. Possibly the most startling erotic motif to emerge in colonial settings is that of male rape. Dilating on the dangers of the Sotadic Zone for Western travelers, Richard Burton writes:

> A favourite Persian punishment for strangers caught in the harem or Gynaeceum is to strip and throw them and expose them to the embraces of the grooms and negro-slaves. I once asked a Shirazi how penetration was possible if the patient resisted with all the force of the sphincter muscle: he smiled and said, "Ah, we Persians know a trick to get over that; we apply a sharpened tent-peg to the crupper-bone (os coccygis) and knock till he opens." A well-known missionary to the East during the last generation was subjected to this gross insult by one of the Persian Prince-governors, whom he had infuriated by his conversion-mania: in his memoirs he alludes to it by mentioning his "dishonoured person"; but English readers cannot comprehend the full significance of the confession. About the same time Shaykh Nasr, Governor of Bushire, a man famed for facetious blackguardism, used to invite European youngsters serving in the Bombay Marine and ply them with liquor till they were insensible. Next morning the middies mostly complained that the champagne had caused a curious irritation and soreness in la parte-poste.[56]

The culmination of this motif of interracial male rape, as Eve Kosofsky Sedgwick points out, is, unfortunately, an account of a real rape in T. E. Lawrence's *Seven Pillars of Wisdom*.[57] Many passages in Lawrence's book are devoted to charting the alien yet compelling geography of male homosociality in Arab culture. Lawrence himself had moved from apparently unfulfilling bonds with English men to bonds with Arab men that had, for political reasons, far more space for fantasy and mystification and, hence, for the illusionistic charisma of will.[58] The rape occurs at a point when Lawrence, taken prisoner as a possible spy, refuses the advances of a Turkish commander, who "half-whispered to the corporal to take me out and teach me everything":

> To keep my mind in control I numbered the blows [of a whip] but after twenty lost count, and could feel only the shapeless weight of pain, not tearing claws, for which I had prepared but a gradual cracking apart of my whole being by some too-great force whose waves rolled up my spine till they were pent within my brain, to clash terribly together. Somewhere in the place a cheap clock ticked loudly, and it distressed me that their beating was not in its time. I writhed and twisted, but was held so tightly that my struggles were useless. After the corporal ceased, the men took up, very deliberately, giving me so many, and then an interval, during which they would squabble for the next turn, ease themselves, and play

unspeakably with me. This was repeated often, for what may have been more than ten minutes . . .

At last when I was completely broken, they seemed satisfied. Somehow I found myself off the bench, lying on my back on the dirty floor, where I snuggled down, dazed, panting for breath, but vaguely comfortable. I had strung myself to learn all pain until I died, and no longer actor, but spectator, thought not to care how my body jerked and squealed. Yet I knew or imagined what passed about me.

I remember the corporal kicking with his nailed boot to get me up; and this was true, for next day my right side was dark and lacerated . . . I remembered smiling idly at him, for a delicious warmth, probably sexual, was swelling through me; and then he flung up his arm and hacked with the full length of the whip into my groin. This doubled me half-over, screaming, or, rather, trying impotently to scream, only shuddering through my open mouth. One giggled with amusement. A voice cried, "Shame, you've killed him." Another slash followed. A roaring, and my eyes went black; while within me the core of life seemed to heave slowly up through the rending nerves, expelled from its body by the last indescribable pang.[59]

Lawrence experiences a profound loss of the sense of time, of personal identity, and, indeed, of life itself. Sedgwick observes that for Lawrence "the racial and cultural foreignness of the Turks (in relation to 'his' Arabs, as well as to himself) seems an emblem for the wrenching disjunctions in his ability, as a man, to master the map of male homosocial desire . . . For Lawrence, the unprepared-for and hence unmasterable confrontation with yet another, arbitrarily different, brutally contradictory way of carving up the terrain of male bonding, sexuality, and domination, made the self-contradictory grounds of his previously costly and exciting poise too rawly obvious."[60] In a brutal instance of the empire striking back Lawrence's chilling account returns the figure Freud repressed so assiduously in his theories of gender and sexuality—the figure of a man being (ab)used "like a woman." By focusing on the rape of a white man, the account also conceals a different scene of homosexual exploitation in which the subaltern Oriental male is ravished by a lustful European. Such a refiguration of rape is available in the self-censored "kanaya" memoir of E. M. Forster's *The Hill of Devi*.[61] Forster's depiction of homosexual rape provides a more appropriate metaphor for the dynamics of a homosocial colonialism founded on the economic and political exploitation of brown men by white men.

Such direct representations are, however, rare in Anglo-Indian literature, in which the theme of white male penetration and ravishment is more commonly expressed through metaphoric and disguised images of supernatural invasion, possession, regression, and decline. These images are manifested most starkly in the genre of colonial fiction Patrick Brantlinger has called the "Imperial Gothic."[62] In the demonic universe of the Imperial Gothic, a genre favored by Rudyard Kipling, the sexual and racial anxieties of Victorian and Edwardian imperialism are externalized in the form of supernatural, mystic, or occult forces that threaten the white man's physical and psychological integrity. In chapter 5 I examine the motif of male ravishment in Kipling's Indian tales and consider its historical link to the weakening of Britain's imperial hegemony. The pervasiveness of male sexual fear in the Imperial Gothic suggests that, by the end of the nineteenth century, rape may have come to condition the minds of white men almost as much as it had the minds of white women in the colonies.[63]

The homosocial economy of colonialism, however, ensures that empire's master metaphor—rape—is inscribed as a heterosexual viola-tion of the innocent white woman by the dark Indian rapist. Yet, despite the wide currency of the stereotype of the dark rapist, the Indian male, unlike the black male in America, was not portrayed to any marked extent as a phallic figure or as a sexual rival to the white male. While the myth of the black rapist supposes a potent Negro bestiality, the stereo-type of the Oriental rapist hinges on an assumption of Asiatic duplicity derived from British perceptions of Hindu degeneracy and Mughal decadence. Thus, in the case of the Indian male sexual aggression itself becomes a symptom of weakness rather than of virility.

Effeminacy as Mimicry

Anglo-India thus found its most seductive metaphor for racial, physical, moral, and cultural weakness not in the vulnerability of womanhood but in the weakness of colonized manhood. Colonialism was justified, naturalized, even legitimized, through an ideological distinction between English manliness and Indian, particularly Bengali, effemi-nacy. But, as Mrinalini Sinha points out, Bengali effeminacy is not sim-ply the complete opposite of Victorian manliness; rather, like homosex-uality, it was constructed as the fallen, failed, bastardized, or incomplete form of manliness.[64] The construction of effeminacy as a distorted or degenerate version of a pure original, Sinha suggests, was extremely effective, because it captured the element of what Homi Bhabha has called "mimicry," or "hybridization." She goes on to argue that the depiction of the Westernized Bengali male as a mimicry of the white male reflects an ideological contradiction, or, in Bhabha's terminology, an "ambivalence," that shaped colonial policy in India. In the early decades of the nineteenth century Thomas Macaulay and others successfully argued for the promotion of Western education and Western values as a means of civilizing the native. But by the late nineteenth century, when Westernized Indians began to question the exclusionary policies of the imperial government, the task of redeeming the native was declared to be an impossible one. Thus, through a "splitting of the Self" imperialism's universal imperative to remake the Other in the image of the Self produces a "distortion of similarity," so that the project of remaking could then potentially go on for ever.[65]

Sinha's elaboration of effeminacy usefully historicizes Bhabha's concept of mimicry, or hybridization, by treating it not as a general theory of subject constitution under colonialism but as an explanation of how a particular segment of the Indian population (elite, educated, Bengali) came to be defined by the exigencies of late-nineteenth-century colonial politics. Sinha also grounds the notion of ambivalence in colonial reality by relating its ideological function to political practices that ensured continued imperial dominance. In doing this, however, she overlooks or minimizes, what I consider to be a crucial aspect of hybridity: the potential for subversion or resistance. Bhabha elaborates this aspect of colonial mimicry in his later theoretical formulations. Although mimicry imposes a flawed identity on colonized people, who are then obliged to inhabit an uninhabitable zone of ambivalence that grants them neither identity nor difference, Bhabha argues that there is a slippage between identity and difference that throws the "normalizing" authority of colonial discourse into question. The dream of post-Enlightenment civility is alienated from itself because in the colonial state it can no longer parade as a state of nature. Mimicry becomes "at once resemblance and menace."[66] Bhabha recognizes that ambivalences of colonial subjectivity need not always pose a threat to dominant power relations and may, in fact, "exercise them pleasurably and productively."[67] But elsewhere he develops the notion of mimicry less as a self-defeating colonial strategy than as a form of anti-colonial resistance. Mimicry here "marks those moments of civil disobedience within the discipline of civility: signs of spectacular resistance."[68] Hybridity "unsettles the mimetic or narcissistic demands of colonial power but reimplicates its identifications in strategies of subversion that turn the gaze of the discriminated back upon the eye of power . . . If discrimina-

tory effects enable the authorities to keep an eye on them, their prolifer-
ating difference evades that eye, escapes that surveillance . . . It
[hybridization] reveals the ambivalence at the source of traditional discourses on authority and enables a form of subversion, founded on that
uncertainty, that turns the discursive conditions of dominance into the
grounds of intervention."[69] This elaboration may be usefully compared
to Luce Irigaray's feminist theorization of mimicry as a subversive strategy employed by the disempowered.

Challenging the phallocentrism of orthodox psychoanalysis, Irigaray makes an important distinction between masquerade and mimicry, between a nonparodic imitation of a role and an ironic hyper-
bolization of that role, between an unconscious assumption of
femininity and a deliberate performance of femininity as a survival
strategy in a world colonized by male desire.[70] Irigaray suggests that
under certain conditions, women deliberately assume or put on the
mask of femininity—an act that discloses the constructedness or "artifi-
ciality" of gender and enables women to "convert a form of subordination into an affirmation."[71] But in making this bold and provocative
challenge to Lacanian masculinism, Irigaray inscribes mimicry as an
essentially female strategy and thereby not only overlooks the possibilities of male masquerade/mimicry but also elides the categories of class
and race. By the same token, Homi Bhabha's theory of colonial mimicry
focuses on race but ignores the categories of class and gender. As Anne
McClintock observes, "The ironically generic 'Man' in Bhabha's title
('Of Mimicry and Man') both conceals and reveals that Bhabha is really
only talking about men. By eliding gender difference, however, Bhabha
implicitly ratifies gender power, so that masculinity becomes the invisible norm of postcolonial discourse. By eliding racial difference, Irigaray, in turn, ratifies the invisibility of imperial power."[72]

Despite the rich and valuable insights contained in both Irigaray's
and Bhabha's theorizations of resistance, these two notions of mimesis,
as Diana Fuss points out, "cross, interact, and converge in ways that
make it increasingly difficult to discriminate between the mimicry of
subjugation and a mimicry of subversion, or at least to know with any
degree of certainty their possible political effects."[73] If, as Bhabha suggests, the ever-present possibility of slippage between unconscious
assumption and self-conscious performance enables the mimicry of subjugation to open up unexpected opportunities for resistance and disruption, then the mimicry of subjugation, Fuss notes, can find itself reinforcing rather than eroding conventional power relations. Recent

studies on the subject position of whites in black masks (exemplified in such historical figures as Lawrence of Arabia and such fictional figures as Kipling's Kim) reinforce Fuss's cautionary argument that "the dream of a playful mimesis cannot be so easily or immediately recuperated for a progressive politics" if we take into account the "multiple axes of difference that cross-cut, interfere with, and mutually constitute each other," as evident in instances of cross-cultural impersonations that work in the service of colonial imperialism.[74] Highlighting the difficulty of locating or identifying colonial resistance, Jenny Sharpe had, quite early on, criticized Bhabha for ignoring the material violence of colonialism and making resistance inhere in the discursive or textual dynamics of empire's ironic and parodic representations.[75] Similarly, questioning theories that locate agency in the internal fissures of discourse, Anne McClintock has, more recently, observed that for Bhabha, "colonial authority appears to be displaced less by the shifting social contradictions or the militant strategies of the colonized than by the formal ambivalence of colonial representation itself."[76]

Keeping in mind these problems and pitfalls, I shall attempt to selectively deploy Bhabha's rich insights into the play of fantasy and desire in colonial contests to theorize the subversive potential of effeminacy not as an intrinsic or internal effect of colonial mimicry as such but, rather, as a strategy historically available only to elite Indian men in their struggle against colonialism. In so applying his idea of subversive mimicry exclusively to elite Indian men, I am perhaps taking Bhabha far more literally than he intends. My discussion highlights two specific ways in which effeminacy becomes subversive: first, as an "everyday form of resistance"; and second, as a programmatic rescripting affected by Gandhian nationalism. I shall, however, argue that, to the extent effeminacy or cultural hybridity was a specific attribute of urban, western-educated, elite, mostly Hindu men, both the parodic possibilities of effeminacy in everyday life and the Gandhian deployment of effeminacy actually served to ensure elite male hegemony in an emerging postcolonial order. In other words, I attempt to show that effeminacy was simultaneously a mimicry of subversion that successfully disrupted colonial authority in certain contexts as well as a mimicry of subjugation that kept the lower castes, religious minorities, and women under elite male control. Context, therefore, is decisive in my determination of whether and when effeminacy may be considered subversive.

The subversive potential of mimicry becomes visible in the unexpected, ironic effects of colonial effeminism. The violent intervention of the West into the East, not to mention colonialism's ideological project of remaking the Other in the image of the Self, inevitably needed and produced culturally hybrid subjects among the colonizers as well as the colonized. By the late nineteenth century many Anglo-Indian families with a tradition of colonial service involving long periods of residence in the colony included many who, like Kipling, had been born in India and nurtured by Indians during the initial impressionable years of childhood. The Anglo-Indian practice of sending children away to England for schooling—a practice born as much out of a fear about physical health as about cultural purity and, as in Kipling's case, one that would prove psychologically harrowing—was aimed at erasing or at least diluting the effeminizing influence of colonized culture by instilling the manly virtues of Englishness. The typical product of such practices was, like Kipling, a split subject, a bicultural sahib alienated from manly England and effeminate India alike. This subject position is somewhat different from the "white skin, black mask" position taken up by Lawrence of Arabia. Kipling, unlike Lawrence, tried very hard to repress and deny that part of himself that, without his conscious choice or will, had become Indianized. In fact, one might say that what Kipling really desired but was never sure he possessed was the self-conscious, manipulative hybridity emblematized in Lawrence. Indeed, as I will argue later, Kipling's characterization of Kim is driven by an anxiety that mimicry, instead of becoming a willed performance of hybridity that reinforces racial difference, might well become a paralyzing, unwilled, mongrelization of identity that would collapse all difference. This is why the syncretic possibilities of Kim must necessarily atrophy into the pseudo-hybridity of a colonial spy. Colonialism required of every white man a denial of cultural androgyny. "Colonialism," as Ashis Nandy notes, "took away the wholeness of every white man who chose to be a part of the colonial machine and gave him a new self-definition which, while provincial in its cultural orientation, was universal in its geographical scope."[77]

Bound together by mimicry, the Anglicized Indian and the Indianized English man represent mirror images of each other. Yet it was the Indian's hybridity that was systematically stressed and ridiculed, while the biculturality of the Anglo-Indian was silently suppressed. Thus, the quintessential embodiment of cultural hybridity in the post-Mutiny era was the Bengali babu, a figure stereotyped by Kipling as pathologically effeminate, ridiculous, and inauthentic. What Kipling despises most is the babu's inability (his refusal?) to be a proper victim, to stand up boldly, fight in manly fashion, and pay back the tormentor in his own coin. In story after story he mocks the babu for adopting such effeminate tactics as noncooperation, flattery, obsequiousness, evasion, shirking, irresponsibility, lying, avoidance, and refusal to value face-to-face fights. But at key moments, Kipling's fiction registers a keen awareness of the subversive potential in the babu's passive-aggressive modes of resistance. The crafty babus, Kipling recognizes in disgust, adopt but adapt English ways to suit their own ends; they bow down obsequiously before the white man only to subtly manipulate him for their own purposes. Indeed, I shall be arguing that Kipling's *Kim* not only exposes the terrifying similarities between the androgynous wonder-boy Kim and his effeminate partner Huree babu, it also contains an implicit acknowledgment of the subversive potential of effeminacy, or cultural hybridity.

The figure of the Westernized Indian, in spite of its pathology and its tragicomic core, may be viewed, Ashis Nandy suggests, as an assimilated form of an other civilization that gate-crashed into India. For what looks like Westernization may actually be a means of domesticating the West, sometimes by reducing the West to the comic or the trivial.[78] The process of cultural osmosis in colonial India was highly complex, not always unidirectional, not always involving conflict, not always producing a sense of loss. The uncanny art of survival perfected by an ancient society experienced in absorbing and adapting foreign influences taught Indians to bend to colonial rule without completely breaking. The performance of effeminacy or the practice of hybridity in everyday life allowed Indians to assimilate and conform while preserving subterranean spaces of escape and refuge.

My understanding of effeminacy as an "everyday form of resistance" is grounded in recent studies that seek to move away from the conventional focus on extraordinary, often violent, moments of collective protest toward those forms of struggle present in the behaviors and cultural practices of subordinated peoples at times other than those of overt revolt. The writings of James Scott have, most notably, questioned the common assumption that in "normal" times, when there are no dramatic collective upheavals, the relations of power remain largely intact, and the identities and cultural practices of the dominant remain firmly in place.[79] Pointing to the presence of "hidden transcripts" or parodic rejections of the claims of the colonizing culture, Scott eloquently argues that the appearance of hegemony is only the "public script" that serves the purposes of both the colonizer and the colonized in situations of near total domination: "In this respect, subordinate groups are complicitous in contributing to a sanitized official transcript, for that is one way they cover their tracks."[80] Such an understanding obviously goes against a Foucauldian view of panoptic hegemony but is quite compatible with Michel de Certeau's notion of *la perruque,* a term which metaphorically refers to the little ruses and tricks practiced by dominated groups.[81]

Extending Scott's insights, historians of South Asia have, in recent years, focused on the myriad ways in which the social relations of daily existence in colonial India were enmeshed in and transfigured by contradictions and contestations that seem quite innocent or innocuous. This means, as Douglas Haynes and Gyan Prakash, editors of an important collection of essays on everyday social relations in South Asia, point out, "consciousness" need not be essential to resistance.[82] Although this provocative theoretical assertion also does not fully address the issue of reception (whether something is resistant even if it is not perceived or treated as such), it differs not only from the implicit intentionality Scott ascribes to his "hidden transcripts," but also from all those theorists of identity and resistance (e.g., Fanon, Bhabha, Irigaray, and Althusser) who tend to make resistance and agency contingent upon an ironic or self-conscious intention.[83] Colonial ideology itself, as my discussion of Flora Annie Steel and Kipling will demonstrate later, differentiated the mimicry of the colonizer from the mimicry of the colonized precisely by claiming self-consciousness, agency, and individual will exclusively for the colonizer while attributing a paralyzing lack of consciousness to the colonized. My point here is not simply to show up the obvious bias in such a claim by pointing to instances of deliberate or willed colonized agency—something already done quite forcefully by Fanon, Bhabha and Irigaray. Rather, it is to suggest that consciousness is neither a necessary nor a sufficient ground of resistance.

To view the babu's effeminacy as a lived or everyday form of passive resistance does not, therefore, imply that he consciously adopted cultural hybridity as a form of protest against the colonizer. Far from it. In fact, the self-image of Indian, especially Bengali, men in the nineteenth century was deeply conditioned by a negative view of effeminacy. Whether they urged their fellow Indians to cultivate a robust physique or advocated violent military resistance to imperial rule, whether they undertook to revitalize Hinduism along the lines of muscular Christianity or attempted to reform the lives of women, many Bengali writers, reformers, political and religious leaders of the time—men like Michael Madhusudan Dutt (1824–73), Dayanand Saraswati (1824–83), Bankim Chandra Chatterjee (1838–94), and Vivekananda (1863–1902)—were simply reacting to being labeled effeminate.

Effeminacy, or rather femininity-in-masculinity, however, had not always been given such a negative scripting in precolonial Hindu society. Although Brahmanical masculinity, which emphasized a hard asceticism, renunciation, and sublimation, and Kshatriya masculinity, which emphasized a hard aggression, pleasure, and good living, remained the dominant contending models of masculinity, a third model that involved androgyny, particularly for men, had evolved out of Puranic traditions and had been held up as a spiritual ideal by various medieval Bhakti movements. Beginning in the eighth and ninth centuries in South India, the Bhakti movements, which involved an impassioned, frequently eroticized intimacy with god, had, by the thirteenth century, spread to most parts of India and remained a powerful force well into the nineteenth century. The emergence of the Bhakti movements also interestingly coincided with the rise of goddess-centered cults, especially in Bengal, where they served as a powerful site of anticolonial resistance during the nineteenth century. Bhakti, however, stands in clear contrast not only with Brahmanical Vedantic Hinduism but with Tantric Hinduism as well. In Vedanta the worshiper is the godhead; in Tantrism the worshiper can either identify with the goddess or entertain an erotic relationship with her; however, the Bhakti cults (more so in the Vaishnava cults than in the Saivite ones) generally envisioned a male diety and placed the devotee in a paradigmatically feminized position. The bhakta, or devotee (paradigmatically male), visualizes himself as a woman not only because god is male but also because the stance of the ideal devotee is identical with the stance of the ideal woman, for the goal of the bhakta is to become completely open to being penetrated and possessed by the male diety. While this resolutely heterosexual paradigm replicated the conventions of male dominance–female subordination and respected the taboos on overt homosexuality, it required the male worshiper to renounce masculinity and embrace femininity.[84] This requirement, which in extreme and rare cases involved an actual change of sex, more often took the form of transvestism, as in the case of Chaitanya (1486–1538) and Ramakrishna (1836–86), two of the most prominent saints of Bengal, whose spiritual practice combined Bhakti and Tantric traditions.

The bias toward femininity in the stance of the worshiper is also an effect of the nature of the diety when it is visualized as female. Except in

Tantrism, in which a fairly straightforward erotic relationship is entertained between male worshiper and female deity, most other forms of goddess worship are driven by a need to avoid an erotic union that is apprehended as an annihilation. To avoid the fate of lascivious demons, beings typically dominated and killed by the goddess, male worshipers sometimes became transvestites or even eunuchs, just like the bhaktas of male deities. Thus, the male worshiper must become female either to unite with a male god or to avoid uniting with a female mother goddess. Even in the Shakta religion, in which the relationship between male devotee and female deity is conceived in nonerotic terms, the male worshiper becomes female in order to serve the goddess.[85]

In an interesting letter to Freud (Nov. 1929) G. Bose, the first Indian Freudian (and one who actively worked to establish the Indian Psychoanalytic Society), wrote about the necessity to rethink castration anxiety in view of goddess worship in India: "The real struggle lies between the desire to be a male and its opposite the desire to be female . . . The Oedipus mother is very often a combined parental image and this is a fact of great importance. I have reason to believe that much of the motivation of the 'maternal deity' is traceable to this source."[86] Kalpana Seshadri-Crooks characterizes Freud's response to Bose as "nominal and evasive," because Freud's theory "could not accommodate a mother-worshipping polytheist as analyst or subject."[87] Nor could Freud's heteronormatizing theory accommodate the picture Bose was painting of a male desiring *to be* rather than *to have* a female.

Hindu androgyny, however, was widely understood as a symbolic transcendence of gender division rather than as a lived experience of bisexuality that was tolerated more in local folk traditions than in the pan-Hindu traditions. But even in the symbolic realm androgyny was presented as an ideal primarily for men, not women. In Hindu mythological representations androgyny is a predominantly male phenomenon. Thus, contrary to Ashis Nandy's view, Ardhanarishwara, literally "the lord (iswara) who is half (ardha) woman (nari)" is always regarded as a form of Siva, not a form that represents an equal synthesis of Siva-Parvathi. As in Hindu marriage, when Parvati fuses with Siva, she generally becomes half of his body, losing half of her own substance, while he usually becomes enriched by her without losing any of his own substance. Similarly the iconography of the linga (phallus) is regarded as a form of Siva alone even though the linga is always surrounded by the yoni, symbolizing the goddess's sexual organ. Again the Hindu conception of shakti or energy as feminine traditionally refers to the energy of the male.[88] Even in the Bhakti movement, despite the active participation of several women saint-poets, there was a greater tendency to present androgyny as an ideal for the male worshiper.[89]

As this ideal of Hindu masculinity weakened and eroded under colonial assault, androgyny got rescripted as effeminacy, and Hindu men felt forced to reform themselves and their religion in the image of a muscular, monotheistic, heterosexual, masculine Protestantism. Here we see a situation of what James Scott characterizes as genuine or total hegemony—a situation where, the oppressed group hopes it will eventually exercise over others (not its present oppressors, though) the domination it endures today, where there are "strong incentives to legitimate patterns of domination," thus cancelling the hidden transcripts of contempt for the oppressor and turning into self-contempt.[90] The shift from a positive notion of androgyny toward a negative image of effeminacy is most sharply dramatized in the difference between Ramakrishna and his star disciple, Vivekananda. Ramakrishna was perhaps the last prominent Hindu saint to embrace androgyny credibly both as a spiritual goal and as a method for achieving transcendence. His performance of Hinduism, involving explicit transvestism and implicit homoeroticism, did not really engage colonialism in a contest of manliness. By contrast, Vivekananda's virile Hinduism, like his hard gendering, was locked in a Manichean battle with colonialism and, consequently, carried with it all the normative trappings of colonial masculinity. Attributing contemporary Hindu weakness or emasculation to loss of textual Brahmanism and social Kshatriyahood—a loss that had robbed Hindus of those original Aryan qualities they shared with Westerners—he tried to turn Hinduism into an organized monotheism (albeit a goddess-centered one), complete with The Book (the Vedas and the Gita), priests (order of monks), and even missionaries.[91] Echoing the novelist Bankim Chandra Chatterjee, this activist monk, who declared manliness to be his "new gospel," preached that the androgynous motifs of Hindu mythology were dissolute, enervating and effeminate.[92] "Who cares what your scriptures say?" he asked defiantly. "I will go into a thousand hells cheerfully if I can arouse my countrymen, immersed in darkness, to stand on their own feet and be men inspired with the spirit of Karma yoga."[93] Attempting to arouse his followers to action, Vivekananda admonished them: "No more weeping, but stand on your feet and be men. It is a man-making religion I want. I want the strength, manhood, kshatravirya or the virility of a warrior."[94] Musing that "the older I grow, the more everything seems to me to lie in manliness,"[95] this stellar student of Ramakrishna prayed, "O Thou Mother of the Universe, vouchsafe manliness unto me—Make me a man!"[96]

The Bengali male's self-perception of effeminacy was also an effect of the struggle for hegemony by an elite community under the conditions of nineteenth-century colonialism. Manhood in colonial society, as Tanika Sarkar shows, was based on a particular relationship to property—a relationship that was gradually eroded for the Bengali middle class in the second half of the nineteenth century. Combined with the gradual decline in the fortunes of the landed classes, Bengali elites were being defined more and more in terms of professional and administrative employment. The majority found their horizons severely contracted by petty clerical work. Indeed, the ignominious experience of petty clerical work, according to Tanika Sarkar, underpinned the self-perception of effeminacy among the Bengali elites. Thus, at a time when the Bengali elite still refrained from direct criticism of colonial rule, it expressed its hegemonic aspirations not by assuming economic and political leadership but by attributing to the male physique all the ravages and despair of colonial rule.[97] Ashis Nandy is therefore quite correct in his perception that most pre-Gandhian reform and protest movements ended up legitimizing the very model of masculinity they sought to resist because they accepted, rather than altered, the terms of colonial discourse.[98]

Effeminacy, as mimicry or hybridization, however, did provide an opportunity for tactical intervention—an opportunity that Gandhi was to use very effectively. Benita Parry has pointed out that Bhabha's theory of mimicry effectively renders "visible those moments when colonial discourse already disturbed at its source by a doubleness of enunciation, is further subverted by the object of its address; when the scenario written by colonialism is given a performance by the native that estranges and undermines the colonialist script."[99] Gandhi's tactical reformulation of effeminacy as androgyny represents just such an estrangement or undermining of a colonialist script. In contrast to the early militant phase of Indian nationalism, Gandhian nationalism, Ashis Nandy contends, undermined the imperialist ethos of hypermasculinity by delinking courage and activism from aggression and violence and making them compatible with certain forms of femininity.[100] Or, as I would like to argue, with certain forms of effeminacy. In other words, I am suggesting that Gandhi strategically drew upon premodern Christianity (he claimed to have taken nonviolence from the Sermon on the Mount) as well as traditional Hindu images of positive androgyny and dynamic womanhood to elaborate an alternative model of masculinity,

not femininity. Contrary to Nandy's view, Gandhian androgyny is neither an equal bisexual fusion of male and female nor an asexual transcendence of male and female; rather, what Gandhi devised was a coun-
termodel of masculinity, one that selectively incorporated certain Hindu
conceptions of femininity for use by Indian men in their fight against
colonialism. Its effect on the material lives of Indian women therefore
proved to be both uneven as well as limited.

Contrary to what Nandy implies, Gandhian gender ideology did
not radically alter Indian conceptions of womanhood or wholly liberate
Indian women from conventional roles. In Gandhian nationalism, as in
various forms of anticolonial Hindu militancy and subaltern insurgency, femininity, particularly maternity, serves as an important discursive site for the mobilization of male interests and aspirations. The
maternal figure in Hindu iconography incorporates a dialectical tension
between the virulent, potently sexual Kali and Durga, her docile,
domesticated counterpart. Most varieties of elite Hindu militancy and
subaltern insurgency had traditionally embraced the more aggressive
symbol of female energy; Gandhi, on the other hand, upheld the domestic ideal, emphasizing moral qualities such as patience, self-sacrifice,
and suffering. In challenging nationalist historiography, which typically
subsumes female liberation under the grand narrative of national liberation, Indian feminist scholarship has identified the domestic ideal as an
important inhibiting factor in Gandhian gender ideology.[101] While
Gandhi's maternal domestic ideal clearly inhibited radical change in
Indian women's lives, it is important to note that neither elite nor subaltern insurgent movements that worshiped man-eating goddesses did
much better. Instances of goddess-worshiping communities vehemently
opposing female leadership can be found in the historiography of the
Subaltern Studies collective, although the historian, like the subaltern
male himself, remains indifferent to the critical disjunction between the
symbolic and historical roles of women. In a sympathetic critique of
Subaltern Studies Gayatri Spivak demonstrates that the tropological construction of the subaltern as insurgent produces a model of agency that
cannot accommodate the sexed subaltern.[102] Thus, while goddesses as
icons of worship and women as objects of exchange appear at crucial
moments in the historiography of the Subaltern Studies collective for
explaining the mobilization of peasants across villages, the historians do
not raise questions about the absent text of subaltern women's consciousness as they do about peasant insurgency in elite historiography.

The problematic of the Indian woman as signifier in heterogeneous discursive sites, it would appear, must necessarily take into account her function as a transactional token in the homosocial struggle between English imperialism and Indian nationalism. I therefore view Gandhian ideology as an effort to construct an oppositional model of masculinity for Indian men, rather than as an intervention into the lives of Indian women. When viewed this way, Gandhi's selective utilization of femininity makes strategic sense, since it incorporates precisely those qualities imperial culture had devalued as effeminate. What Gandhi managed to do was tap the ambiguities and contradictions that mimicry produced in the economy of effeminism and turn them to political advantage.

Women and Homosocial Colonialism

Absolutely necessary yet eminently dispensable, women are the circuitry through which colonial desire flows, the conduit through which collusions and collisions between colonizing and colonized men are conducted. Nineteenth-century colonial ideology and politics are marked by the historic emergence of womanhood as the most powerful signifier of cultural superiority. Indeed, one of the most common liberal justifications for the extension of colonial rule and for the maintenance of the civilizing mission is the imputed barbarity of the treatment of women within the culture under attack. The social status of women thus became the ultimate and unequivocal measure of civil society. In his influential *History of British India* James Mill, one of the foremost exponents of moral imperialism, contrasts the "exalted" status of British women with the degraded condition of Indian women as a way of establishing the unmanliness of Hindu society.[103] The treatment of widows in Hindu society and the practice of sati became the most spectacularly visible signs of colonized female oppression. By making the treatment of women an important determinant of manhood, and therefore a critical sign of civilization, the imperial project was narrativized in moral terms as a case of "white men rescuing brown women from brown men."[104] From Jules Verne's *Around the World in Eighty Days* (1873) and Flora Annie Steel's *On the Face of the Waters* (1897) to M. M. Kaye's *The Far Pavilions* (1978), the ideological production of a chivalric model of English manhood invariably involves the rescue of the Indian woman, particularly the sati, from the clutches of a barbaric Indian patriarchy.[105] Sati continued to exercise the European imagination long after it was legally abolished in 1929, and, interestingly, sati continues to dominate post-colonial perspectives of India.

In projecting themselves as champions of women, the British were far more concerned with emasculating or effeminizing Indian men than with emancipating women. Feminist historians have shown that nine-teenth-century social reforms aimed at improving the lives of Indian women were motivated more by political expediency than by humani-tarian concern. Moreover, since colonial lawmakers were acting in accordance with Victorian gender ideologies when legislating over such matters as sati, child marriage, and widow remarriage, in many cases they effectively "rescued" Indian women from one form of male domi-nance only to subject them to another. Lata Mani has persuasively argued that Indian women were neither the subjects nor the objects of colonial discourses on sati but, rather, the ground upon which coloniz-ing and colonized men confronted and negotiated the moral challenges of colonial rule. Similarly, Mrinalini Sinha's discussion of the 1891 Age of Consent Act, which sought to regulate child marriages in India, shows that the moral principle of female emancipation was not the real concern of legislators, who were always willing to subordinate the women's question to the pursuit of economic and political power. Despite its liberal and humanitarian rhetoric, Sinha shows, the Age of Consent Act became an arena in which English men exhibited their dis-dain of Bengali manhood, while Bengali men, in turn, tried to reassert their masculinity. To the colonizer the Indian woman was primarily a tool for demonstrating the inferiority of indigenous masculinity. To the colonized she became an instrument for reclaiming their lost manhood, a device for renewing a defunct patriarchy.[106]

While the social reforms that emerged out of the homosocial strug-gles between English and Indian men incidentally ameliorated the Indian woman's life to an extent, imperial intervention often had a con-tradictory and ironic effect upon her material life. Not only was she newly subjected to the control of British patriarchy, her subjugation in Indian society was perpetuated, albeit in a modified or altered form. The disarming and disempowering presence of the colonial state shut out Indian men from public political authority and denied them access to the main instruments of state power. Yet out of this general disempow-erment the British rulers found a variety of means through which to re-empower groups of Indian men at different levels of colonial society. In fact, the colonial construction of the Indian male as effeminate actually led to an intensification of indigenous patriarchal structures as Indian men, denied participation in the public arena, began to exercise increasing authority in the private realm. Through a gradual severance of Hindu social relations and ritual practices from politics, the state produced a depoliticized socioreligious sphere, implicitly defined in terms of contemporary Western distinctions between public and private domains and explicitly defined, especially after the Sepoy Mutiny of 1857, by state assurances of noninterference in the private socioreligious concerns of Indian subjects. In Western political contexts the distinctions between private and public were employed ideologically to emphasize the personal freedoms of the individual. In the colonial context these distinctions juxtaposed the realm of the state's competence not with that of individuals but of Hindu communities. This historical process had some important consequences for gender relations and gender ideology in colonial society. On the one hand, it pushed Indian women ever more deeply into the privatized domain of the home over which Indian men were assured complete and unqualified control. On the other hand, it effeminized Indian men by mystifying and essentializing the newly constituted private domain as the true site of Hindu/Indian identity, which was nevertheless defined in feminine terms as excessive, passive, inert, conservative, dependent, and irrational.[107]

Constituted as the privileged object of colonial salvation, the Indian woman also served as an important site for nineteenth-century English feminist individualism. Rather than contesting the moral superiority and the concomitant desexualization imposed upon them by Victorian patriarchy, early English feminists empowered themselves as "mothers of the race" and as "companionate colonialists."[108] By casting themselves in the role of maternal saviors, they adopted the secluded Indian woman as the object of their own unique female salvationist project and thereby negotiated an acceptable, albeit limited, entry into public life.

The entry of white women in large number into the homosocial arena of colonial India signals the emergence of an anomaly in colonial hierarchy, since the English woman embodies a contradictory combination of sexual subordination and racial domination. These contradictions are most sharply visible during the Sepoy Mutiny of 1857, an important historical moment that constituted the English woman as the innocent sex victim of a degenerate and rapacious Indian male. The tropology of rape highlights in a particularly stark manner the simultaneous exploitation and exclusion of women in colonial politics. The positioning of white women as sex victims of dark indigenous males allowed English men to crush a challenge to colonial rule ruthlessly by casting themselves in the role of righteous avengers and chivalric protectors. Describing white woman as the "absent center" around which colonial allegories of rape and race revolve, Jenny Sharpe has suggested that "a crisis in British authority is managed through the circulation of the violated bodies of English women as a sign for the violation of colonialism." Sharpe thus finds English womanhood emerging as "an important cultural signifier for articulating a colonial hierarchy of race."[109] Within the interpretive parameters of colonial homosociality the rape of English women by Indian men is both intended and interpreted as a political challenge to English men. Indian nationalists shared the masculinist understanding of rape as an assault on men rather than as a violation of women. The "Ravishment Proclamations," issued by Indian nationalists in the aftermath of the Amritsar massacre of 1919 in which unarmed Indians were shot down by the imperial army, equates the sexual humiliation of women with an indirect attack upon men. Tactically deploying the image of the dark rapist against the British, Indian nationalists put out incendiary posters calling for the "dishonor" of English "ladies." The violated white female body could thus serve as a mobilizing site not only for imperialists but for nationalists as well.[110]

By becoming both a public spectacle and an object of white male salvation during the mutiny, the English woman in India ironically came to occupy a position similar to that of the Indian sati, functioning, like her, as a transactional token in the homosocial power struggle between colonizing and colonized men. The question of whether the Indian man could be trusted to exercise political or judicial power over English women dominates debates in post-Mutiny India, debates in which the women themselves often played an active and public role. The Illbert Bill controversy of 1883–84 represents one such important moment in which the sexual vulnerability of the white female body was used to deny Indian men access to political participation. Thus, the presence of the English woman at once emasculated the Indian male and constituted him as a sexual threat.

White male response to the increased visibility of their women in the public life of the colony was typically ambivalent. While the decline in sexual liaisons between British men and Indian women brought on by the arrival of British wives had been viewed approvingly by evangelicals, colonial administrators saw the women, especially after 1857, as obstacles to intimate contact with Indian culture and society. From the administrator's perspective a wife and family made demands upon a man's time and took him away from his colonial duties. The literature of the Raj reflects this attitude toward English women in India. Although most Anglo-Indian novels maintain the decorums of hetero-sexuality—men marry, have affairs, visit prostitutes—the women in-volved in colonial transactions, when they are not hollowed out into conduits for interracial male friendships, are typically devalued as dis-tractions to masculine pursuits or marginalized as impediments to male solidarity. Thus, in Kipling's *Kim* (1901) the young hero loquaciously complains, "how can a man follow the Way or the Great Game when he is so always pestered by women?"[111] And in E. M. Forster's *A Passage to India* (1924) Turton, the district collector, retains "a contemptuous affec-tion for the pawns he had moved about for so many years, they must be worth his pains," but is annoyed at the women whom he silently blames for making "everything difficult out here."[112] Turton's feelings are echoed loudly in the literature and historiography of the Raj. And even in recent years English men have blamed the women for the loss of empire.[113]

The Raj, as many have recognized, was founded on an intimate bond between English administrator, soldier, or spy and the Indian men they ruled, subjugated, and controlled.[114] Ashis Nandy points out that the ambivalence of white males often compelled Anglo-Indian women to regard themselves as the "sexual competitors of Indian men, with whom their men had established an unconscious homoeroticized bond-ing."[115] At the same time, the racial fear of rape that the Sepoy Mutiny had produced led to an intensification of patriarchal controls over En-glish women in India. Consequently, the Anglo-Indian woman often found herself confined in homes, hill stations, cantonments, com-pounds, and clubs, living a life of segregation that was not very differ-ent from that of the Indian woman she deplored. Based on a reading of Flora Annie Steel's *On the Face of the Waters,* I will argue that the intense resentment and rivalry between English and Indian women that such unacceptable contiguity provoked, stage-managed by an interested patriarchy, marks out the extent and limit of late-nineteenth-century British imperial feminism.

The writings of Anglo-Indian women like Flora Annie Steel amply attest to the fact that these women, like their Indian counterparts, found themselves caught in the homosocial crossfire between colonizing and colonized men. While I draw attention to this symbolic or structural similarity in order to highlight the instrumentality of both Indian and English women in colonial society, I hasten to add that it does not warrant an equation between the historical positioning of white and brown women, because English women's access to domestic companionship and social independence, the norms of nineteenth-century feminism, is in fact grounded in and guaranteed by the negative presence of the silent, passive Indian woman. Their histories, neither same nor separate but intersecting, point to contradictions in the categories of race and gender that homosocial colonialism thrived upon.

3

Manufacturing Masculinity

The Beginnings

The cult of masculinity, which was a dominant element of late-nine-teenth-century British colonialism in India, is a historical product overdetermined by various intersecting ideologies that are metropolitan as well as colonial. From the eighteenth-century onward English masculinity grounds itself in a paternal code of hygiene expressed in terms of a fundamental opposition between the hoarding of energy—sexual, economic, political—and its vital squandering, leading to dissolution or death. Parliamentary debates over England's role in India dramatize a profound struggle within English society between those who wished to pursue an aggressive, unrestrained policy of imperial expansion and those who advocated a more disciplined, controlled approach to colo-nization. This conflict reflects, in part, a class struggle between the aris-tocracy and the emerging classes, which saw the empire as a means to quick riches. The charges brought first against Robert Clive and later against Warren Hastings for rapaciously plundering India exhibit a volatile mixture of jealousy, anxiety, and guilt over England's belligerent and voracious policy of colonial expansion. In *The Rhetoric of English India* Sara Suleri has drawn attention to the way in which Edmund Burke's speeches invoke the categories of class and gender to indict Hastings. The social aggression of returning Indian "nabobs" and the threat it poses to the class hierarchy is one of the points Burke implicitly emphasizes. In another instance colonized women supply Burke with a powerful rhetorical weapon against Hastings. In his lurid descriptions of physical tortures and sexual assaults perpetrated by Hastings's minions upon vulnerable, virginal, female bodies, Suleri finds the figure of rape functioning both as a deflector from and a facilitator of male embattlement.[1]

As the English middle class gained economic and political muscle, it attempted to establish its sociocultural identity by specifically rejecting what it saw as aristocratic profligacy and decadence and by defining itself in terms of respectability, moderation, frugality, and common sense. With the rise of evangelicalism, English masculinity began to be firmly cast in bourgeois terms of duty, discipline, and restraint, although the aristocratic code of chivalry was strategically assimilated to fit the needs of a rising class in an expanding empire. British colonialism also began to acquire the definite ideological underpinnings of the civilizing mission. The historical producers and products of evangelical masculinity are men like Charles Grant and Thomas Babington Macaulay, men noted for turning away from the more "Orientalist" colonial policies of Warren Hastings toward a more interventionist policy aimed at producing a culturally/linguistically homogeneous English India. In fiction the ideals of evangelical manliness are perhaps best exemplified by the coldhearted, duty-bound, self-immolating St. John Rivers in Charlotte Brontë's *Jane Eyre* (1847). "Evangelical manhood, with its stress on self-sacrifice and influence, came dangerously close to embracing 'feminine' qualities," explain Leonore Davidoff and Catherine Hall, and so manliness was reinforced through a control of emotions, the religious duty of work, and, above all else, the separation of a "woman's sphere."[2] Thus, while Jane Eyre (opposing herself to the passive Hindu sati) asserts her individuality and will by rejecting St. John's attempts to coerce her into joining the India Missions as his "incorporated wife,"[3] she finally gains access to agency only (as Rochester's wife) within a space that, although reorganized, is nevertheless still segregated as feminine. As woman, Jane does not have access to the heroic Christian allegory of self-sacrifice and martyrdom that St. John writes himself into. So, resigning the moral imperative of the civilizing mission to St. John, Brontë's novel carves out a domestic sphere for Jane by conflating the feminine virtue of self-sacrifice with self-fulfillment.

Although *Jane Eyre* leaves the gendered division of spheres intact, domesticity provides a condition of possibility for women's entry into public life, as in decades to come middle-class English women expanded the domestic ideal in a manner that permitted them to take on duties outside the home, including the larger arena of empire.

Encouraged by evangelicals, Victorian women used the idiom of motherhood to empower themselves as moral mothers and social redeemers. In this capacity they adopted the colonized races as ignorant wayward "children" in need of maternal guidance. Enthusiastically absorbing evangelical values such as moral purity, nurturing, and childcare as intrinsically "feminine" virtues, Victorian women deliberately cultivated the civilizing responsibility as their own special burden because it affirmed an emancipatory role for them.[4] Thus, by mid-nineteenth century an increasing number of women were going out on civilizing missions, often with a husband or brother and, at times, even alone.

But, if collusion with evangelical imperialism expedited English female emancipation, it also freshly recontained women, especially those in the colonies, within the material and ideological structures of patriarchal imperialism. Missionary work was considered particularly dangerous for women, since it involved close contact with native populations. It was believed that women who lacked sufficient religious fervor would succumb to the allure of the East or disintegrate in the hot tropical climate. In India arguments for racial purity and female vulnerability, when yoked with stereotypes of native decadence, forged strong chains to imprison English women within hill stations, cantonments, and clubs. Moreover, the Anglo-Indian practice of employing native nurses to care for infants, while sending older children away to be educated for colonial service in England, deprived white motherhood of its progeny. The women who had used the idiom of motherhood to gain access to the public arena of empire thus found themselves unable to influence the lives of the children they produced for the empire. The physical and psychological damage caused by the separation of mother and child is a subject to which Anglo-Indian writers from Mary Martha Sherwood and Harriet Tytler to Flora Annie Steel and Rudyard Kipling repeatedly return. The idiom of motherhood (along with childhood) thus emerges as a deeply divided emblem of colonial power in Anglo-Indian writing.[5]

The white woman in India is an anomalous figure who embodies a contradictory combination of superior race but inferior sex. In this she curiously mirrors the Indian man as superior sex but inferior race. Rather than trying to "resolve" these contradictions by collapsing the categories of race and gender, I shall attempt to examine the ways in which these anomalies were elaborated and used to consolidate the image of colonial masculinity at a critical juncture in the history of the Raj.

The Crystallization of Colonial Masculinity

The Sepoy Mutiny of 1857 marks an important historical moment in which the contradictions of race and gender in colonial India were brought to a crisis. Colonial historiography produced in the aftermath of the event generated a whole mythology of excess and restraint to rationalize and justify colonial violence. Shutting out the possibility of widespread discontent with colonial rule, the mutiny was depoliticized into a mythic conflict between gods and demons, heroes and villains, between the forces of good and evil, civilization and savagery, order and chaos, faith and fanaticism, reason and superstition, knowledge and ignorance, light and darkness, manliness and effeminacy. In this discursive process the ideological categories of race, class, and gender were freshly elaborated, transformed, and reconstituted to fit the changing needs of colonial rule.

The mutiny, which quickly spread to many parts of northern and central India, began on May 10, 1857, with the revolt of the Bengal Army in Meerut against its officers. The British community was taken unawares as the mutineers marched from Meerut and seized Delhi. At Delhi they proclaimed Bahadur Shah, a weak old Mughal king, as emperor of Hindustan. The most notorious instance of insurrection was at Cawnpore (Kanpur), where, under the leadership of Nana Sahib, the mutineers surrounded the British garrison and forced a surrender in return for safe passage to Allahabad. But news of a British advance on a rescue mission reached Cawnpore, resulting in the execution of about four hundred English soldiers, and about three hundred and seventy-six women and children, who were put to death in the Bibighar, or the "House of the Ladies."[6] This rather exceptional event, enshrined in the collective British imagination as "the Cawnpore massacre," came to symbolize three powerful ideas: white female vulnerability, Indian excessiveness, and the need for white men to extract revenge but to do so without abandoning their sense of restraint and civility.

By September 1857 British forces had rallied and recaptured Delhi. By the summer of 1858 they had regained control of Lucknow and Oudh, and, even though large-scale fighting continued in many parts of the country, British success was assured. In the early stages of the mutiny, however, a strange and horrifying tale spread throughout Anglo-India and even found its way back to England. According to the story, the mutineers were committing "unspeakable atrocities" on "our countrywomen." Natives, the story had it, were systematically raping

English women and dismembering their ravished bodies. Although the rumors were quickly discredited as having no factual basis, the events of 1857, quickly reduced to "the Cawnpore massacre," went on record as a barbaric attack by dark Indian savages on innocent white women and children. The stories of rape, although seldom proved, served to inflame public opinion in Anglo-India and England, particularly because they constituted the white woman as the paradigmatic sex victim of the dark Indian male. While Indian rumors of being raped by British soldiers were dismissed as gossip and lies, Anglo-Indian rumors were transformed into facts, as English newspapers, journals, and pamphlets printed the rape stories without even investigating their sources. Hiding behind a code of decency, the reports withheld details about the unspeakable atrocities even as they generated, through hints and innuendoes, enormous desire and fear around what they did not say.[7] The official colonial understanding of the mutiny as the desecration of English womanhood continues to be reproduced by contemporary writers such as Pat Barr, who in *The Memsahibs: The Women of Victorian India* writes that in Cawnpore "one of the most revered of Victorian institutions, the English lady, was slaughtered, defiled and brought low."[8]

Challenging such a colonialist interpretation, Jenny Sharpe's study *Allegories of Empire: The Figure of Woman in the Colonial Text* demonstrates how a violent reproduction of gender roles in stories of rape—stories that first emerged during the Sepoy Mutiny and resurfaced during subsequent crises in colonial India—appropriates the English woman as the sex victim of anticolonial rebellion in order to manage or contain political challenges to British authority. The circulation of the violated bodies of English women as a sign for the violation of colonialism, Sharpe argues, prepared the ground for new modes of domination even as it allowed preexisting ones to be reestablished ever more firmly. Sharpe thus finds English/Victorian womanhood emerging as an important cultural signifier for articulating a colonial hierarchy of race.[9] Sharpe's argument about the instrumentality of English women/womanhood in colonial rape stories strongly supports my reading of British colonialism as a homosocial transaction because the basic ideological function of the colonial rape narrative is to establish the Indian male's failure to behave in accordance with the code of chivalry, a preeminent Victorian index of civil society. What I am attempting to do here, however, is to trace how the production of white-woman-as-rape-victim in mutiny narratives helped to elaborate and reconstitute the ideologeme of effeminacy to fit the changed needs of colonialism in post-mutiny India.

When the uprisings began in 1857, the British, lulled by long-stand-ing stereotypes of sepoy loyalty and Hindu passivity, had been taken completely by surprise. The notion of Indian, especially Hindu, effemi-nacy had served to explain the history of India's subjugation to a series of invaders including the Mughals, even as it allowed the British to cast themselves as simply the latest yet fittest of conquerors who would lead India, with the consent of the natives, out of the jungle of Oriental despotism into the garden of self-government. The idea of English colo-nialism as a "civilizing mission based on rule by consent" not only served to distinguish the British from other previous conquerors, but it also produced among a section of Indians a desire for Western knowl-edge and, by extension, for British rule. Thus, in the decade preceding the mutiny the English-educated urban Bengali elite, with access to the publishing businesses, constituted, for all practical purposes, "the native public opinion."[10] And, not surprisingly, this Westernized Ben-gali elite openly opposed the 1857 revolt, thereby providing an ideolog-ical alibi and a moral justification for colonial rule.

The Sepoy Mutiny was not simply the military insubordination its name suggests but, rather, a wave of uprisings, fought on several, often relatively autonomous fronts, in which Indian soldiers, princes, reli-gious leaders, and peasants all played a role.[11] Historians have shown the rebellion to be a culmination of Indian resentment against colonial policies and practices in spheres ranging from annexation of territories, military recruitment, and agrarian reforms.[12] The dramatic display of widespread indigenous discontent, which the uprisings signified, not only challenged the image of English colonialism as civilizing mission based on consent, but it brought deeply held beliefs in Indian passivity to an impasse. Colonial historiographers often tried to draw on preex-isting stereotypes of Asiatic effeminacy to explain or accommodate the violence of anticolonial insurgency. Writing in 1858, Alexander Duff observes: "Throughout all ages the Asiatic has been noted for his duplic-ity, cunning, hypocrisy, treachery; and coupled with this . . . his capacity of secrecy and concealment. But in vain will the annals even of Asia be ransacked for examples of artful, refined, consummate duplicity, sur-passing those which have been exhibited throughout the recent mutinies."[13] The contradiction presented by the mild Hindu as a perpe-trator of crimes against defenseless English women and children is vis-ible in a Bombay letter writer's exclamation: "But, oh, the savage mind never yet conceived the atrocities which these civilized savages have committed . . . The exquisite nature of the torture they inflict has something awful in it."[14] Since the Hindu male was considered to be cruel yet physically weak, duplicitous rather than savage, colonial historiographers often identified the Muslim as the perpetrator of the most violent crimes. As members of an imperial race deposed by the British, the Muslims were suspected of harboring a secret desire to take revenge and restore Mughal despotism. Scapegoating the Muslim could not, however, completely restore British confidence in the sepoys, many of whom were Hindu. So, the repertoire of effeminacy was expanded by casting the Hindu as an incorrigibly conservative, excessively religious, emotionally volatile, morally misguided child.

Accordingly, the origins of the uprising were attributed to an unfounded rumor about religious pollution. Sepoys, who were otherwise loyal and trustworthy, had gone on a rampage because they had been deceived by a false belief that the cartridges of a new Enfield rifle had been greased with beef and pork fat. In a widely read account of the 1857 uprisings Ascott Hope writes that "many [mutineers], if not most, were hurried into it by panic or excitement, or the persuasion of the more designing, and their hearts soon misgave them when they saw the fruit of their wild deeds, still more when they considered the punishment likely to follow."[15] Colonial historiography typically traces English victory and Indian defeat to personal character rather than to military might. Even in initial defeat the British are seen to display qualities that foreshadow their final victory. In his monumental history of the mutiny John Kaye describes the mutineers as weak and impulsive, while he attributes to the British soldier "that calm confidence which betrays no sign of misgiving, and the very quietude that indicates a consciousness of strength."[16] The quick disintegration of the rebellion and the anarchy that followed is attributed to the emotional temperament of the native, who is portrayed as being inconsistent both in loyalty and in rebellion. Reproducing the colonialist view, Christopher Hibbert, author of one of the most popular modern histories of the mutiny, describes the sepoys as being "misled by rumours," instigated by prostitutes "taunting them with their failure," and joined by "badmashes from the bazaar" and "bands of marauders . . . from the surrounding villages."[17]

Stories of a British conspiracy to sabotage the religious proscriptions of both Hindus and Muslims, like the many rumors and prophecies that circulated in the bazaars during the mutiny, are not so much the signs of superstitious fears as expressions of distrust or dissatisfaction with colonial rule and, more importantly, a statement of communal alliance. Rumors, Ranajit Guha has shown, are an effective form of com-

munication and mobilization in preliterate societies. Due to their anonymous origins and ambiguous signification, rumors can be rearticulated
at any point along their line of transmission. The dismissal, devaluation,
and delegitimization of rumor as mere gossip springs from an official
view of truth that is inevitably blind to the sign systems of subaltern
resistance.[18] Guha has also identified the switch from a religious to a
militant code as critical to the operations of anticolonial insurgency.
Thus, popular rebellions in colonial India often began as religious fundamentalism and later adopted the code of political militancy. Colonial
authorities, slow to recognize this process, invariably dismissed signs of
unrest as religious conflict. Guha sees this cognitive failure as symptomatic of the inertia that make it difficult for an alien authoritarian
regime to grasp promptly enough the meaning of a quick change in tem-
per among a habitually docile mass of peasantry.[19] He points out that
colonial discourse is marked by a reduction of the semantic range of
many words and expressions to which specialized meanings are
assigned in order to identify rebellious peasants as criminals. Thus,
dacoit village would indicate the entire population of a village united in
resistance to the armed forces of the state; *contagion*, the enthusiasm and
solidarity generated by an uprising among various rural groups within
a region; *fanatics*, rebels inspired by some kind of revivalist or puritani-
cal doctrines; *lawlessness*, the defiance by the people of what they had
come to regard as bad laws; and so on.[20]

The main focus of colonial histories and newspaper reports of the
Sepoy Mutiny is the sexual vulnerability of English women. In these
accounts, which repeatedly stage the ravaged white female body as a
public spectacle, English women are reduced to the vulnerability of
their sex. Even when women are occasionally praised, it is their moral
fortitude that is stressed. Jenny Sharpe points out that the mutiny narratives demand the victim be a "lady," a class-specific term with a definite
notion of female chastity that confines female agency to a woman's
choice of death over dishonor. Indeed, what determines a woman's
membership in the English race, Sharpe suggests, is less her racial or
class origin than her choice of death over dishonor.[21] Female moral fortitude thus becomes the sign of racial purity. The feminized place of
what it means to be rapable in the mutiny reports bears not only a class-
specific but also a race-oriented inscription of what it means to be an
English lady. So, on one level the ideological production of white
woman as victim excludes working-class white women, who "appear
only as an absence, between the interstices of a chivalrous code that

demanded the victim be a lady."[22] On another level it also eliminates the possibility of Indian women being targets of British attacks. Not only do mutiny reports remain silent about the treatment of Indian women by British troops, but some go to great lengths to prove that, unlike the treacherous sepoys, British soldiers exhibited great restraint and did not assault or murder defenseless women.[23] In fact, contrary to Western stereotypes of Oriental female passivity, Indian women appear in the mutiny reports as the instigators of the worst offenses. As colonial representations of the warrior queen of Jhansi, considered responsible for a massacre second only to that at Cawnpore and known to the British as the "Jezebel of India," illustrate, the paradigmatic Indian woman of the mutiny is a decidedly masculine one. Sir Hugh Rose, the officer who finally defeated the Rani, reportedly said of her that "the Indian Mutiny has produced but one man, and that man was a woman."[24] Jenny Sharpe quotes a report in the *Bombay Times* that shows the Rani ordering her soldiers to rape, humiliate, and torture English women. The Rani exercises a power of speech that is capable of violating English womanhood, even though, as a woman, she herself cannot perform that violence. The difficulty in transforming a stereotypically passive Indian woman into a killer and a rapist, Sharpe observes, is overcome by sexually positioning her as the inciter of male lusts.[25] Thus, behind the rapes and mutilations carried out by Indian men on white female bodies looms the monstrous figure of the masculine Indian woman.

If, as Sharpe contends, the discursive positioning of the white woman as rape victim and the white man as her savior violently "reproduces" gender roles,[26] the construction of the Indian woman as an unwomanly virago and the Indian man as her passive agent, I suggest, violently *reverses* gender roles in ways that have two important ideological effects. First, the process of masculinization *excludes Indian women* from the gendered category of "woman" as such and thereby forecloses the possibility of her sharing the space of "innocent victim" alongside the English lady. Second, the reversal of gender roles *neutralizes anticolonial insurgency by "unmanning" the Indian male.* Even as Indian men were brutalized for allegedly raping English ladies, the military/political threat their mutiny posed to colonial authority was contained, if not negated, by casting them as weak puppets jerked around by unwomanly women. Indian masculinity was thus discredited by the double move of either highlighting the unnatural influence of women/femininity in Indian culture or emphasizing the Indian devaluation of women as evidenced by misogynistic practices (such as sati) in Indian society and confirmed by the treatment of English women during the mutiny. The differential treatment of women was offered as explanation, even justification, for the brutality with which the mutiny was crushed. In a contemporary version of this understanding Christopher Hibbert writes: "To the mid-nineteenth century British mind, this ruthless murder of women and children was a crime of unspeakable, blasphemous enormity. Englishmen regarded women in a light quite different from that in which the Indians did, as creatures not merely of another sex but almost—if they were not mere drudges—of another form of creation, as (in T. H. Huxley's phrase), 'angels above them.' "[27]

Mutiny accounts also largely bypass the mutilation of white men at the hands of the mutineers to linger over the details of what was done to the women. The almost exclusive focus to be found in the mutiny reports on the terrifying crimes against women, Sharpe rightly argues, displaces attention away from the image of English men being dismembered and slaughtered by insurgents, since the fragmentation and death of the male body would symbolically place British men in the objectified space of the rape victim—a status that would negate colonial authority at the precise moment when it needed reinforcing.[28] Yet this repressed content, as I will show in my discussion of Kipling's tales, returns with increased force in the "Imperial Gothic" of the 1880s and 1890s. Produced during a time when the empire, "seemingly so stable, was growing ever more fragile,"[29] these tales of possession, dismemberment, and death make available a startling thematic of white male rape in colonial literature.

But in 1857 the ideological production of the English lady as the sole sex victim of a barbaric Indian male effectively provided a rationale for white men to extract revenge and helped consolidate the image of English men as chivalric champions of the weak and defenseless. The code of chivalry legitimized retribution and repression, allowing English men to exercise increasing authority over Indian men in the name of victimized womanhood. Mutiny historiography depicts the brutality with which the rebellion was crushed as the uncontrollable rage of honorable men who were responding to the knowledge that the sanctity of their homes had been violated. Pointing to the ways in which Colin Campbell's *Narrative of the Indian Revolt* forces the reader to experience the horror of sexual violence from a male perspective, Jenny Sharpe suggests that what is significant to the author is not that any woman has been subjected to "native atrocities" but that "*women who are the property of English men*" have been violated.[30] Acting as fathers, brothers, and husbands, English men reasserted their claim over what was "rightfully theirs" by protecting the victims and punishing the offenders. The victims' honor was defended by making the punishment fit or exceed the crime. For instance, when a British force under General Henry Havelock stormed Cawnpore, they punished the sepoys deemed responsible for the killings by forcing them to lick the bloodstains of the murdered Britons before being hanged.[31] Conducted as highly ritualized affairs and articulated in terms of "duty" and "punishment," such spectacular acts of revenge simultaneously served to maximize native terror and restore colonial authority.[32]

The excessive brutality with which British forces retaliated and crushed the Sepoy Mutiny, however, posed a problem, since it contradicted colonial claims of civility and restraint. As the following passage illustrates, the hysterical "panic" driving the imperialist to imitate the very intemperance he claims to control produces enormous cognitive and textual strains in colonial historiography: "in the English, as well as in all Imperial races, there is an element of the wild beast. There is a disposition which has shown itself, once and again, in the hour of provocation or of panic to indulge in wild reprisals or even in deliberate revenge long after all justification, or even excuse for it, has ceased."[33] The picture of the British as royal beasts, magnificent even in revenge, unwittingly exposes the underlying congruence between colonial strategies of insurgency and counterinsurgency, between the modalities of strength and weakness, between the manifestations of hypermasculinity and effeminacy. It also points to a cognitive failure or frustration, suggesting that effeminacy marks the tropological boundary of colonial representation.

Colonial historiography does not so much censor the excessive brutality of colonial response as attempt to symbolically "resolve" the ideological contradiction of restoring civility through brutality. It does this by generating a whole mythology that dramatizes a romantic but tragic struggle within the British character between the opposing forces of passion and reason, spontaneity and restraint, heart and head, poetry and prose. In scriptural rhetoric John Kaye writes of those impassioned English men who were prepared "to strike at once, smiting everywhere, hip and thigh, like the grand remorseless heroes of the Old Testament."[34] Repeatedly pointing out that it was the excessiveness of Indian brutality that stretched English restraint to the breaking point, Kaye and other historians celebrate the English soldier as an indignant avenging angel. But, at the same time, they almost always underscore the dangers of such spontaneous passion. Colonial representations of John Nicholson, who led a ruthless victorious march against the mutineers at Delhi, are frequently inscribed with this ambivalence. As the greatest military hero of the mutiny, and one of its foremost martyrs, Nicholson soon became a legendary figure in the collective imagination of Anglo-India. John Kaye reports of a group of Muslim fakirs in the frontier district of Hazara, whose worship of "Nikkul Seyn" could not be discouraged even with flogging and imprisonment.[35] In Flora Annie Steel's *On the Face of the Waters* Nicholson is the belligerent spirit who embodied England's outraged sense of justice. In Kipling's *Kim* the loyal old soldier recalls his hero "Nikul Seyn" with pride. But, while Nicholson is deified as the protector of innocent women and children, he is simultaneously portrayed as a somewhat obsessive character who pushed his men a little too much and a little too far. In *Bound to Exile: The Victorians in India* Michael Edwardes describes Nicholson as "a violent, manic figure, a *homosexual bully,* an extreme egoist who was pleased to affect a laconic indifference to danger."[36] Stressing the violent aspect of Nicholson's character, Kaye reports that the general proposed a bill for "the flaying alive, impalement, or burning of the murderers of the women and children at Delhi," because "the idea of simply hanging the perpetrators of such atrocities is maddening."[37] Nicholson's death on the battlefield at the hand of the rebels is presented not only as a heroic martyrdom but also as an avoidable tragedy resulting from his own inordinate passions. In this way both imperial power as well as imperial excess get individualized or psychologized as an attribute of personal character rather than as an aspect of systemic military strength. Such a view rationalizes the brutal treatment of the mutineers as a momentary fit of rage rather than as an exercise of raw power licensed by martial law.

The dramatic fraternal struggle between Henry and John Lawrence, two of the most powerful figures in turbulent mid-nineteenth-century India, provided colonial historians with an even more spectacular parable for the conflict between spontaneity and restraint.[38] Henry's benevolent paternalism and his intensely emotional relationships with Indians frequently brought him up against his bureaucrat brother, who favored a policy of aloofness and restraint. With the support of Governor-General Lord Canning (called "Clemency Canning" by those who wished harsher punishment for the mutineers), John Lawrence managed to marginalize his brother politically. Henry's subsequent death at the hands of Indians during the mutiny allowed Anglo-Indian historians to martyrize him in the manner of Nicholson while magically subsuming his passion into the reticence of John Lawrence, who then emerged as the ideal synthesis of poetic passion and prosaic reason, decisive action and judicious restraint. Under the stewardship of Lawrence and Canning the law became an incarnation of these "English" qualities. The idealization of the law embodied the force of evangelical and Utilitarian doctrines, now invested in the notion of order and efficiency as the ultimate political ends to which the Raj was dedicated.[39]

The Consolidation of Colonial Masculinity

Immediately after the mutiny the Crown took over from the East India Company, and the viceroy became the direct representative of the queen empress. The betrayal and cruelty of the sepoys, the British felt, justified the racial and moral condemnation of Indians. Shaken by the ferocity of the insurgency, the rulers reconstituted the army and the government on a stricter and stronger basis. Although the queen's proclamation of 1858 committed the colonial government to providing equal access for all races, the procedural and practical barriers set up by the bureaucracy effectively prevented Indians from competing for influential posts. Recruitment of Indians to both army and government was thereby restricted. Strict caste distinctions were maintained and encouraged by enforcing orthodox behavior. The overt policy of Westernization was abandoned, and a spectacularly dictatorial "Oriental" approach to colonial policy was restored, as more suited to the conservatism in Indian society. Reform was abandoned in favor of rule. Although the government continued to advocate "progress," its method of achieving it focused on practical and efficient administration rather than on political or social reform. The British turned their attention to such "safe" areas such as sanitation and transportation, stressing the need for an efficient bureaucracy that could implement these changes.

Because the Sepoy Mutiny brings colonialism to a crisis, it allows us to chart the flow of colonial desire in a particularly sharp manner. In the first half of the nineteenth century colonial politics had revolved primarily around issues of social reform, especially those that ostensibly aimed at rescuing Indian women from the clutches of a cruel native patriarchy. Sati, or widow burning, had served as a particularly spectacular sign for the barbarism and misogyny in Indian society. During the mutiny, however, Anglo-Indian women became, like their Indian counterparts, victims of Indian patriarchy and, consequently, objects of white male salvation. In the post-mutiny years a real or imagined sexual threat to the white female body, interpreted as a challenge to white male authority, could and would be invoked in times of political crisis to rationalize colonial repression. Political debates such as the Illbert Bill controversy of 1883–84 turn precisely upon the issue of whether Indian men could be trusted to exercise power over English women.

The mutiny also left Anglo-Indians with ever more exaggerated notions of Indian conservatism, religiosity, apathy, and passivity, reinforcing colonial constructions of Indian, particularly Hindu, tradition as peculiarly feminine. Declaring a policy of noninterference in the social and religious affairs of its subjects—affairs that colonial policies had gradually relegated to a depoliticized, privatized sphere and reified as the essential core of Hindu identity—the colonial state found safe ways of re-empowering groups of politically disenfranchised Indian men by inducing them to appoint themselves as the privileged spokesmen of a depoliticized tradition that colonial officials nevertheless continued to identify with the feminine. This peculiar position of authoritative identity in and disassociation from a feminized tradition offered divergent groups of elite Indian men public participation in the moral and judicial discourses, many of which concerned Indian women. In and through these debates a generalized Hindu tradition was defined, represented, and made the basis not only of colonial legislation but also, in different forms, of contemporary nationalists' own efforts to construct a cultural equivalent for India as a political entity. The Indian woman and the feminized tradition she was made to embody thus continued to serve as transactional tokens in the homosocial struggle for hegemony.

The Sepoy Mutiny enriched, elaborated, and reconstituted the stereotype of effeminacy, transforming it from a simple metaphor for Hindu passivity and Muslim decadence into a complex and powerful ideological weapon in post-mutiny politics. One important way in which the stereotype of effeminacy was reconstituted was by making aggressive sexual behavior a symptom of effeminacy rather than an expression of manly virility. The production of the Indian male as rapist thus did not impute a dangerous sexual potency to colonized manhood; instead, even as rapist, the Indian male was seen to be exhibiting a characteristic racial debility. In viewing sexual aggression as evidence of effeminacy, colonial writers were giving a distinctly racial orientation to the class-specific paternal code of hygiene that defined English masculinity.

Victorian imperial systems of education placed inordinate emphasis on the body as the site to be disciplined by sexual, class, and race power. The colonizer's body is a microcosmic embodiment of society's macrocosmic body and therefore a political reality that must be schooled into order and discipline. In *Race, Class and Sex under the Raj* Kenneth Ballhatchet notes that, while Victorian society expected the upper and middle classes to affirm its manliness through sexual control and abstinence, it required the lower class to establish its manliness by demonstrating sexual prowess.[40] The distant intimacy that was officially promoted and, in fact, systematically institutionalized between British soldiers and Indian prostitutes is a manifestation of such a class-based code of sexual conduct. From this perspective the determination with which Kipling maintains his soldiers' innocence by denying any sexual contact with Indian women constitutes a kind of disavowal, or negation, that points to the possibility, if not the actuality, of such contacts. Official attitudes toward the prostitute herself were typically ambivalent. Although she was considered to be playing a necessary, even somewhat positive, role, in satisfying the soldiers' manly needs, she was viewed as a threat to the health of the soldiers as well as to the racial purity of the rulers. Nevertheless, the British soldier who satisfied his sexual desires by visiting Indian brothels was assumed to be merely acting in a natural way. But the Indian male who acted in a similar manner was regarded as a depraved creature who could not be expected to show any self-control and therefore could not be trusted with self-government.[41] In this manner a class-specific concept such as the "English gentleman," and the ideal of masculinity it implies, produces racial divisions that go far beyond that of class. The use of class and gender categories to express race points to the emergence of a more explicitly race-oriented idiom being mediated through a semiosis of manliness.

Systematically opposed to the manly restraint of the English, the sexual excessiveness of the Indian male was seen as both the cause as well as the result of effeminacy. Such circular logic characterizes the Age of Consent Act of 1891, which sought to reform Hindu child marriage. The assumption underlying the legislation was not only that premature consummation causes moral and physical effeminacy but that effeminate men were more likely to indulge in premature consummation.[42] Early sexual experience, it was believed, would not only corrupt the moral fiber of men but actually sap the vigor of the race by producing weak and sickly offspring. In addition to child marriage, the sexually overcharged atmosphere of the zenanas in princely courts were seen to be the cause of degeneracy and impotence among Hindu as well as

Muslim royalty. The British believed that a king who lived in such circumstances could never control himself or his subjects. The Indian male was caricatured as a physical and moral weakling who had lost the taste or capacity for leadership. Working on the assumption that premature consummation occurs only among effeminate people, ethnologist H. H. Risley of the Bengal Civil Service observes: "As we leave the great recruiting ground of the Indian Army and travel south eastward along the plains of the Ganges, the healthy sense which bid the warrior races keep their girls at home until they are fit to bear the burden of maternity, seems to have been cast out by the demon of corrupt ceremonialism ever ready to sacrifice helpless women and children to the traditions of fancied orthodoxy."[43] The distinction Risley makes between the "martial" and the "nonmartial" races points to an important development in colonial sexual ideology.

Based on an elaborate classification of Indian castes and communities, a hierarchical distinction was manufactured between the martial (understood as manly) and the nonmartial (understood as effeminate) races of India. By the end of the century this distinction was fully developed into a justification for the selective recruitment of Indian soldiers in the post-1857 army. Even though the distinction was not deployed with full force until the latter half of the nineteenth century, colonial rule had long favored certain sections of the native elite, which included the martial, aristocratic, landowning, and noncommercial groups. This preference perhaps points not only to the economic, political, and ideological needs of colonialism in India but also to the influence of aristocratic values in British society.[44] Although the colonial government claimed to be perpetuating an Indian tradition that distinguished between martial and nonmartial castes, scholars of colonial India have, in recent years, shown that the British view of the caste system represents a specifically colonial understanding of an indigenous institution, while the martial/nonmartial criterion for military recruitment reveals a specifically colonial understanding of the ways in which certain attributes of masculinity were supposedly distributed in traditional Indian society.[45]

As reflected in the contrast Kipling draws in *Kim* between Huree Babu and Mahbub Ali, the distinction between martial and nonmartial was most conventionally rendered as a division between the sturdy, wild, "pure" Pathan and the allegedly intelligent, educated, but mongrelized Bengali. The urban middle-class Bengali Hindu was ridiculed as a rootless hybrid and primarily in contrast with the sturdy traditionalism of the rural Pathans, who were Muslims. If the Bengali was the spoiled child of British India—spoiled, as Kipling suggested, on the sweets of Western education—the Pathan was the child of nature, an unregenerate noble savage.[46] Western education was seen as compounding the Bengali's inherent cowardliness to produce personal malice and political sedition. Dina Nath, the vapid student of Kipling's story "The Enlightenment of Pagett, M.P.," represents the stereotypical Bengali. "Married three years," and the "father of two weaklings," Dina Nath is a bombastic "school-boy" incapable of honest work.[47] Unlike the weak and cowardly Bengali, the Pathan seemed bold, manly, and courageous. Although the British denounced the Pathan's ferocity and utter disregard for restraint, they admired his rebellious spirit, for it had no threatening political consequences for the British.[48] By contrast, the Bengali middle class was growing increasingly restless. Despite Lytton's efforts to muzzle the native press through the Vernacular Press Act of 1878, the increasingly articulate, politically self-conscious, Western-educated Bengalis continued to press for a greater role in the colonial administration. Consequently, the Bengali was portrayed as the real enemy of the Raj; his willingness to compromise with the imperialists aroused as much scorn as his efforts to resist them.

The viceroyalty of Lord Curzon from 1898 through 1905 marks the culmination of the autocratic trend in post-mutiny colonial policy. The authoritarianism, expressed through spectacular Mughal emblems of power, was said to satisfy the Oriental need for benevolent despotism and attraction to strength. Extravagant durbars, such as Curzon's Delhi durbar of 1903, were held as magnificent displays of power. The native aristocracy, which had lost much of its authority during the pre-mutiny years, was strengthened by Lord Canning's land tenure policy. This succeeded in containing the peasants by restoring a loyal landholding class. It also served to protect the British against an increasingly restive emerging middle class. Curzon redoubled efforts to diffuse political aspirations with administrative reforms. The Indian Civil Service became the cornerstone of the Raj, with its officers, responsible for the day-to-day administration, acquiring a reputation for dedication to duty, honesty, sincerity, and a paternal devotion to their native subjects. These are the heroes of empire celebrated by Flora Annie Steel and Rudyard Kipling.

The emergence of the dutiful, disciplined, restrained, civil servant as the paradigmatic emblem of late-nineteenth-century English imperialism is overdetermined by the class conflicts within British society as well. As empire opened up unexpected economic opportunities for the

British lower classes, the unvarnished material motive they brought to colonization inevitably undermined its moral imperative. In Flora Annie Steel's *On the Face of the Waters* the Gissings are crass and vulgar merchants who prefer India, where they are rich and respectable members of white society, to England, where they would have been poor outcasts. In the end both husband and wife are martyred through their deaths at the hands of Indians, an act that indirectly serves as punishment for low-class waywardness, economic as well as sexual. The close contact that often existed in the colony between the lower classes and the natives was also a source of great anxiety to imperial policies of aloofness and racial purity. From this perspective the identity of Kim as a poor Irish orphan becomes ideologically significant in Kipling's novel. Clearly, it is the boy's lowly origin that enables his initial intimacy with Indians. Yet in the end Kim is "punished" for his lack of discipline, as his joyous spontaneity is relentlessly refigured into empire's paternal code of duty and restraint. Undisciplined lower-class looters like Dravot and Carnehan in Kipling's story "The Man Who Would Be King" are brutally punished, especially when they yield to the sexual temptations offered by Indian women. Praise is usually reserved for the dutiful and disciplined administrators, who toil tirelessly without expectation of reward. When they do succumb to fears or fantasies, Kipling's idealized upper- and middle-class colonialists are mercilessly shamed and embarrassed, if not mortally wounded or killed.[49] Late-nineteenth-century English imperialism thus found its rationale in a class-specific, racialized cult of masculinity.

4

Imperial Feminism in an Age of Homosocial Colonialism: Flora Annie Steel's *On the Face of the Waters*

Feminist Resistance and Feminine Complicity

> The year 1857 had been fateful to many. The waves of horror that had spread through Great Britain as one after another of the Great Mutiny tragedies came through reached even the nurseries and schoolrooms. Nana Sahib was hung, drawn, and quartered by children hundreds of times . . . I burned and hanged and tortured Nana Sahib in effigy many times. In truth he really was a scoundrel; and as my eldest brother was going out to Civil Service in 1858, it was only natural that the personal element prevailed over soft-heartedness.[1]

It was with such memories and personal associations that Flora Annie Steel went out to India in 1867 as the wife of an Indian Civil Service officer posted in the Punjab. In her best-known novel, *On the Face of the Waters* (1896),[2] a work she considered to be "the epic of the race,"[3] Steel returns to the turbulent upheavals of 1857. Steel was able to gain access to certain confidential official documents but only on condition she exercise the patriotism and discretion expected from a woman of her rank and prestige.[4] Steel immersed herself in her research, living on a rooftop like her heroine, roaming the streets of Delhi and pouring over official records and histories. She considered the highest praise for *On the Face of the Waters* to have come from a stranger who told her that the novel had allowed him to forgive Indians for the murder of his wife during the rebellion.[5]

Despite the glowing tributes Steel received from her English readers, her account does not deviate from the standard imperialist interpretation of the Sepoy Mutiny. Although she avoids the lurid sensationalism of typical mutiny stories and reports, Steel, too, traces the rebellion to a failure of British authority, due in part to an ignorance of Indian culture and an insensitivity to Indian conservatism. The British, she feels, should have realized the folly of preaching Christianity to native regiments. She faults colonial officials for being complacent and dismissing signs of native discontent as bizarre rumors. Steel also implies that they should have been more sensitive to the humiliation felt by the Mughals, whom she identifies as the prime instigators of the mutiny. Throughout the novel, when native discontent with colonial rule is not assimilated to natural phenomena like storms and earthquakes, it is presented as a revival of religious fanaticism, ranging from sepoy fears over greased cartridges to a more pervasive resentment over the 1829 abolition of sati and the 1856 passage of the Widow Remarriage Act. The popular base of anticolonial sentiment is discounted through descriptions of a fundamentally content and submissive peasantry, unaffected by the mutiny, carrying on the immemorial routines of daily life.

And, although authored by a woman, *On the Face of the Waters*, does not refrain from either demonizing Indian women or effeminizing Indian men. Following masculinist colonial historiography, Steel's novel identifies Indian women as the chief instigators of sepoy atrocities. The spark that kindles the flames of rebellion is a bazaar whore who taunts the sepoys to prove their manhood by storming the jails. As Jenny Sharpe observes, "the narrative function of the harlot—who, like the Rani of Jhansi, speaks violence into being—is to delegitimate the religious discourse of prophesy that was so crucial for spreading the revolt."[6] Reproducing the circular logic of effeminism, Steel offers the unnatural influence of women in Indian society as both the cause as well as the result of effeminacy. Her portrait of Zeenut Mahil, the Mughal queen, reflects a popular stereotype in colonial literature that strips the Indian woman of her conventional passivity and transforms her into a monster behind the veil. Enlarging on the despotic power wielded by the Indian woman behind the walls of the zenana, Fanny Parks writes in her pre-mutiny journal that "to induce a native woman to give way to any reasons" that are "contrary to her own wishes" is "quite out of the power of mortal man."[7] Such attitudes persist in Maud Diver's 1909 account of life in India. Attempting a "true and terrible picture of the scope and unscrupulousness of feminine tyranny behind the veil,"

Diver describes the secluded woman as "a shrill-tongued virago; a tyrant unassailable in her own domain."[8] In the same vein Steel's novel also presents the Mughal queen as a scheming witch who controls both her husband, the king, as well as the young heir to the Mughal throne. Bahadur Shah, the old dottard under whose banner the mutineers gather in Delhi, is a weak puppet manipulated by the cunning Zeenut Mahil. The effeminate king sits around dreaming and writing poetry when the need is for manly action. And young Prince Abul, the heir to the Mughal throne, is a decadent, pleasure-loving "idler," "content to be the best musician in Delhi, the boldest gambler, and the fastest liver" (OFW 236). Steel is quick to distinguish the Mughal queen who spins a web of intrigue, spreading jealousy, fanaticism, and confusion among the ranks of rebels, from that other "mysterious woman across the sea, who reigned over the Huzoors and made them pitiful to women" (92). Rather than question white male understanding, Steel represents the massacre of English women as yet another spectacular illustration (along with sati and female infanticide) of the Indian male's disregard for women. The status or the treatment of women thus emerges as the fundamental factor that separates the English from the Indians.

What makes *On the Face of the Waters* different and more interesting than the formulaic mutiny fiction then is its "feminist" recasting of the memsahib as "companionate colonialist." By telling a remarkable story about an English woman who survives the fall of Delhi, Steel's novel refigures the racial memory of the mutiny to fit the emerging needs of late-nineteenth-century English feminism. Kate Earlton, the heroine, lives for three months on the rooftops of the besieged city with an English spy, disguised as his Persian wife, until finally, with the help of her Indian maid servant, she manages to escape to the cantonment on the ridge outside Delhi. By literally placing the Anglo-Indian in the Indian woman's position, the novel stages an interracial contest that establishes the racial superiority of the Anglo-Indian woman over her Indian counterpart. The experience allows Kate Earlton to gain a new sense of self-confidence and self-reliance that liberates her from the alienated, stifling, space of domesticity she had occupied at the beginning of the novel. Afraid that her story would be dismissed as "incredible," Steel underscores its plausibility by explaining in the preface that her account is nothing more than a fictionalized version of a real survival story. Yet this cautionary explanation does not seem to have kept contemporary (male) readers from criticizing Steel for introducing the "sex problem" into a historical novel or for being far too modern in her approach to the "woman question."[9] What interests me about Steel's novel, however, is the way its feminism is infected with homosocial desire. Not only is Steel's critique of traditional gender roles in Anglo-Indian society sharply defined and delimited by the economy of effeminism, but her feminist "resistance" actively enters into the very processes by which white male domination persists and even renews itself.

The Making of the Memsahib

Steel's attempt to restore the memsahib to the colonial historiography from which she is absent significantly coincides with the increased visibility of Anglo-Indian women in public life. The publication of *On the Face of the Waters* in 1896 was preceded by a decade in which English women found themselves at the center of a protracted and bitter political debate about the role Indian men could be given in the colonial government. This time, however, the women did not remain just spectators.

The historic entry of Anglo-Indian women into the public arena of colonial politics took place over the Illbert Bill controversy, also called the "white mutiny."[10] On February 9, 1883, Courtney Peregrine Illbert, the law member in the viceroy's Executive Council in India, introduced a bill that sought to appease Indian nationalists by granting Indian judges the right to try European offenders in rural areas, where until that time Europeans had been privileged to be tried by judicial officers of their own race. The bill was furiously opposed by the Anglo-Indian community, especially by the tea and indigo planters of Bengal, who feared that Indian judges would be more likely to prosecute them for mistreating their workers.[11] These fears were, however, articulated in a homosocial rhetoric that centered on two specific ideas: Indian male effeminacy and white female vulnerability.

The effeminacy of the Indian male, it was argued, made him unfit to sit in judgment over men and women of a more civilized race. Many Anglo-Indians felt that native men had never had the opportunity of enjoying the company of cultivated members of the opposite sex. Mr. J. Munro, the officiating commissioner of the Presidency Division in Bengal, wrote, "The training of natives from their childhood, the enervating influence of the zenana on their upbringing, early marriage, a low moral standard resulting from caste distinctions and the influence of centuries of subjugation all tend to hinder the development in Bengalis of those manly and straightforward qualities which under other conditions are found in Englishmen."[12] It was alleged that Indian men were unmanly because they held barbaric views about the female sex. R. H. Wilson, the magistrate of Midnapore, observed that the Indian male's "ideas on the subject of women and marriage are not European but Oriental."[13] The *Civil and Military Gazette,* for which Kipling worked, joined the storm of protest and voiced its contempt for the effeminate Bengali character in no uncertain terms. Not surprisingly, Anglo-Indian women expressed similar attitudes toward Indian men. "In Bengal," wrote one woman, "the men are notoriously destitute of manliness and are most harsh and cowardly in their treatment of the weaker sex."[14] Another suggested that Indian men were rendered unfit by the upbringing they received at the hands of uncivilized women: "Hindoo women are degraded, they are totally devoid of all delicacy, their ideas and language are coarse and vulgar, their terms of reproach and abuses are gross and disgusting in the extreme. Although they manifest much shyness and outward modesty there is little real virtue of the higher order among them."[15]

The second idea repeatedly invoked by Anglo-Indians opposed to the Illbert Bill was the potential mistreatment English women would suffer at the hands of Indian judges, especially in cases involving rape charges. It was feared that isolated white women, particularly in rural areas, would become victims of unbridled native lust. The suggestion that Bengali magistrates might deliberately misuse their powers over white women was hinted at frequently in letters and meetings. A senior Anglo-Indian officer in the Indian army wrote: "Many English officers have English servant girls attached to their families; a native Magistrate, puffed up with importance might set eyes upon one of the girls and make overtures to her. If she refused, as she probably would do, what would be easier than for this native, acting under the smart of disappointment, to bring a case against the girl to be tried in his court. A few annas would bribe all the native servants of the household and we might guess the result."[16] Rumors circulated about Indians, emboldened by the Illbert proposal, attempting to rape an English woman in Calcutta.[17] Numerous cases of assaults or attempted assaults on white women were reported in the Anglo-Indian press. These fears took on alarming proportions in the minds of white women who lived in the midst of a large native population. The argument that liberal reform would threaten the sanctity of white womanhood found its greatest support among Anglo-Indian women. A letter written to the *Englishman* by Flora McDonald dramatically captured the prevailing sentiment among Anglo-Indian women:

Englishmen try to picture to yourselves a mofussil court, hundreds of miles away from Calcutta—in that court a Native Magistrate is presiding with the supercilious assurance that a native assumes when he has an Englishman in his power. Before that man stands an English girl in all her maidenly dignity; she has been accused by her ayah of revenge of a loathsome crime, a crime that is common among native women; the Court is crowded with natives of all castes who have flocked to hear an English girl being tried for an offense; this motley crowd laugh and jeer; and stare that English girl in the face; and spit on the ground to show the contempt they have for the female sex; scores of witnesses are present to give evidence; a native Doctor has also been hired for that occasion; witnesses are cross-examined by a native pleader; the most irrelevant questions are asked, questions that only a native dare to ask. Picture to yourself that girl's agony of shame! By her stands her only protector, a widowed mother, who has not the means wherewith to secure the protection and counsel of her countrymen. That innocent girl so kind, so affectionate, so loving, the stay of her widowhood, must go from the court with shame, with a blighted name . . . It cannot be that Englishmen renowned for chivalry are willing to subject even the humblest of their countrywomen to dishonour.[18]

McDonald's image of white female vulnerability and her assumptions about Indian male sexuality legitimize her appeal for white male protection. The image of the degraded Indian woman played a key role in Anglo-Indian propaganda against the Illbert Bill. Many white women claimed that their opposition was no "unwomanly animosity against [their] fellow subjects the natives" but that they opposed the bill only in the name of the long-suffering native woman.[19] A case in point was the scathing attack on the Illbert Bill that appeared in the *Englishman,* a Calcutta daily, under the title "A Lady's View of Mr. Illbert's Bill." Its author was Annette Ackroyd Beveridge, an idealistic young woman who had gone out to India in 1872, in response to the request of the Bengali reformer Kesub Chundra Sen for female educators in Bengal. Subsequently disassociating herself from Sen, whose notions about women she found unacceptable, Ackroyd started her own Anglicized boarding school for Bengali girls. After struggling for several years to keep the school running, she quit her job in a cloud of controversy and went on to marry Henry Beveridge. The letter Mrs. Beveridge wrote to the *Englishman* on March 6, 1883, brought her into unusual public conflict with her husband, who was a stout defender of the Illbert Bill, and forced her to acquiesce publicly to his views, although she held her own privately. In the letter that received much attention Mrs. Beveridge wrote:

Englishwomen have been forgotten while their rulers are busied in adding a new terror to their lives in India . . . Six-and-twenty years do not suffice to change national characteristics . . . I am not afraid to assert that I speak for the feelings of all Englishwomen when I say that we regard the proposal to subject us to the jurisdiction of native Judges an insult. It is not pride of race which dictates this feeling, which is the outcome of something far deeper—it is the pride of womanhood. This is a form of respect which we are not ready to abrogate in order to give such advantages to others as are offered by Mr. Illbert's Bill to its benefactors. In this discussion, as in most, *Il y a question de femmes*—and, in this discussion, the ignorant and neglected women of India rise up from their enslavement in evidence against their masters. They testify to the justice of the resentment which Englishwomen feel at Mr. Illbert's proposal to subject civilized women to the jurisdiction of men who have done little or nothing to redeem the women of their own race and whose social ideas are still on the outer verge of civilization.[20]

Reviving mutiny fears of rape, Mrs. Beveridge makes an implicit appeal to the Victorian code of chivalry, calling on English men to guard their women against a degenerate Indian patriarchy. She productively deploys the anomalies of race and gender in colonial society in ways that both exploit and exclude Indian women. On the one hand, Mrs. Beveridge erases racial difference by pointing to the shared gendered suffering of Indian and English women at the hands of Indian men. But, on the other hand, she intensifies racial difference by separating the "civilized" English woman from her uncivilized Indian counterpart. The "pride of womanhood" Mrs. Beveridge invokes in place of "pride of race" refers exclusively to the pride of white womanhood and, as such, at once silences native women and reinforces the colonial racial hierarchy. Mrs. Beveridge's argument thus contributes to a racial discourse that commodifies the female body into an ambiguous and overdetermined site of struggle between colonizing and colonized men.

The sexual vulnerability of white women served to mobilize the Anglo-Indian male community against the Illbert Bill. At the Calcutta Town Hall meeting J. H. A. Branson, one of the most notorious speakers of the evening, invoked the code of chivalry to urge English men to resist any move by the government that would place their female dependents at the mercy of native males. Branson reminded his countrymen that protecting white women was "more than a sentiment; it is a sacred charge of a sacred duty."[21] The *Pioneer* printed a resolution approved by three thousand residents of Calcutta that charged the Illbert Bill with stirring up racial antagonisms and jealousies "such as have never been aroused since the Mutiny" and warned that passage of the bill would jeopardize the liberty and safety of British subjects, especially their wives and daughters.[22] The vociferous opposition to the Illbert Bill forced the viceroy to retreat and revise the controversial clauses, killing any impetus for reform. It was not until 1923 that Indian judges were finally given jurisdiction over European offenders through an amendment of the Indian Criminal Procedure. Thus, Adela's case in *A Passage to India* (1924) could be tried by an Indian judge, although the Anglo-Indian community is still "convulsed" by "wrath" at the idea of an Indian man having legal power over an English woman.

Even though they too shared the racial animosity of Anglo-Indian men toward Indians, the mobilization of Anglo-Indian women on their own initiative against the Illbert Bill posed a challenge to the homosocial structure of colonial society founded on a denial of white female agency. Anglo-Indian women's contribution had taken various forms, from writing letters of protest and attending meetings to organizing a successful social boycott against supporters of the bill. The men responded to this unprecedented phenomenon with characteristic ambivalence. The numerous letters to newspaper editors written by men under female pseudonyms suggests that, while Anglo-Indian men appreciated the strategic value of having the opposition to the Illbert Bill assume a female voice, they clearly resented the intrusion of women in what was considered to be an exclusively male domain. As a result, the women who organized a Ladies' Committee to protest the bill encountered resistance and ridicule from the very men whose opinions they shared. The home member of the viceroy's Executive Council, James Gibbs, observed that the female was "far more unreasonable and active in opposition than the male."[23] Even the viceroy, Lord Ripon, expressed the opinion that "the ladies are as is often the case hotter than the men."[24] Indians expressed a similar view of the white woman's role in the Illbert Bill agitation. Some native newspapers suggested that the natives had lost the fight over the bill because of the vitriolic campaign of the "white kalis," "white in complexion [but] . . . black at heart."[25] In a parodic but shrewd commentary on the agitation, one popular native weekly wrote that the government had backed away from the bill because white women had refused to "submit to the jurisdiction of Calibans lusting after the Mirandas of Anglo-India."[26] Public statements made by women like Annette Ackroyd Beveridge, who was later rebuked for contributing to racial discord in India, fed the stereotype of the racist memsahib.

Best known through the caricatures of Kipling and Forster, the memsahib is a notorious figure who looms large during the post-mutiny period. Historically a class-specific term of address used for the wives of high-ranking civil servant and officers, the memsahib is stereotyped as an idle, frivolous social snob who tyrannically rules over a household of servants and refuses to associate with Indians. This stereotype, Jenny Sharpe suggests, is none other than the defenseless "mutiny lady" stripped of her innocence. In the jingoistic discourse of the mutiny, Sharpe shows, English women were represented as abused victims so that English men could be their heroic avengers. During the post-mutiny years of liberal reform, however, the women themselves were held responsible not only for the excesses of the mutiny but also for the subsequent deterioration of race relations.[27] In *Ideas about India* (1885) Wilfred Scawen Blunt declares that "it is a fact that the Englishwoman in India during the last thirty years has been the cause of half the bitter feelings there between race and race. It was her presence at Cawnpore and Lucknow that pointed the sword of revenge after the Mutiny, and it is her constantly increasing influence now that widens the gulf of ill-feeling and makes amalgamation daily more impossible."[28] This sentiment is echoed by the police superintendent of Chandrapore, McBryde, who, in E. M. Forster's *A Passage to India*, secretly blames the women for all the racial troubles in Chandrapore. And such sentiments continue to be expressed well into the twentieth century. Kenneth Ballhatchet explains: "Improved conditions encouraged more Englishwomen to live in India, and in various ways their presence seems to have widened the distance between the ruling class and the people . . . As wives they hastened the disappearance of the Indian mistresses. As hostesses they fostered the development of exclusive social groups in every civil station."[29] And Sir David Lean is reported to have said in 1985: "It's a well-known saying that the women lost us the Empire. It's true."[30] Even V. S. Naipaul claims that "no other country was more fitted to welcome a conqueror; no other conqueror was more welcome than the British. What went wrong? Some say the Mutiny; some say the arrival in India afterwards of white women. It is possible."[31]

The widely held view that English women were responsible for the problems faced by an empire under siege may be traced to what Margaret Strobel has called "the myth of the destructive female."[32] This myth posits an idyllic past of racial mixing before the arrival of white women. Interestingly, this belief seems to have been shared by English as well as Indian men—a fact that attests to the homosocial basis of colonialism. Thus, in *A Passage to India* Aziz shares McBryde's repressed resentment toward English women in India, and V. S. Naipaul concurs with David Lean in blaming women for the disintegration of the empire. Although early Indo-British relations were certainly not as friendly as the proponents of the myth suggest, there are indeed certain historical reasons for associating the deterioration of race relations with the arrival of English women in India. Although concubinage was regarded by the British as an important contributor to race relations, its fruits— Eurasians—were seen as a threat to the racial gap so critical to colonial rule. The importation of white women to the colony during the early decades of the nineteenth century was, in fact, aimed at reducing the problem Eurasians presented to the racial policies of the colonial government, particularly to the hiring procedures of the East India Company. When racial mixing was further discouraged after the sexual hysteria unleashed in 1857, the confinement of Anglo-Indian woman to the domestic sphere became all the more a sign of the racial and moral superiority of the ruling race.

The stereotype of the memsahib is not only a distortion of real women but also a sign of the symbolic value of domesticity. In keeping with the Victorian domestic ideal the British reproduced in the colony, Anglo-Indian society emphasized the restriction of middle-class women to the home as a sign of national integrity and moral supremacy. But, in addition to these virtues, the sphere of colonial domesticity was also a space of racial purity that the housewife guarded from contamination from outside. Racial segregation thus became part of domestic work, with the colonial woman being given the duty of enforcing a strict separation of the races. Yet, paradoxically, it was precisely this function of ensuring racial segregation that also deposited blame upon the colonial woman for undermining race relations. Thus, it is within the contradictory arena of colonial domesticity that the stereotype of the memsahib may be located.

Flora Annie Steel herself embodies the memsahib in all her contradictions. In her best-selling guide for Anglo-Indian housewives, she strategically redraws the boundaries of the Anglo-Indian home itself: "We do not wish to advocate an unholy haughtiness, but an Indian household can no more be governed peacefully without dignity and prestige than an Indian Empire."[33] Steel's startling analogy presents the empire itself as nothing more than an expanded household. The management of empire is seen as essentially home management on a larger scale. There are doors to be locked, corners to be dusted, rooms to be fumigated, children (or natives) to be doctored, educated, clothed, and disciplined, accounts to be kept, and fences to be mended. Colonial housekeeping, in turn, is viewed as a military campaign. Noting that "life in India always partakes of the nature of a great campaign,"[34] Steel goes on to discuss the daily duties of the housewife, duties such as daily supervision of servants, which she describes as "an inspection parade" that should be punctually conducted at ten o'clock.[35] Steel also strongly recommends the learning of Indian languages as an effective way for English women to control their servants. The essence of housekeeping, as the essence of imperialism, is the learning of racial privilege. Redefined thus, good housekeeping skills could be extended into selective areas of public life in the colony. Steel herself refused to conform to a conventionally gendered role of domesticity. Not only did she learn to read and write several languages, she also assumed the post of inspectress of mission schools and served as vice president of the "Victoria Female Orphan Asylum." Indeed, much to the consternation of the Indian Civil Service, which was quick to voice its disapproval, she even lived apart from her husband for a year so that she might complete the term of her own public appointment in a different part of the country. While in her autobiography Steel presents herself as a model of the emancipated Anglo-Indian women, there is little recognition of how much her own social status was derived from her husband's rank in the Indian Civil Service.

Feminists who explain the stereotype of the racist memsahib as a purely male creation that distorts the relative powerlessness of white women in the colony try to show how European women were victims of a system not of their own making or attempt to demonstrate that women contributed a nurturing, maternal alternative to the masculine ethos of empire.[36] What they fail to acknowledge is the role of colonial women as both pawns and players in maintaining—even elaborating, extending, and reinforcing—the racial hierarchies and homosocial ideologies of empire. The centrality of femininity, motherhood, and domesticity to the discourse of the civilizing mission calls for an explanation not so much of how European women transformed colonialism as of how colonialism has molded European women.[37]

To chart the colonial production of the discourse of domesticity is to map the contradictory pressures of English imperialism upon an emer-

gent feminist individualism. The coalition of convenience that emerged
between evangelicalism, imperialism, and feminism during the early
decades of the nineteenth century had given birth to certain shared
themes and ideas that gradually gained great symbolic value in colonial
discourse, even though they were deployed by the various forces to different, even opposing or contradictory, ends.[38] The theme that Victorian
women, with the enthusiastic support of evangelicals and imperial policy makers, seized upon was one that expanded or extended the domestic role of child rearing to include religion and education in ways that
gave them a dignified entry into public life. Victorian women thus
entered the colonial arena in the capacity of missionaries and educators.[39] The colonies provided an attractive and convenient place for
"emancipated," tough-minded Victorian women, who at first went out
on civilizing missions with a brother or a husband and, later, even
alone.[40] One area of reform that particularly opened up opportunities
for European women reformers was female education. The "Ladies
Association for the Promotion of Female Education among Heathen"
was formed in 1866, and even the Indian missions that had previously
discouraged single women from joining began to actively recruit
women missionaries for educating secluded upper-class/caste zenana
women. Missionary work soon had greater appeal for British women,
who considered teaching the zenana women more prestigious than
working with poor, low-caste native converts (which missionary wives
continued to do as before). Middle-class English women who were
hired as governesses, as zenana and missionary schoolteachers, generally found the higher wages and professional status overseas preferable
to employment in England. Thus, ironically, English women came to
recognize themselves and were recognized as national subjects primarily outside the national boundary. Indeed, as Rosemary Mangoly
George has provocatively suggested, in some sense the English woman
who went out to the colony was further along the route to "full individualism" than her counterpart back home.[41]

But, while they slaved for the Lord's cause and the Raj's cause,
female missionaries were regarded with great anxiety by the Anglo-
Indian community, which saw their contact with Indians as a source of
racial and cultural contamination. The position of the single woman was
particularly delicate, as the case of Miss Pigot confirms.[42] When Miss
Pigot, a Church of Scotland missionary running an orphanage and a
zenana mission in Calcutta, refused to accept the control of Rev. William
Haste, she was accused of sexual misconduct with Babu Kali Charan

Banerjee, a Bengali convert who taught at her orphanage. Although Miss Pigot took Hastie to court and was acquitted after much delay, her case drew public attention to the role of women missionaries. The response of an anonymous "District Judge" published in the *Friend of India* reflects popular sentiment. The judge himself thought it morally dangerous for "young unmarried ladies to proceed, alone or unprotected, to the houses of middle-class Hindoos to impart elementary instruction to the ladies of the household." It was time that missionary societies realized they were putting their young ladies at the mercy of lascivious Hindu men: "the system of family life among the secluded females of a Hindoo household is quite inconsistent with the idea of any protection from familiarity or insult from the male members of the household being afforded by the ladies of the zenana."[43]

As the writings of Mary Martha Sherwood, Fanny Parks, Harriet Tytler, Flora Annie Steel, and others amply attest, the colonial wife frequently found herself living a life of isolation and seclusion not unlike that of the Indian woman she displaced and deplored. The wife of a senior Anglo-Indian official once wrote: "You must understand that most Europeans of the old school would not allow a lady to accept an Indian gentleman's proffered hospitality. They would not permit her to drive through an Indian town, be a spectator of tent-pegging, or receive an Indian as a visitor, far less dine with him. They would, in short, prefer her to be as wholly absent from every kind of society as are the inmates of zenanas."[44] The contradictory pressures of race and gender in colonial society placed colonizing and colonized women in an uneasy contiguity that compelled Anglo-Indian women to explore their own caged condition through the confinement of the Indian woman.

Jenny Sharpe has drawn attention to a polemical two-part essay by J. E. Dawson in which the author, defending the "right to work for India," requests that the same compassion and sympathy shown toward the cloistered Indian lady be extended to her Anglo-Indian counterpart.[45] Dawson paints the picture of a lonely and bored housewife who, not unlike Kate Earlton at the opening of Steel's novel, has nothing to occupy her mind. The English woman who went out to India as the wife of an Indian civil servant not only had to leave her family behind but was constantly separated from her husband and children even in India. Anglo-Indian wives, Dawson explains, are regularly sent off to the cool hill stations during the summer months, while their husbands remain on the plains, carrying on the duties of imperial civil service. And as soon as they come of age Anglo-Indian children are sent back to England for schooling. Indeed, the physical discomforts, disease, death, maternal anguish, and emotional and psychological deprivation described by Anglo-Indian women often make the zenana's limited solaces such as the companionship of children and other women seem almost preferable. Anglo-Indian women are discouraged from having any contact with Indian society because it is believed they need to be protected from a culture that shows little respect for women. They are not permitted to engage in philanthropic work or even learn an Indian language for fear of racial and cultural contamination. The absence of social duties other than "calling" or preparing for balls, Dawson concludes, forces Anglo-Indian women into a superficial lifestyle, centering on fashion, flirtation, and frivolity. Dawson ends the first part of her essay with the reminder that the frivolous memsahib who leaves her children in the hands of the *ayah* (Indian nurse) risks producing a generation of Anglo-Indians that are more Indian than Anglo.

The similarities between the cloistered inmate of the zenana and the secluded colonial wife do not, however, lead the Anglo-Indian woman writer to ally herself with her Indian counterpart and denounce their shared oppression within patriarchal structures. Rather, as Dawson does in the second part of her essay, she typically asserts the superiority of English domestic institutions, presenting herself as a role model to and a savior of Indian women. Sharpe points out that even a feminist understanding of female infanticide and sati as drastic measures consciously adopted by Hindu women to alleviate their miserable condition (and not, as colonial officials would have it, unconscious expressions of ignorance and religious delusion) does not make Dawson grant agency to the Indian woman. Instead, she calls upon Anglo-Indian women to serve as moral examples for native women to imitate. Nothing short of the emancipation of Anglo-Indian women, she argues, will encourage Indian men to improve the status of their women. She concludes her essay with the hope that English women will one day become the "cherishers," "protectors," and "mothers" of the empire.

Jenny Sharpe suggests that, like Dawson, Flora Annie Steel also regarded the Indian woman as an inferior being.[46] In making this argument, she follows the lead of Antoinette Burton and other feminist scholars who have focused attention on how Victorian and Edwardian feminists increased their gender status by establishing themselves as the authorities of Indian women, whom they regarded as inferior beings in need of civilization. "Both in practice and in theory," Burton has argued, "the Indian woman acted as a foil against which British feminism gauged its own progress. Thus, not only did British feminists of the period reproduce the moral discourse of imperialism, they embedded modern western feminism deeply within it."[47] It is indeed true that Flora Annie Steel, like most English women of her time, looked down on Indian women because she believed they were hopelessly caught up in perpetuating their own oppression. Sharpe's reading of *On the Face of the Waters*, however, overlooks an important fact: Steel actually concedes a certain moral value to a particular ideal of Indian womanhood—the sati—offering her not only as a signifier of absolute Otherness but also as a model the English woman must emulate and excel. This concession, I suggest, marks the limits of imperial feminism in an age of homosocial colonialism.[48]

The Subject of Sati

The frequency with which comparisons between English and Indian women are routinely drawn by men as well as women, colonizers as well as colonized, marks it as an important ideologeme that feeds into various colonial discourses on gender. The figure of sati plays a particularly significant role in mediating these comparisons. In 1817 James Mill observed that, "of the modes adopted by Hindus of sacrificing themselves to divine powers, none . . . has more excited the attention of Europeans than the burning of wives upon the funeral piles of their husbands."[49] Sati had generated intense popular, even literary, interest in Europe in the eighteenth century. In England it was sensationalized in early Romantic texts such as Southey's best-selling *Curse of Kehama* (1817) as well as in several lesser-known "oriental tales."[50] French writers of diverse leanings also appropriated sati to a variety of concerns. Voltaire used it to attack both priestly control and female constancy; the traveler Pierre Sonnerat (cited by Southey) initiated a persistent European tradition of eroticization, in which sati represented a "fallen" woman's redemption, as she proved an undiminished femininity by following her lover's corpse into the flames.[51]

As the "Indo-Western encounter became largely an Indo-British encounter,"[52] sati became an important ideological element in the vindication of English imperialism. The criminalization of sati in 1829 was a significant marking of how sati had been read by the British. Gayatri Spivak has pointed out that among available classifications for the act of sati were religious martyrdom and warlike heroism, "with the husband standing in for sovereign or State, for whose sake an intoxicating ideology of sacrifice can be mobilized. In the event, it was categorized with murder, infanticide and the lethal exposure of the very old. The dubious place of the free will of the constituted sexed subject as female was successfully effaced."[53] Official attempts to regulate sati, Lata Mani has shown, frequently hinged on the enigmatic question of the burning woman's free will. Depending on whether the woman was defined as one who chose to die or as one who was forced to die, a distinction was made between "illegal" and "legal" burnings.[54]

Criminalization appears to have increased the power of sati as a cultural symbol in Victorian England. Arvind Sharma traces two related features that characterized the English response: "It became necessary for British writers to sensationalize Suttee on the one hand, and for British historians to monopolize the credit for having abolished it on the other."[55] Throughout the mid-nineteenth century sati continued to provide justification both for colonialism and for missionary penetration. Meanwhile, English art indulged in picturesque arrangements of the moment of immolation.[56] James Atkinson's famous painting of a supplicant and bare-breasted sati looking to heaven (and England) for deliverance was exhibited as late as 1841. So pervasive was this tendency to romanticize that Paul B. Courtright characterizes the nineteenth century as the era of the "picturesque sati."[57]

In a finely nuanced essay on the representation of sati Rajeswari Sunder Rajan has argued that traditions of representation tend to glorify or eroticize sati by ignoring or eliding its primary aspect of pain.[58] Discussing British representations of sati in the nineteenth century, Sunder Rajan points out that British society maintained two different views of the act of burning, depending on whether the Indian woman was assigned an object position or a subject position. Objectified as the paradigmatic victim of Indian patriarchy, the sati provoked implicit comparisons with the freedom and privileges of British women, thus offering further proof of the superiority of English civilization and providing moral justification for colonial rule. But the sati was also seen positively as the ultimate exemplar of female chastity and conjugal fidelity. Viewed not as a woman forced to die but as a woman who chooses to die, the subject of sati was presented as a model to British women, who were beginning to deny the superior advantages ascribed to their social status.[59]

In fact, sati was a key figure for feminist polemic in Victorian England. Many women writers, such as Fanny Parks, used it as an emblem of female oppression in British society. Attempting to understand the practice of widow burning more as a method of ensuring patriarchal property rights than as a performance of religious ritual, Parks makes some revealing comparisons between the Indian woman and her English counterpart: "The laws of England relative to married women, and the state of slavery to which those laws degrade them, render the lives of some few in the higher, and of thousands in the lower ranks of life, one perpetual *sati*, or burning of the heart, from which they have no refuge but the grave, or the cap of liberty—i.e., the widow's and either is a sad consolation."[60] Eliding cultural Otherness and erasing the crucial difference between burning to death and living in oppression, comparisons such as those made by Parks served to produce an enhanced and universal female suffering. Dorothy Stein's examination of the role of sati as a "normative institution" in Victorian England parallels Fanny Parks's:

> Suttee did not occur in England, but many manifestations of the attitudes and anxieties underlying the practice did. Nineteenth-century respectability in both Britain and India divided women into exalted and degraded classes, not only on the basis of actual or imputed sexual behavior, but also on the basis of whether that behavior was at all times controlled supervised, preferably by a male connection . . . Both societies agreed to disadvantage those women who could not obtain suitable male protection. These were not simply shared general attitudes. They found expression in numerous specific parallels . . . Most revealing of all, however, was the discussion that arose out of the recognition that England too possessed a sizable group of unmarriageable, and hence anomalous, women of good breeding.[61]

It is for the express purpose of managing various kinds of anomalous women that the powerful Victorian ideology of the "woman's sphere" was developed in England. "Within this ideological structure," Rajeswari Sunder Rajan observes, "the Indian widow as subject of sati could be selectively admired as exemplifying chastity, fidelity and sacrifice—important components of the model of behavior that was being constructed for English women."[62] The ideological power of this view of sati is evident in the fact that, in the end, even such a forcefully feminist narrative as *Jane Eyre* (1847), which self-consciously and systematically repudiates the seductive invitation to female self-immolation, rhetorically collapses feminist self-fulfillment into feminine self-sacrifice. And in Dickens's *Dombey and Son* (1848), as Rajeswari Sunder Rajan has pointed out, the resonant ambiguity inscribed in the figure of sati shows how in popular usage "sati could be raised above its cultural and gender specificity" to convey qualities such as courage, determination, and zeal.[63]

As Fanny Parks, J. E. Dawson, and others did, nineteenth-century feminists countered the official glorification of sati by arguing that the Hindu widow chose to burn not so much out of blind devotion as out of a knowledge of the life that awaited her. Indeed, some went so far as to suggest that, in the absence of more extensive reforms regarding widowhood, the colonial abolition of sati was nothing more than a cruel restriction of the widow's meager options. Yet even such a sympathetic understanding, Rajeswari Sunder Rajan suggests, introduced the dangerous possibility of rationalizing the act of burning as a voluntary suicide: "an exclusive focus on choice and motivation in constructing the subjectivity of the sati in some representations leads either to mystification or cognitive closure."[64] Steel's ambivalent and contradictory deployment of sati, I propose to show, produces precisely such "mystification" and "cognitive closure."

The tropology of sati is a crucial component in Steel's production of the companionate colonialist. Before she can stake her claim to companionate status, the female colonialist in *On the Face of the Waters* must not only demonstrate courage and determination, but she must voluntarily undergo a symbolic sati to prove her superiority to her rival, the Indian woman. The impact of homosocial desire on imperial feminism is nowhere more sharply manifested than in this event Flora Annie Steel stages at the very heart of *On the Face of the Waters:* the contest of purity between the English and the Indian woman. Focusing on the shifting and contradictory function of the Indian woman as a signifier in Steel's text, I shall argue that the novel's thematic of white female liberation is insufficient to counter completely the force of masculine desire invested in the sati.[65] Steel's deployment of the figure of sati reveals how the negative and the positive views of sati could be played off in ways that simultaneously further the cause of feminist individualism and also recontain it within the safe bounds of those patriarchal institutions and imperatives that were necessary for the maintenance of colonial rule. My reading of *On the Face of the Waters* will thus emphasize the manner in which the novel's feminist intent to write white female agency into colonial historiography is deeply split by the exigencies of colonial homosociality—a split that is coded into the novel's dual perspective on the Sepoy Mutiny: an unofficial feminist perspective that exposes the derangements and dislocations of white women in a male dominated, racialized society; and an official masculinist perspective that presents a predictable tale of heroism and chivalry in which British manhood avenges white womanhood and triumphs over Indian effeminacy.

Feminist Plottings, Homosocial Plots

Like most mutiny novels, Flora Annie Steel's *On the Face of the Waters* is a romance but one with a feminist twist: although the hero risks his life to save a woman while she nurses him back to life, the English woman in question is not saved by the man but, rather, by her own ingenuity. The Sepoy Mutiny becomes an opportunity for Kate Earlton to escape domestic confinement and to prove her independence. As the feminist plot moves toward a predictable resolution, true love is offered as the just reward for female courage and independence. The energy of Steel's narration goes into demonstrating that, contrary to male belief, English women are quite capable of taking care of themselves and need neither protection nor saving. This bold critique of British patriarchal authority is, however, countered by the novel's firm endorsement of the masculine code of chivalry. Although Steel refuses to characterize English women as helpless victims, she will not question the colonial logic that explains British retribution as the response of righteous English men to the massacre of innocents by unlawful Indians. To do so would obviously undermine the moral imperative of the civilizing mission, but not doing so clearly dilutes the force of Steel's feminism.

As the novel opens, we find the female protagonist, Kate Earlton, estranged from a disloyal husband upon whom she is financially, legally, and socially dependent. In addition to marital incompatibility and infidelity, Kate is condemned to bear the anguish of maternal deprivation in solemn silence. Trapped in an unhappy marriage, Kate continues to maintain a dignified front for the sake of her absent child (sent away to England in accordance with Anglo-Indian custom) by suppressing her sorrow in religion and nostalgia. Through an elaborate "cult of home" (OFW 22) Kate reproduces a Victorian ideal of domesticity that both hides the emptiness of her life and insulates her from the Indian society she regards with repulsion.

The beginning of the mutiny coincides with Kate receiving a letter from her husband informing her that he is leaving her for Alice Gissing, the vivacious and voluptuous wife of a low-class trader. Unlike Kate, who lives in India like an exile in a foreign land, Alice adopts a "nabob-and-pagoda-tree style" of life, for "the Gissings preferred India, where they were received into society, to England, where they could have been out of it" (OFW 48). Steel represents Alice's lower-class sexual exuberance with characteristic ambivalence, viewing it as emancipating and liberatory on the one hand and as dangerous and threatening on the other. *On the Face of the Waters* insistently draws attention to the double standard by which the sexual conduct of men and women are regulated and judged in Anglo-Indian society: "this tale of Fate—the man's excuse for the inexcusable which will pass current gaily until women combine in refusing to accept it for themselves" (140). Steel takes a certain delight in using Alice to expose the hypocrisy underlying the sexual decorums of Victorian society: "if she had more to give she would probably have been less generous than she was; being of that class of women who sin because the sin has no appreciable effect on them. It leaves them strangely, inconceivably unsoiled. This imperviousness, however, being, as a rule, considered the man's privilege only, Major Earlton failed to understand" (51). To the refined and repressed Kate Earlton, who lives strictly in accordance with upper-class codes of conduct, Alice is, however, a source of sexual anxiety: "Why, briefly, had she failed to make him what Alice Gissing had made him—a better man? And yet Alice Gissing did not love him; she had no romantic sentiment about him. Did she really lay less stress—she, the woman at whom other women held up pious hands of horror—on that elemental difference between the tie of husband and wife, and brother and sister than she, Kate Earlton, did, who had affected to rise superior to it altogether? It seemed so" (202–3). Kate seems unable to make her husband happy precisely because she is the ideal wife who sacrifices all her passions and ambitions for her family.

The sexual threat the lower-class woman poses to Kate is eliminated in the novel by martyring Alice as a maternal warrior in the imperial cause. Even as Kate confronts her rival about the affair, the mutiny breaks out, and Alice Gissing dies bravely trying to protect an English boy from an Indian rebel. The tragic and heroic death of Alice Gissing transforms her into a symbol of English womanhood that British soldiers carry into battle. Jenny Sharpe observes that, "by having the adulterous yet courageous Alice Gissing serve as the feminine ideal that soldiers are willing to die for, Steel wrests the 'mutiny lady' away from a sacred image in which a woman's chastity is the sign of her moral value."[66] Yet, at the same time, Alice's death must also be read as punishment and atonement for lower-class female sexual waywardness. And, as a final solution to the problematic of lower-class white female sexuality, her timely demise, I will argue a little later, becomes ideologically significant in the novel for the way it at once resembles yet differs from the fiery fate meted out to the Indian woman.

After the death of Alice Gissing, Kate is forced into hiding along with Jim Douglas, a gallant spy for the colonial government who had nine months earlier done her a personal favor that saved her husband's reputation. Arriving too late to prevent Alice's death, Jim Douglas finds Kate concealed in the Gissing house dressed as an Indian woman. He brings her to live with Tara Devi, a high-caste Rajput woman whom he had rescued from the flames of her husband's funeral pyre. Kate spends three months in Delhi with Tara, who teaches her how to speak and act like a native so she will not arouse suspicion. The English woman in hiding may be considered as a female counterpart to Jim, who, as spy, practices the same skills of disguise in order to travel back and forth between the city and the garrison. Being a woman, however, Kate is not free to transgress the borders that a British army spy does. Jim considers it too risky to take her out of the city, but he is haunted by the need to rescue her, especially because he had not been able to save Alice Gissing's life. For him it is not a matter of losing one woman but of contemplating the hundreds that must have died because men like himself were unable to save them. Inspired by General Nicholson, Jim Douglas determines to "save Kate, or—*kill somebody*. That was the whole duty of man" (OFW 305). The narrator, however, concerned about not endorsing this masculine discourse of revenge, quickly informs us that Kate "had already been found, or rather she had never been lost." Steel's heroine is so concerned that Jim not return to Delhi to rescue her that she places her own life in danger to save him. He does come back for her, only to discover that she has already made her escape with the help of Tara and other Indians.

Not only does Kate manage to escape without white male help, but she is never confronted with any sexual danger. At the same time, exaggerated rumors of English women being raped and tortured spread through the Anglo-Indian community and drive British soldiers into a frenzy of revenge. Caricaturing masculinist thinking, Steel wryly comments, "all women were alike in this, that they saw the whole world through the medium of their sex; and that was at the bottom of all the mischief. Delhi had been lost to save women; the trouble had begun to please them" (OFW 259). *On the Face of the Waters* questions the historical use of white women as an excuse for colonial violence. Yet this questioning does not lead to a condemnation of the severity with which the Sepoy Mutiny was crushed. In fact, John Nicholson, the general who led the successful charge against Delhi, is depicted in mythical terms as a belligerent avenging angel meting out rewards and punishments on the day of judgment. As the symbol of imperial patriarchal authority, Nicholson appears "kinglike" and "heroic" (359), cutting through doubts, hesitations, and red tape, as he declares in sonorous tones, "If I had them [the rebels] in my power today . . . and knew I was to die tomorrow, I would inflict the most excruciating tortures I could think of on them with an easy conscience" (356). Following the logic of colonial historiography, Steel rationalizes Nicholson's obsessive desire for revenge as a character flaw. She portrays him as a tragic figure who allows his passions momentarily to get the better of his English restraint: "a symbol of the many lives lost uselessly in the vain attempt to go forward too fast" (469). In the end the novel equivocates between criticizing British men for blaming their military excuses on women and reifying these women into symbols of male inspiration: "But if women had lost Delhi, those who lay murdered about the little cistern had regained it . . . the strength of the Huzoors lay there. The strength of the real Master!" (263).

The Trope of Chivalry

Like the abolition of sati in 1829—the first major legislation passed by the East India Company in India—the series of laws that were subsequently enacted on "women's issues" like widow remarriage, were homosocial acts through which white men could prove their superiority over brown men. *On the Face of the Waters* replicates this homosocial (ab)use of Indian women, portraying the white man as the savior of hapless Indian women caught in the clutches of a cruel and abusive native patriarchy. Although he is not allowed to save Kate Earlton, Jim Douglas, the gallant hero, not only buys Zora, his Indian mistress, out of prostitution but rescues Tara, the Rajput maid, from being burned on her husband's funeral pyre. At the same time, Steel strains to maintain the fiction that Jim Douglas's gallantry toward Indian women is motivated more by "romance" than by "passion." Unlike some English men who had combined the two lives, Jim, the author insists, is racially "fastidious" and will not be "content to think half-caste thoughts, to rear up a tribe of half-caste children" (OFW 35). Even the memory of the child Zora had borne him repulses Jim as he guiltily recalls the sense of relief he had experienced at the death of both child and mother. By contrast, when he and Kate rescue a little English boy during the mutiny, Jim realizes that "because Sonny's skin was really white beneath the stain that he thought of him as something to be proud of possessing; a boy who would go to school and be fagged and flogged and inherit familiar virtues and vices instead of strange ones" (OFW 324). As Jim's relationship with Kate and Sonny deepens, he recalls his life with Zora with increasing distaste: "the mystery of fatherhood and motherhood, which had nothing to do with that pure idyll of romantic passion on the terraced roof at Lucknow, yet which seemed to touch him here, where there was not even love; yet it was a better thing. The passion of protection, of absolute self-forgetfulness, seeking no reward, which the sight of those two raised in him, was a better thing than that absorption in another self" (OFW 324–25). The vocabulary of protection and possession used in many such passages throughout the novel to eroticize male-female relationships not only blunts Steel's feminist resolve to make the English woman independent but also restores the English woman to a position strangely similar to that of the Indian woman she seeks to displace.

Because of the public humiliation English women suffered at the hands of Indian rebels in 1857, they became, like the Indian sati, spectacular victims of Indian patriarchy and objects of British male protection. If the ideology of chivalry mobilized English men and justified colonial terror, it also inscribed English women within a code of chastity that valued female sexual purity over and above female life. As already noted, the Victorian code that venerated womanhood over women has frequently prompted comparison to the orthodox upper-caste Hindu code that demanded a widow's self-immolation as the essential expression of female purity. Steel's mutiny novel mediates this historical irony by staging a confrontation between the two women's worlds.

The "Good Wife" Contest

Living on the rooftops of Delhi in the disguise of Jim Douglas's Indian wife, Kate Earlton predictably discovers true love. But Steel will not gratify the English woman's desire until she has first elaborately set up and then eliminated the Indian woman as a potential sexual rival. Through a phantasmatic substitution of the Anglo-Indian woman for the Indian woman, *On the Face of the Waters* attempts to define certain distinguishing racial and cultural qualities that identify the white woman as uniquely suitable for the role of companionate colonialist. There are two major rivals Kate Earlton must both literally and symbolically displace before she can legitimately take her place by Jim Douglas's side: Tara, the Rajput woman who serves Kate out of gratitude and love for Jim Douglas; and, indirectly, Zora, the Muslim courtesan with whom Jim had led a secret Indianized life and whose death facilitates his return to an English life with Kate.

The sexual threat that Indian mistresses historically represented to Anglo-Indian women underwrites the narrative struggle between the Kate Earlton and her Indian counterparts. Living a life of seclusion in Delhi disguised as Jim Douglas's Indian wife, Kate Earlton once again finds herself physically and emotionally confined to a domestic space but now in the company of Tara, the servant woman whose loyalty to Jim Douglas alone ensures her safety and survival. A mutually disempowering relationship develops between the two women segregated together from the historic site of masculine struggle. Kate's enforced proximity to and dependence upon Tara reflects the derived and disempowered status English women shared with their Indian counterparts in a society shaped predominantly by male antagonisms. There are several instances when Steel's narrative registers with pain and anguish the troubling similarities binding colonizing and colonized women together in a common gendered disempowerment: "But God save all women, black or white, say I! Save them from men, and since we be all bound to Hell together by virtue of our sex, then will it be a better place than Paradise by having fewer men in it" (OFW 253). But since such insight exposes an unacceptable resemblance between Indian and English patriarchy and threatens to collapse the racial difference on which the colonial civilizing mission rested, Steel quickly reasserts an absolute difference between the two women: "Tara was spinning calmly, and Kate wondered if the woman could be alive. Did she not know that brave men on both sides were going to their deaths? And Tara, from under her heavy eyelashes, watched Kate, and wondered how any woman who had brought Life into the world could fear Death . . . So the two women waited, each after her nature" (OFW 283).

Kate Earlton finally renders her Indian counterparts redundant by making Jim Douglas realize how much "the mystery of such womanhood as Tara Devi's and little Zora's oppressed him. Their eternal cult of purely physical passion, their eternal struggle for perfect purity and constancy, not of the soul, but the body, their worship alike of sex and He who make it, seemed incomprehensible" (OFW 72). By comparing and contrasting Kate Earlton with Tara (and Zora), Steel elaborates a racialized distinction between an ungovernable and scorching "Eastern passion" and a refined and elevated "Western love." The difference is most powerfully framed through Tara's jealous gaze:

> In truth Tara had grown restless of late. Kate, looking up from her game of chess—at which her convalescent [Jim] gave her half the pieces on the board and then beat her easily—used to find those dark eyes watching them furtively. Zora Begum had never played *shatranj* with the master, had never read with him from books, had never treated him as an equal. And, strangely enough, the familiar companionship—inevitable under the circumstances—roused her jealousy more than the love-making on that other terraced roof had done. That she understood. That she could crush with her cry of *sutee*. But this—this which to her real devotion seemed so utterly desirable—what did it mean? So she crept away, when she could, to take up the saintly role as the only certain solace she knew for the ache in her heart. (OFW 315)

The political unconscious of this crucial passage forces us to read English feminism and social reform in nineteenth-century India in the context of colonialism. The companionate "equality" of women is offered as the foundation of English and hence of civil society. Kate's independence, courage, tact, and ability mark her out as a fit companion for the male colonialist. But, at the same time, the rhetoric of companionship used to represent white domesticity is contained within patriarchal norms of behavior and desire inscribed in the text. The code of chivalry that dictates Jim's behavior toward Kate, the code of submission that determines Kate's feelings for Jim, point unequivocally to the homosocial origins of Steel's sexual myths. In fact, male dominance and female submission are eroticized in several symbolic gestures in the text: Jim gives Kate half the pieces and then easily beats her at chess; he puts on her arm Zora's gold bracelet as a mark of ownership, making Kate feel a "flush, half of resentment, half of shame, still on her face. In such surroundings how trivial it was, and yet he had guessed her thought truly. Had he guessed also the odd thrill which the touch of that gold *fetter* gave her?" (OFW 258; emph. added).

In the end Kate Earlton moves from an incompatible loveless marriage into a relationship not of economic and intellectual equality but of reciprocal love. As the female colonialist articulates herself in shifting relationship to domestic companionship and social independence, the "native woman" is systematically excluded from any share in these emerging norms of Victorian feminism.[67] Although Tara finds the "familiar companionship" enjoyed by the English woman utterly desirable, she remains intrinsically incapable of comprehending it or gaining access to it. Even at the very end, when Jim falls ill a second time, Tara tries to copy Kate's actions in a pitiful attempt to recreate an English-style atmosphere. Since Jim fails to respond to her treatment, Tara is forced to accept her failure and fetch Kate (who had escaped to the English camp even before Jim returns to rescue her). The Indian woman is consigned to the margins, from where she jealously watches the English woman save the life of the man they both love.

The exhibitionistic quality of colonialism that made the master's identity dependent on the recognition of the slave is evident in the relish with which Steel parades scenes of companionate domesticity before the "hungry, passionate eyes" of Tara, whose presence at once testifies to and threatens the romance between Kate and Jim (OFW 331). Kate's jealousy toward Tara, which springs in part from her belief that it was her own lack of passion that had driven her husband into the arms of Alice Gissing, inscribes a gendered fear that the restrained, repressed upper-class white woman may not be woman enough to stave off the sexual threat embodied less fearfully by the lower-class white woman and far more fearfully by the brown woman. Kate Earlton's disguised life as an Indian wife may therefore be seen as a symbolic cannibalism that allows the Anglo-Indian woman to appropriate (in a "refined" form) the passion and power of Indian femininity so that the sexual threat posed by Indian women may be effectively eliminated.

Steel returns to this theme of sexual inadequacy in *The Law of the Threshold*, a lurid romance about India in which the sexual rivalry between Lucy Morrison and Maya Day is cast as a struggle between opposing versions of femininity—between Eastern passion and Western restraint. Although Lucy Morrison is too proud to admit it, she feels threatened by the attraction her fiancé, Charles Hastings, feels toward the sensuous Maya Day. Professor Anderson, the novel's symbol of benign British paternal authority, warns Maya: "Lucy Morrison is, as you know, a dear girl, a charming girl, who when she is his wife, will realize a lot that she doesn't understand at present. She has taught herself to hate what she calls nonsense—She is Western—cold as ice—you're Eastern, hot as fire—Yes! you are for all your idealism."[68] The implication is that the Anglo-Indian woman must somehow learn to combine passion with refinement in order to compete with the Indian woman for white male attention. Laughing at Maya's determination to suppress her inherited sensuality, Professor Anderson remarks: "You are simply woman—woman more than most—waiting as every woman waits, consciously or unconsciously, for a lover."[69] In the end the Indian woman delivers the white man into the safe custody of the white woman, declaring, "he is yours by right of birth, by right of creed, by right of love,"[70] and sacrifices herself in a supreme act of self-immolation. Similarly, in the final chapters of *On the Face of the Waters* Jim's rejection drives Tara to throw herself into the fires of Delhi, thus symbolically performing the sati she had been rescued from eight years earlier.

As a woman rescued from her husband's funeral pyre, Tara is objectified in the novel as a paradigmatic victim of Indian patriarchy and a passive recipient of the white man's chivalry. Since his intervention makes her an "out-cast" in her own community, Jim Douglas employs her as a servant to his Persian mistress, Zora, whom he had purchased from a brothel. But, having survived, the rescued widow's life, framed by her desire for death, becomes a deferred sati. Throughout the novel Tara expresses disappointment at having been denied the honor of sati, although it is unclear whether her disappointment stems from a deep devotion to her dead husband or from a rejection of her ignominious status as widow. After Zora's death Tara shaves her head, puts on the white sari of a widow, and goes down to the Ganges to drown herself. While praying at the holy river, she is struck by fire that leaves the "sacred scars" (OFW 112) of sati on her limbs. As a result of this miracle, Tara is both a widow who survives her husband and one who dies with him, a lowly out-cast as well as a heroic saint. As a living sati, Tara embodies the contradictory condition of death in life—a contradiction that is resolved only when she finally throws herself into the fire.

Tara Devi's death ensures Kate Earlton's survival and clears the way for her subsequent marriage to Jim Douglas. But, before her Indian rival can be eliminated, the English woman is required to undergo a rite of passage to prove that she is indeed the better woman of the two and, hence, the more suitable companion for Jim Douglas. Kate's test comes when Tara, believing that no English woman would make this ultimate sacrifice for a man, challenges her to disguise herself as a sati, a role for which she would have to shave her head, remove all her jewelry, and wear a widow's shroud. Tara herself had resisted when her head had been shaved and her jewelry removed. But, to the Rajput woman's astonishment, Kate readily agrees to do whatever she asks in exchange for assurances of Jim Douglas's safety. She begins hacking away at her hair and actually comes to enjoy the whole procedure: "for, in truth, she was becoming interested in her own adventures, now that she had, as it were, the control over them" (OFW 400)

The purpose of Kate's entry into the place of sati is obviously to establish an absolute racial difference between English and Indian women by giving the former agency precisely in the place most paradigmatic of female subjection. Steel's novel thus makes individual will the basis of racial difference. Unlike the Indian woman who is a passive slave to her domestic role, the English woman has agency to freely and voluntarily enter the space of sati. And, because she has access to free will, the English woman can escape the excesses of martyrdom: she will not burn to death like her Indian counterpart but, rather, will have an "adventure" playing sati (a masquerade that repeats the movements of the military spy across enemy lines) and thereby live to remarry. Thus, on one level Jenny Sharpe is quite correct to read the burning of Tara Devi in *On the Face of the Waters*, like that of Bertha Mason in *Jane Eyre*, as the orchestration and the staging of the self-immolation of the colonized woman that enables the emergence of the English feminist individualist.[71] But we cannot ignore the fact that in Steel's novel the sati, or good wife, is also presented as a model the English woman must emulate, even excel.

It seems as though Steel's companionate colonialist has the free will to reject not the ideal of the good wife as such but only the excesses implied by this ideal. In other words, Kate Earlton does not have to commit suicide like the Indian woman, but she must still prove her superiority over the Indian woman by exemplifying the feminine virtues of purity, loyalty, and, above all, self-sacrifice. Only after she proves this does Steel reward Kate with a companionate marriage to Jim Douglas. The fact that Steel enters her companionate colonialist into such a contest at all not only reveals Anglo-Indian women's internalization of patriarchal standards of female behavior, but it also makes them players in a colonial economy that uses women as currency to extend the reach and strengthen the hold of white men over brown. As such, I see the interracial good wife contest as a boundary post of imperial feminist individualism in an age of homosocial colonialism. On the one hand, the contest allows Steel to redefine the role of the Anglo-Indian woman in the home by transforming her from a passive moral symbol into an active moral agent of civilization. But, on the other hand, the white female moral agency Steel manufactures functions primarily as a privileged transactional token in the struggle between British and Indian patriarchies. That is, the purpose, or effect, of white female moral agency in Steel's novel is not so much to dismantle patriarchal ideologies as to uphold the racial superiority of English domestic institutions and thereby provide continued justification for colonial rule. By offering the sati simultaneously as a signifier of absolute Otherness and as a model, as inimitable and exemplary, as eminently dispensable and utterly indispensable, Steel furthers the cause of imperial feminist individualism yet effectively recontains it within those ideological structures through which colonial rule was affirmed and extended.

In the final analysis Steel's novel provides a measure of the psychological and emotional cost of internalizing Anglo-India's paternal codes and its concomitant ambivalence toward women. At the very moment of victory, when the English woman has proved her independence by surviving and escaping, she is forced to recognize the limitations of that independence. A rough reminder from John Nicholson that English men had "sacrificed too much for women" is sufficient to make Kate Earlton denigrate herself as an obstacle to imperial endeavor. She finds "a sudden sense of being a poor creature" come over her: "It flashed upon her that she could imagine a world without women—she was in one, almost, at that very moment but not a world without men; and yet that ceaseless roar filling the air had more to do with women than men; it went more as a challenge of revenge, than as a stern recall to duty" (OFW 392). The female colonialist's anguished awareness of her own superfluousness seeps through precisely at a moment in history when the Raj was consolidating its power with a vengeance. Produced in the aftermath of the Illbert Bill controversy, which revived mutiny fears of rape and constituted English women as objects of white male protection, *On the Face of the Waters* makes visible the uneasy yet productive links between English imperial feminism and homosocial colonialism.

5

Cartographies of Homosocial Terror: Kipling's Gothic Tales and *Kim*

Kipling's White Man

Rudyard Kipling has been a profound embarrassment to generations of literary critics. Ever since Oscar Wilde and Max Beerbohm began ridiculing his fiction in the late nineteenth century, Kipling has been read and condemned as the bard of empire by critics on the Right as well as on the Left of the political spectrum. Whether he was denounced as "the Hooligan" who wrote not about "the true spirit of our civilization" but about "the vulgarity, the brutality, the savagery" of "what the mob is thinking"[1] or dismissed as the prophet of British imperialism whose "imperialism is reprehensible not because it *is* imperialism but because it is a puny and mindless imperialism,"[2] Kipling has generally been viewed as an unproblematic and transparent producer of imperialist discourse. Critics who tried to defend Kipling's reputation as an artist did so mainly by separating his artistry from his imperialism and focusing on the "permanent human and moral themes" in his fiction rather than on its "politics."[3]

When Edward Said restored politics to the study of literature, he placed Kipling squarely within the discursive tradition of Orientalism.[4] Kipling's White Man is, for Said, the paradigmatic producer and product of Orientalism. Claiming that the White Man, like Orientalism itself, commanded a "field" that entailed certain peculiar modes, even rituals, of behavior, learning, and possession, Said observes: "Only an Occidental could speak of Orientals, for example, just as it was the White Man

who could designate and name the coloreds, or nonwhites. Every statement made by Orientalists or White Men (who were usually inter-
changeable) conveyed a sense of the irreducible distance separating
white from colored, or Occidental from Oriental; moreover, behind each
statement there resonated the tradition of experience, learning, and education that kept the Oriental-colored to his position of *object studied by
the Occidental-white,* instead of vice versa."[5] Said goes on to point out
that being a White Man in the colonies involved

> speaking in a certain way, behaving according to a code of regulations,
> and even feeling certain things and not others. It meant specific judg-
> ments, evaluations, gestures. It was a form of authority before which non-
> whites, and even whites themselves, were expected to bend. In the institu-
> tional forms it took (colonial government, consular corps, commercial
> establishments) it was an agency for the expression, diffusion, and imple-
> mentation of policy toward the world, and within this agency, although a
> certain personal latitude was allowed, the impersonal communal idea of
> being a White Man ruled. Being a White Man, in short, was a very concrete
> manner of being in the world, a way of taking hold of reality, language,
> and thought.[6]

I wish to problematize Said's monolithic and omnipotent conception of the Kiplingesque White Man by drawing attention to the
homosocial terror that fractures Kipling's cartographies of colonial
desire. Through an analysis of some early Gothic Indian tales (primarily
from the 1880s) and the picaresque novel *Kim* (1901), I shall demonstrate
that Kipling entertains a complex, often antagonistic, relationship to the
colonial ideal of manliness. Indeed, his tales of transgressions and
breakdowns, of slips and confusions of gender and race, display the
colonial body revolting against imperial technologies of discipline and
surveillance through impermissible, freakish, behavioral excess such as
unmanly hysteria and unacceptable sexuality. These narratives often
blur, overflow, or even undermine the boundary between the rational,
restrained, manly West and the irrational, excessive, effeminate East. In
these stories the White Man emerges not as an omnipotent embodiment
of imperial authority but, rather, as a deeply divided, culturally androgynous figure torn between the opposing demands of imperial manliness
and Indian effeminacy, between "going native" and "being sahib."

Kipling's representations and contestations of colonial masculinity
proves that English manliness was not only a race and class specific construct but one torn by severe tensions and contradictions. The narrow

ideal of manliness officially espoused and promoted by empire as the appropriate model required many Anglo-Indians, including Kipling himself, to brutally repress or deny certain aspects of their experience, identity, and self-image. Ironically, the official model of masculinity called for a repression or denial of precisely those aspects of experience that, by the 1880s, had become the capillaries of colonial power in India. It is in this context that Kipling's historic "failure" to come to terms with cultural hybridity becomes significant, making his representations of Self and Other deeply disruptive and burdening his White Man with a gloomy sense of fragility and futility about the civilizing mission.

The simplest way of explaining Kipling's ambivalence toward cultural hybridity is to see it as an effect of psychobiography. Thus, reading Kipling's "life" as a "textual system of characteristic behavior,"[7] Angus Wilson traces the fictional ambivalence to the conflict between Kipling's primary, unconscious, emotional identification with a maternal India, the land of his childhood, and his conscious rational adult masculine role as imperialist.[8] The problem I have with such psychobiographical explanations is that they tend to reify the ideological separation between the public and the private by reading the familial, the personal, the emotional, and the unconscious as the source of the social, the political, the rational, and the conscious. My use of biographical information in this chapter (as in others) is different in that it stresses the historical constructedness or the political basis of psychobiography. I therefore see the split at the core of Kipling's self-representation as an effect or a trace of the politics of post-mutiny India. As my analysis will demonstrate, the inexorable realism of Kipling's best stories involve complex mechanisms that link fantasy and reality, desire and history, in such inconceivable ways that no easy solutions to the anxieties of the colonial self are readily available.

In emphasizing the split at the core of colonial self-representation, I do not wish to suggest that colonial authority is any the less effective but, rather, that it is effective differently. In the historical context of late-nineteenth-century English colonialism in India, power is renewed and extended through novel more sophisticated discursive strategies that involve ambivalence, opposition, and contradiction. As recent studies have shown, late-nineteenth-century Orientalism actually relied upon contradiction and discontinuity to maintain, renew, even extend, its power as a discourse of dominance.[9] Thus, Kipling's fiction rejuvenates colonial authority as it opens up new, more efficient means of exercising power by appropriating for colonialism the language of defiance of its victims.

Kipling's India

When Kipling returned to India in October 1882, he found "a society which politically, nervously, physically, spiritually quivered on the edge of a precipice."[10] The 1883 controversy over the Illbert Bill provides a measure of both the force of Indian dissent and the ferocity of a government under siege. Kipling himself was neither then nor later a public supporter of "liberal" reforms in India. When the *Civil and Military Gazette,* for which Kipling worked as reporter, initially appeared to support the Illbert Bill, the members of the Punjab Club hissed at the bewildered young Rudyard as he entered the dining halls. The gazette subsequently joined the storm of protests against the bill, voicing its contempt for the Bengali character in no uncertain terms. Although the Illbert Bill was effectively neutralized, Indian nationalists were gathering force. By 1883 A. O. Hume had once again begun agitating for a parliamentary government for India. Hume was a controversial figure trusted both by English officials and elite Indian nationalists until he broke ranks with the British and joined Indian leaders like W. C. Bonnerjee, G. S. Iyer, and P. Mehta to become the cofounder of the Indian National Congress in 1884–85. The pamphlets Hume published in the 1880s brought upon him the wrath of officials who thought he aimed at becoming the "Indian Parnell."[11] Although Kipling, unlike Hume, took a decidedly conservative public stance on colonial policies, he was also accused by the English of consorting too closely with Indians. It is therefore not surprising that the problematic of how a sahib could become Indianized without losing his racial and cultural identity as an English man should become one of the major preoccupations of Kipling's fiction.

The viceroyalty of Lord Curzon from 1898 to 1905 signals the culmination of the autocratic trend in post-mutiny policy. The paternalistic authoritarianism of British rule expressed through Mughal emblems of power was said to satisfy the Oriental need for benevolent despotism. Extravagant durbars (such as Curzon's Delhi durbar of 1903) were held as spectacular displays of power. The Indian aristocracy, which had lost much of its authority in the pre-mutiny years, was strengthened by Lord Canning's land tenure policy. This successfully contained anticolonial peasant insurgency by restoring a loyal landholding class to power. The restored aristocracy also provided a measure of protection against an increasingly restive middle class. Curzon redoubled the effort to defuse political aspirations with administrative reforms. The Indian Civil Service became the cornerstone of the Raj and its officers, who were responsible for the day-to-day administration, the heroes of empire.

Many of Kipling's short stories feature these heroes of empire. They are typically faceless unindividualized middle-class characters like Bobby Wick ("Only a Subaltern") and George Cottar ("The Brushwood Boy") whose days are spent in unrelenting "duty" to the imperial mission without expectation of personal recognition or reward. They rarely deviate from the policy of aloofness Anglo-India officially adopted in the post-mutiny years. By contrast, lower-class looters like Dravot and Carnehan ("The Man Who Would Be King") are brutally punished for lacking restraint, emotional as well as political. And Kipling celebrates the common soldier as an unsung hero of empire only after sanitizing, domesticating, and romanticizing him from a decidedly middle-class perspective. These monolithic, unified constructions of colonial identity must, however, be placed alongside Kipling's compelling chronicles of colonial disintegration. The Gothic tale becomes a powerful artistic tool with which Kipling probes the anxiety and terror underlying Anglo-India's authoritarian paternalism.

The Imperial Gothic

Kipling's choice of the Gothic as the genre for conveying colonial terror is ideologically significant for several reasons. The Gothic, Eve Kosofsky Sedgwick points out, was the first novelistic form in England to have close, relatively visible links to male homosexuality, at a time when styles of homosexuality, and even their visibility and distinctness, were markers of division and tension between classes as much as between genders. But when homosexuality is not explicitly thematized, Sedgwick explains, mostly what seems like homosexual thematics is actually based on homophobia, the psychology of prohibition and control, while heterosexuality constitutes its real subject.[12] The Imperial Gothic emerges as a powerful genre in Anglo-Indian literature at a time when homosexuality was a marker of racial division between English and Indian. As such, the treatment of interracial male relations in Kipling's Gothic tales, which clearly exhibit no visible links to homosexuality, stems from a homophobia that is visible only as an effect of race. In these resolutely homosocial stories the obligatory female middle term either facilitates or deflects attention from intense interracial male antagonisms.

Transposed into the colonial context, Kipling's tales follow what Sedgwick identifies as the typical Gothic plot line: one or more males who not only are persecuted by, but also consider themselves transparent to and often under the compulsion of another male. If the sense of persecution represents a repressed homosexual (or even merely homosocial) desire, then the plot can be expected to embody homophobic mechanisms.[13] Kipling's tales are about white men who get caught up in strange situations in which they feel vulnerable to or persecuted by Indian men over whom they are authorized to exercise power. These symbolic reversals make graphic the mechanisms of homosocial panic even as they re-implicate colonial authority in a whole series of new, more efficient, completely naturalized relations of power.

"The Strange Ride of Morrowbie Jukes" (1885) presents what may be considered a typical Gothic plot.[14] A carnivalesque nightmare located on the ambiguous cusp between dream and reality, the story recounts the bizarre experience of Morrowbie Jukes, an engineer who falls into a sand-walled pit that serves as a prison for Indians condemned by the custom of their community to live in exile after having been pronounced dead prematurely. The gendered geography of the pit presents a surreal setting not unlike the Marabar caves in *A Passage to India*. Isolated and alienated among the hostile group of Indians, Jukes is forced to rely on his engineering prowess to measure and map an escape route out of the pit.

Jukes's story is framed by a narrator who subverts its reliability from the very outset. As the voice of colonial reason and authority, the narrator vouches for the sanity and reliability of Jukes's character yet sabotages the authenticity and veracity of Jukes's tale. He opens the story by assuring the reader that "there is no invention about this tale" but proceeds as follows:

> And, since it is perfectly true that in the same Desert is a wonderful city where all the rich money-lenders retreat after they have made their fortunes (fortunes so vast that the owners cannot trust even the strong hand of the Government to protect them, but take refuge in the waterless sands) and drive sumptuous C-spring barouches, and buy beautiful girls, and decorate their palaces with gold and ivory and Minton tiles and mother-o'-pearl, I do not see why Jukes's tale should not be true. He is a Civil Engineer, with a head for plans and distances and things of that kind, and he certainly would not take the trouble to invent imaginary traps. (SRMB 3)

The narrator invokes the opposition between invention and reality only to blur the line between fact and fantasy, reason and emotion, manliness and effeminacy, Self and Other. In thus destabilizing Jukes's authority, the narrator undermines his own credibility and raises troubling questions about the status of colonial knowledge and the potency of colonial epistemology.

Within the "village of the living dead" there is neither law nor custom, and Jukes's status as an English man means nothing: "Here was a Sahib, a representative of the dominant race, helpless as a child and completely at the mercy of his native neighbors" (SRMB 13). In a potentially radical reversal of colonial rule the Indians declare the pit a republic. Appalled, Jukes cries out: "Yes, we were a Republic indeed! A Republic of wild beasts penned at the bottom of a pit to eat and fight and sleep till we died" (18). Jukes's unsuccessful attempt to dominate the Indians and make good an escape involves him in a desperate game of suspicion, deception, and treachery with Gunga Dass, a former employee of the imperial government who takes the white man under his wing and then treats him with utter contempt.

Predictably, the colonialist experiences loss of power as a loss of masculinity and as a fall into femininity (symbolized by the pit into which he has fallen). Unable to outwit Gunga Dass or find any means of escape, Jukes feels "as completely prostrated with nervous terror as any woman" (SRMB 16). "Fallen" colonizers such as Jukes are cultural reminders of nineteenth-century anxiety about the fluidity of sexual and racial Otherness, an anxiety that insulates itself by excluding that which is deviant, dirty, and effeminate. So, instead of "moping" and exhibiting "unmanly weakness," Jukes determines to act aggressively. The measures he relies upon to regain control both over his own panic and over his surroundings—measuring, calculating, cataloging, classifying, reasoning—are classic expressions of colonial manliness. But within the pit Jukes's rituals of control turn out to be as absurd and irrational as the Indian practices he condemns.[15]

Finally, when Jukes has given up all hope of escape and lies unconscious due to a blow dealt by Gunga Dass, he is gratuitously rescued by a faithful servant, the deux ex machina who appears miraculously at the top of the pit, calling him "in a whisper—Sahib! Sahib! Sahib! exactly as my bearer used to call me in the mornings" (SRMB 24). With the restoration of Jukes, the colonial order is allowed to reassert its hegemony. Only now, in contrast to the demonic world of democratized India, colonial order appears even more "normal" and "natural," rather than constructed or imposed. Thus, instead of being subversive, the carnivalesque reversal of colonial power structures actually facilitates or enables the renewal and enhancement of the White Man's authority. "The Strange Ride of Morrowbie Jukes" appeared at the end of 1885, the year the Indian National Congress met for the first time. Kipling's demonic caricature of democratized India therefore provides an ironic index of colonial anxiety at a historic juncture, when Indian resistance was clearly gathering momentum.

As is the case in "The Strange Ride of Morrowbie Jukes," an important figure of colonial ambivalence in many of Kipling's Gothic tales is the ubiquitous frame narrator. The narrator functions as an ironic and unstable locus of authority in stories that tell of disintegration, collapse and, loss of white male identity. The split in narrative consciousness is manifested either through the narrator's relationship with a "fallen" Anglo-Indian double or through his own direct interaction with Indians. As the next two stories I discuss illustrate, the narrator who "survives" to tell the tale about his fallen Anglo-Indian double is characteristically repressed, official, and perfunctory, while the narrator who interacts directly with Indians betrays the cost of denial and division more openly.

Like Kipling himself, the narrator is a newspaperman defined by inaction who operates on the slippery border between English and Indian society. Yet, if Kipling projects himself into the character of the narrator, he does so in a deeply ironic fashion, undermining any simplistic equation between their positions or views. He repeatedly sets up the narrator as an annoyingly all-knowing sahib, only to call his authority and credibility into question. Typically, the narrator attempts to impose an exaggeratedly monologic, recognizably official frame on an embedded story that never quite fits the frame. The embedded story is often a tale of lurid action told by the narrator whose connection with the events is marginal. Kipling's treatment of the narrator's inaction reflects, in some measure, the ambivalence he felt toward his own vocation as a writer, which, in contrast to that of the soldier, he saw as being effeminate in its passivity. The meditations of the reporter-narrator that precede the reported action raise disturbing and unacknowledged questions about himself and his story. Through this method Kipling exposes in varying degrees the denied or repressed desire of the colonial subject.

"To Be Filed for Reference," the climactic story in *Plain Tales from the Hills* (1888),[16] opens with the narrator's moralistic generalizations about colonial transgression: "When a man begins to sink in India, and is not sent Home by his friends as soon as may be, he falls very low from a respectable point of view. By the time that he changes his creed, as did McIntosh, he is past redemption. In most big cities natives will tell you of two or three Sahibs, generally low-caste, who have turned Hindu or Mohammedan, and who live more or less as such" (TBFR 235). The narrator then proceeds to recount the life of Jellaludin McIntosh, a former sahib and an Oxford scholar who has gone native and transgressed the boundaries of race and class through religious conversion to Islam, through sexual association with an Indian woman, and through cultural assimilation to an Indian lifestyle.

The narrator is a smug and cocky reporter who enjoys exploring the Indian bazaars and caravanserais. Through such explorations he has acquired a superficial knowledge of Indian life, which he parades by priggishly pointing out that Jellaludin was going against local custom in allowing his Indian woman to eat alongside her man. The narrator's apparently unconventional behavior is belied by his "healthy" regard for the opinions of other Anglo-Indians. Although drawn to Jellaludin, the narrator is far too concerned about his own respectability to visit his "loafer" friend by day. Jellaludin himself has forsaken all such considerations of social acceptability. He has thereby gained a deep knowledge of India that respectable sahibs, shackled by conventions, could not hope to gain. He even mocks Strickland, the detective whose familiarity with India makes him a model colonialist in many of Kipling's other stories, as being "ignorant East and West."

Jellaludin's Indian experiences are summed up in his masterpiece, *Mother Maturin*, a "new Inferno," which he claims will reveal more about the Indian way of life than any previous work. But before he can complete the manuscript Jellaludin pays for the knowledge he has gained with death. Wracked by drink and disease and without the aid of civilization (warm clothing, medicine), he dies in his squalid hut, mourned only by his Indian woman. As a final gesture of friendship before he dies, Jellaludin hands over the manuscript to the narrator, asking him to "say how it came into your possession. No one will believe you, but my name, at least, will live. You will treat it brutally, I know you will. Some of it must go; the public are fools and prudish fools. I was their servant once. But do your mangling gently—very gently. It is a great work, and I have paid for it in seven years' damnation" (TBFR 241). It is important to note that in the end neither Jellaludin's oppositional lifestyle nor its product (the manuscript) escape the discursive networks of empire. In fact, through the intervention of the narrator both Jellaludin's life and his "censored" book confirm, even reify, colonial stereotypes about Indian society. This is the way in which Kipling's own anomalous identity as a brown sahib or an Indianized

White Man may be seen as becoming productive for colonialism, providing valuable "feedback" that enriched imperial stores of information about India.

Ironically, it is to Strickland, the detective who appears in so many of
Kipling's stories, that the narrator finally turns for an evaluation of Jellaludin's work. The man whom Jellaludin had mocked is thus given the
final word: "Strickland helped me sort them [Jellaludin's papers], and he
said that the writer was either an extreme liar or a most wonderful person. He thought the former" (TBFR 241). Through the divergent positions
of Jellaludin, Strickland, and the narrator, Kipling explores the problematic nature of colonial knowledge and control. Jellaludin's complete and
public identification with India isolates and destroys him, even as it supposedly brings him profound knowledge. Strickland, by contrast, crosses
the border but only in disguise. Disguise enables him to move freely
among Indians, learning their ways and collecting information useful for
maintaining colonial rule. By minimizing his physical, psychological, and
emotional exposure, Strickland achieves a certain spurious autonomy to
move from one society to another without being bound by the constraints
of either one. It is just such a limited autonomy that the narrator finally
endorses. Although he is clearly fascinated by Jellaludin's unconventional ways, he retreats from the dangers of such close encounters with
the Other. Jellaludin's tale is therefore "to be filed for reference" both as a
warning (to Kipling himself) against taking a similar route and as a
reminder of who wrote *Mother Maturin* (an unfinished novel about
Eurasian lowlife that Kipling himself struggled vainly with).

Kipling's construction of the colonizer as an ambivalent figure is
evident in his narrator's admitted ability to occupy dual positions—
simultaneously distancing himself from the inner story of the Other
while inadvertently revealing his vulnerability. The narrator defines
himself as a typical sahib in allegiance with other sahibs who aid in
defining his official social function, thus guaranteeing his sanity and
continuing service to empire. His function as storyteller is to frame and
thereby foreground the fallen sahib, the sahib-gone-native, against
whom he opposes himself. But his allusions, rhetoric, and imagery dismantle the oppositions and implicate him in the story of failure he
chooses to remember and rewrite. By projecting onto the narrative
double that which he desires, denies, or represses in himself, the narrator makes of the inner story a mirror of the outer frame, both reflecting
and contradicting what the outer story implies. The incident chosen for

retelling is always a source of displaced personal or political anxiety. What makes these stories so compelling is the way in which the narrator, despite his stated intentions, fails to provide a unified and ideologically coherent story. That characteristic stylistic incoherence suggests connections between the story's narrative inconsistencies and the contradictions of its larger historical context. This, in Macherey's terms, is a "historical defect" created by the collision between the narrative voice and the colonial enterprise it chooses to describe.[17] For Homi Bhabha it represents the contradictions of a discourse in which mastery, though asserted, is always slipping away.[18] This historical defect, slippage, or "repertoire of conflictual positions" will reveal itself vividly not only in these stories but in almost all of Kipling's stories about India.

"On the City Wall," first published in the collection graphically titled *In Black and White* (1888),[19] is one of the last stories Kipling wrote in India and one of the most revealing. The story, which features the narrator who interacts directly with Indians, contains all the turbulent characteristics of Kipling's Lahore: religious strife between Hindu and Muslim, the canker of Oriental intrigue that gradually permeates the action, and, most important, the inevitable but somehow superficial presence of the narrator. The natives of Lahore gather in the salon of Lalun, a courtesan, to plot a political rebellion against British authority. Wali Dad, the young English-educated Muslim who promises to help Lalun in rescuing an important political prisoner, loses control over himself during the Mohurrum procession and joins in the usual Hindu-Muslim riot. He passionately participates in the procession, beating his breast and chanting, forgetting, in his religious fanaticism, the part he was to have played in the rescue mission. The narrator inadvertently takes Wali Dad's place and ends up helping Lalun, with whom he is secretly enamored.

Structurally (as indicated by the title of the original collection, *In Black and White*), the story is divided into "black" and "white," native desire and British discipline. *White* is represented in a masculine register of work, government, duty, activity, control; *black* in a feminine code of play, eroticism, sexuality, song, intrigue. The narrator occupies an ambiguous position moving in and out of these two symbolic spaces. His fantasies revolve around his erotic desire to displace Wali Dad as Lalun's lover. On the eve of Mohurrum the narrator daydreams that he is made vizier in Lalun's "administration," with Lalun's silver *huqa* for a mark of office (OCW 234). The completion of this sexual "comedy," the movement of the narrator from a restrained romantic dreamer to an active participant, is closely linked to the political aspect of the plot. The story's management of the narrator's sexual fantasy at once raises and represses questions of indigenous resistance and imperial control.

In the beginning the narrator and Wali Dad embody in a fairly unproblematic way the characteristics of English restraint and Indian excess. Although the narrator transgresses the conventions of Anglo-Indian society in befriending Indians, his (ad)ventures into colonized space never really poses a threat to his superior white identity; he remains an aloof spectator. Wali Dad, however, is a mimic man embody-ing the divided colonized subject. As a romantic, cultivated, decadent, witty, and cynical "young Muhammadan who was suffering acutely from education of the English variety and knew it," Wali Dad divides his life "between borrowing books from me and making love to Lalun in the window-seat" (OCW 222). He was "always mourning over some-thing or other—the country of which he despaired, or the creed in which he had lost faith, or the life of the English which he could by no means understand" (226). Wali Dad, a prototypical cultural hybrid, is the ancestor of Forster's Aziz. His cynical response to the narrator's sug-gestion that he give up dreaming and take his place in the world may indeed have suggested to Forster the famous "bridge party" Aziz attends in *A Passage to India*. Wali Dad replies: "I might wear an English coat and trousers. I might be a leading Muhammadan pleader. I might be received even at the Commissioner's tennis-parties where the En-glish stand on one side and the natives on the other, in order to promote social intercourse throughout the Empire" (232–33).

In the end Wali Dad gets emotionally caught up in a religious riot, and it is the narrator who unwittingly assists Lalun in rescuing the polit-ical prisoner. But, by abandoning his passive role as observer and par-ticipating in the action, the narrator inadvertently gets implicated in the plot against the British and, in a sense, comes to share Wali Dad's ambivalent position. Like Wali Dad, the narrator loses control over the situation and gets emotionally caught up in something he comprehends only much later: "Wali Dad was the man who should have convoyed him [the political prisoner named Khem Singh] across the City, or that Lalun's arms round my neck were put there to hide the money that Nasiban gave to Khem Singh, and that Lalun had used me and my white face as even a better safeguard than Wali Dad who proved himself so untrustworthy" (OCW 242). The erotic fantasy that prevents the nar-rator from seeing the truth mirrors the religious fanaticism that destroys Wali Dad's rational faculties. Kipling underscores the ironic position of the narrator in the story's closing lines: "But I was thinking how I had become Lalun's Vizier after all" (243). The profound irony that underwrites the gratification of colonial desire inscribes an unexpected convergence between black and white conduct.

Structurally, "On the City Wall" inscribes colonial desire on two levels: on one level the story reveals an "impersonal" desire for control that is satisfied through the crushing of the religious riot by a superefficient colonial system; on another, more problematic level the tale unfolds a "personal" desire to abandon control and to submit to the seduction of the East—a seduction that is embodied not only in the overt heterosexual attraction Lalun exerts over the narrator but also in the covert homoerotic appeal Wali Dad holds for him. There is undoubtedly a strong wish-fulfilling register in the story's attempt to gratify both levels of desire. The production of this wish-fulfilling register allows us to account for Kipling's ideology, which may be grasped as an axiomatic of the fantasy text, as those narrative presuppositions that one must "believe" in order for the subject to tell itself this particular dream successfully. The intrinsic effeminacy of the Indian male thus becomes an essential assumption for the gratification of colonial desire. Wali Dad must lapse into fanaticism and become impotent in order for the narrator to take his place. The obdurate realism underlying Kipling's fantasy text, however, makes it supremely aware of the strain involved in such dangerous maneuvers. Thus, the narrator's private desire is gratified but only in a deeply ironic fashion, as, in the process of generating the fantasy, the text is compelled to secure its own mode of probability. The inexorable realism in Kipling's best work usually does its preparatory work so well that even his most wish-fulfilling register is confounded by the resistance of the Real.

In general, the issue of knowledge in Kipling's stories is informed by a gendered anxiety to achieve and exercise "manly" control, both over one's own desires and over one's surroundings. However futile such an ambition may ultimately turn out to be, knowledge for the colonialist, and for the narrator most of all, requires insight into the fabric of illusion and allurement on which the seemingly stable world of empire is based. Precariously poised between order and chaos, convention and ritual, Kipling's White Man usually has only a tenuous hold over reality. As in the epigraph to "The House of Sudhoo" (1886),[20] the colonialist is always keenly aware that "a stone's throw out on either hand / From that well ordered road we tread, / And all the world is wild and strange" (IHS 108). "The House of Sudhoo" at first seems to be invoking a weird and bizarre world like "The Strange Ride of Morrowbie Jukes." The story revolves around the eerie display of jadoo, or sorcery, that the reporter-narrator is invited to witness. But, when the jadoo turns out to be a sham, we realize that we are in a different India from those of the other Gothic tales. The reporter uncovers not another counterpart of Juke's pit but, rather, a network of desire, greed, and fraud that is, in a way, far more menacing: Sudhoo, the victim of a seal cutter's plots, instead of eliciting the narrator's sympathy, is an "old dotard," a miser, and a fool who deserves his sordid fate. Although the seal cutter is a rogue and a charlatan, he is skillful enough at his trickery to win the reporter's admiration.

More complex than either of the men is the figure of the Indian prostitute. Like so many other Indian women who appear in Kipling's tales, Janoo evokes strong feelings in the narrator. He describes her as "a lady of free-thinking turn of mind" and "a woman of masculine intellect." The narrator respects her for seeing through the fakery, and yet her rage at the seal cutter stems not from principle but from her frustration at being unable to cheat old Sudhoo herself. Since Janoo has borrowed money from the seal cutter, she is powerless to challenge him. At the end of the story we are told that Janoo will probably poison the seal cutter unless he murders her first.

The narrator finds himself helplessly caught in a web of power and intrigue, unable to denounce the seal cutter for fear of harm to Janoo or Sudhoo and unable to get a witness to support his evidence. The India that Jukes encounters is a nightmare world, marked by extreme and horrible characteristics that seem unreal. But the India of Sudhoo's world, inhabited only by the venal tenants of a decrepit and gullible landlord, is utterly commonplace. Since the jadoo is shown to be fake, the logic of the tale insists that the wickedness is real. The narrator's helpless situation points to the precariousness of a power whose strategies are constantly frustrated by the everyday tactics of the weak. Thus, Western technology, symbolized by the telegraph line, has been perverted by the seal cutter for furthering his fraud; colonial judicial institutions, embodied in the Indian penal code, have been rendered impotent by a conspiracy of local custom, ignorance, fear, and malice. The status of colonial knowledge is highly problematic in this tale: even insight into the mystery and allurement of indigenous life do not enable the narrator to act upon it.

The Indian woman in Kipling's tales typically serves as the obligatory middle term through which white male anxieties over racial and sexual identity, over status, power, and control, are expressed. "Beyond the Pale" (1888)[21] is a Gothic romance that recounts an ill-fated love affair between an English man and an Indian child-widow. The story opens with a frame narrator's moralizing observations: "A man should, whatever happens, keep to his own caste, race and breed. Let the White go to the White and the Black to the Black. Then, whatever trouble falls is in the ordinary course of things—neither sudden, alien, nor unexpected." Embedded within this moralizing frame is the tragic tale of Christopher Trejago, the English man whose excessive knowledge and desire ultimately leads to the horror of excessive lack: "This is the story of a man who willfully stepped beyond the safe limits of decent everyday society, and paid for it heavily. He knew too much in the first instance; and he saw too much in the second. He took too deep an interest in native life; but he will never do so again" (BP 127). With this ominous statement the narrator determinedly sets out to encode Trejago's sexual tragedy into a Victorian cautionary tale for English men in India.

The forbidden zone of transgression that lies "Beyond the Pale" is the sexualized body of the child-widow Bisesa, which is rendered coterminous with the geography of India. Conflating geography with gender in a fairly stereotypical way, the text exoticizes the Orient as a female Other upon which the colonialist performs predictable rape. Confident in his Orientalist belief that the Arabian Nights provides an adequate travel guide to the East, the narrator maps a setting that lies in ominous passivity under his cartographic probe: "Deep away in the heart of the City, behind Jitha Megji's bustee, lies Amir Nath's Gully, which ends in a dead-wall pierced by one grated window. At the head of the Gully is a big cowbyre, and the walls on either side of the Gully are without windows" (BP 127). Paralleling the narrator's discursive mastery is Trejago's successful entry into the domain of colonized domesticity. While such discursive and erotic domination seem to enact standard colonial fantasies of penetration and possession, it is important to note that, as concept metaphor for imperialism, rape is not so much about the penetration and possession of a female body as it is about the emasculation of a male one. In other words, the real purpose of establishing white male domination over colonized female bodies is to humiliate Indian men, who are assumed to be the legitimate owners of Indian women.

The narrative draws attention to the subordinated position of Indian women with an ironic observation about the attitudes of Indian men: "Neither Suchet Singh nor Gaur Chand approve of their women-folk looking into the world. If Durga Charan had been of their opinion he would have been a happier man to-day, and little Bisesa would have been able to knead her own bread" (BP 127). Trejago's entry into this closely guarded territory is presented as a challenge to Indian patriarchy represented in the text by the absent person of Bisesa's uncle. What unfolds is a serialized conquest of the widow by Indian patriarchy and English imperialism. She is victimized not only by her uncle but also by Trejago and the narrator, who Orientalize her into an obscure object of male desire.

Bisesa's anomalous status as a Hindu widow marks the historical moment of Kipling's narrative. One of the most hotly debated issues during the 1880s was the matter of widow remarriage. The Hindu Widows' Remarriage Act of 1856, one of the critical issues around which anticolonial sentiment had been mobilized during the Sepoy Mutiny of 1857, had not only failed to change the attitudes of high-caste Hindus, who continued to hold widow remarriage in disrepute, but its ambiguous applicability to various Hindu castes effectively disinherited remarrying widows.[22] The issue was revived in the early 1880s by Indian male reformers who appealed to the colonial government, which then instituted in 1884 a broad process of public consultation to elicit further opinion on the issue. The invitation to intervene in matters that the colonial state, with the complicity of elite Indian males, had deliberately marked off as the apolitical private feminine realm of Hindu tradition was seen as further proof of Indian ineptitude. At the same time, since the disarming and disempowering presence of the colonial state denied Indian men access to public political authority, they sought, with the encouragement of the government, to reassert their masculinity in the privatized sphere by installing themselves as the guardians of a tradition that, although it continued to be defined in feminized terms, gave the men increased ability to determine the status and control the freedom of Indian women. Conducted almost exclusively among men, the debate over Hindu widows predictably cast the Indian woman in contradictory terms as oversexed, immoral, ignorant, and ungovernable or as sexless, chaste, pure, and self-sacrificing.[23] The widow thus became a symbolic site for a power struggle between colonizing and colonized men. By making a widow the unstable site of contention between Trejago and Durga Charan, Kipling's story symbolically rehearses the ideological roles of white and brown men in a debate that effectively erased the subjectivity of the woman herself. In the end Bisesa is mutilated by her enraged uncle, who cuts off her hands as punishment for sexual transgression. The final image of Bisesa sticking her stumps out of the window inscribes the Indian woman's sexuality as a corrosive, punishing and punished commodity.

Trejago's conquest of Bisesa represents a territorial invasion that emasculates Durga Charan. Yet, in order to enter the "grave" where Indian patriarchy has incarcerated the child-widow (BP 132), Trejago himself is forced to adopt "unmanly" ruses: "In the day-time, Trejago drove through his routine of office work, or put on his calling-clothes and called on the ladies of the Station, wondering how long they would know him if they knew of poor Bisesa. At night, when all the City was still, came the walk under the evil-smelling *boorka,* the patrol through Kitha Meghi's bustee, the quick run into Amir Nath's Gully between the sleeping cattle and the dead wall, and then, last of all, Bisesa, and the deep, even breathing of the old woman who slept outside the door of the bare little room that Durga Charan allotted to his sister's daughter" (130). The contrasting images of day and night, life and death, order and disorder, point to a split in the colonizer's identity. The office and colonial station are identified as the domain of social obligation, respectability, and consciousness; the dead walls and the dark room of Bisesa mark the scene of desire, transgression, and the unconscious. The colonialist thus becomes both the agent of colonial power and the subject of a defiant attempt to cross its racial boundaries. Trejago's secret visits to his beloved's room involves being disguised in a native garment called the *boorka,* which Kipling explains, "cloaks a man as well as a woman" (129). Notwithstanding this somewhat inaccurate ethnographic observation (the *boorka* being a garment usually worn in public by Muslim women), Kipling's figure of cross-dressed manhood inscribes a sexual ambiguity that deconstructs the phallic image of the colonialist.

Trejago's secret visits to Bisesa come to a violent end on the night he is attacked by Durga Charan. As the English man, dressed in a *boorka,* attempts to enter the widow's room through a window, a hidden hand suddenly thrusts a knife into his groin. The crazed Trejago's first act, when he flees in panic from the native quarter, is to tear off the *boorka* in an attempt to reassert his masculine identity. Although the knife is wielded by Durga Charan, the "native quarter" itself, where sexual identity is confused or obscured, becomes the primary source of threat. The story ends by marking the bounds of colonial cartography through Trejago's symbolic castration: the English man is unable to find the way back to Bisesa's window because "he does not know where lies the front of Durga Charan's house." India's topographical impregnability is literally inscribed upon the geography of Trejago's body as he is left with a lifelong limp from the groin wound.

The image of an Indian man's hidden hand "thrusting" a knife into the groin of an English man whose sexual identity is concealed by the *boorka* (the Indian woman's garment) suggestively recodes colonialism's master metaphor of rape in a more homoerotic register. Even such a subtle recasting should remind us of the extent to which, by the end of the nineteenth century, white male sensibilities in the colonies, not unlike white women's, had become structured around images of rape. The availability of male rape as a metaphor in colonial settings is confirmed by the graphic descriptions in Richard Burton's *Thousand Nights and a Night* (1885–88) and T. E. Lawrence's *Seven Pillars of Wisdom*. In Kipling's Imperial Gothic the motif of white male penetration and ravishment is manifested not in such literal terms but through metaphoric and disguised images of supernatural invasion and possession.

"The Phantom Rickshaw" (1885),[24] one of Kipling's earliest stories, tells of Pansay, a young English man caught between his forbidden desire for a married Anglo-Indian woman and his legitimate love for an unmarried one. His choice of legitimacy and propriety results in the death of the married woman, who returns as a ghost to haunt him into madness and death. The absent subject of the story, however, is neither the woman nor the affair but, rather, India itself, an (un)yielding space where white male mastery, though asserted, is always slipping away. The story opens with this ironic comment from the frame narrator: "One of the few advantages that India has over England is a great Knowability" (PR 26). The problem of "knowing" India—a recurrent theme for parody in Kipling's fiction—is so absurd and outside the scope of narrative undertaking that its very possibility is suggested and negated by shifting the issue from an external historical site to an insider's private realm of possibility. The reader is moved in narrowing concentric circles from macrocosmic India, to English men in India, to the microcosmic case of one solitary English mind that disintegrates in India. The epigraph to "The Phantom Rickshaw" suggests that what the colonialist fears most is being "molested" by the "powers of Darkness" that inhabit India. The mysterious and mystic forces that tantalize and trouble Kipling's characters, narrators, and their narratives mark the bounds of white male potency, ingenuity, pragmatism, and rationality.

In "The Mark of the Beast" (1890),[25] in which an English man who desecrates a Hindu temple turns into a werewolf, ravishment in the form of supernatural possession emerges as a significant metaphor for the weakening of imperial dominance in late-nineteenth-century India. This story, like so many others, opens with a perfunctory comment from the frame narrator : "East of the Suez, some hold, the direct control of Providence ceases; Man being there handed over to the power of the Gods and Devils of Asia, and the Church of England only exercising an occasional and modified supervision in the case of Englishmen" (MB 178). The embedded tale that follows bears out the frame narrator's theory but, as always, only in a deeply ironic fashion.

One day a drunken Fleete rushes into the temple of Hanuman, the "monkey-god," and grinds his cigar butt into the forehead of the stone idol. Immediately, a phantasmatic figure emerges from a recess behind the image:

> He was perfectly naked in that bitter, bitter cold, and his body shone like frosted silver, for he was what the Bible calls "a leper white as snow." Also he had no face, because he was a leper of some years' standing, and his disease was heavy upon him . . . the Silver Man ran in under our arms, making a noise exactly like the mewing of an otter, caught Fleete round the body and dropped his head on Fleete's breast before we could wrench him away. (MB 180)

From the time of the Sepoy Mutiny onward official Anglo-Indian discourse had, of course, constituted the Indian male as a potential rapist by imaging the threat of rape as impinging specifically upon the immobile white female body. If the Silver Man's vampiric "ravishment" and "possession" of Fleete conjures up colonial fears of rape, it does so by wrenching rape out of its officially sanctioned heterosexual context and portraying the colonized male body, naked and disfigured, bending threateningly over a helpless white man and biting his breast. What is hidden behind such homoerotic reversals, however, is the reality of the White Man exploiting subaltern Indian men—sexually, economically, and politically. Even E. M. Forster erased this brutal reality by self-censoring the "Kanaya" memoir from *The Hill of Devi.*

Following his encounter with the Silver Man, Fleete mysteriously degenerates into a state of bestiality. His condition confounds the Anglo-Indian doctor, who functions solely within the logical parameters of Western science. Only Strickland, the detective, realizes that Fleete has been bewitched by the Silver Man as punishment for defiling the image of Hanuman. An agonistic homosocial battle for control over Fleete's body and soul ensues between Strickland and the Silver Man.

With the help of the narrator, Strickland eventually overpowers the leper and tortures him until he agrees to return Fleete to a state of normalcy. But the final image of the colonialist the story presents belies the finality of Strickland's victory over the Silver Man. Recalling the grotesqueness of the whole affair and their own roles in it, Strickland and the narrator suddenly collapse into tumultuous laughter: "But Strickland did not answer. He caught hold of the back of a chair, and, without warning, went into an amazing fit of hysterics. Then it struck me that we had fought for Fleete's soul with the Silver Man in that room and had disgraced ourselves as Englishmen for ever, and I laughed and gasped and gurgled just as shamefully as Strickland, while Fleete thought we had both gone mad" (MB 190). Beneath the brash manly front and the stiff upper lip lurks the face of a frightened child. The ineluctable logic of hybridity makes it impossible for the colonialist to achieve even an illusion of control without breaching his masculine code of restraint. The resultant sense of shame causes the colonialist to display "womanly" hysteria and "effeminate" weakness. Laughter, practical jokes, schoolboy pranks and antics, are an important apparatus through which Kipling conveys colonial anxieties about alienation and impotence. In his sensitive study of the "jest" in Kipling's fiction David Bromwich points out that the rhetorical effect of a jest lies precisely in the fact that it is not required to resolve the conflict to which it claims closure.[26] Instead, what is achieved is a suspension in which no single side is accorded precedence. This kind of deep brutal laughter rings throughout Kipling's stories on India and, occasionally, approaches the stature of tragic insight.

Fleete, the English man who turns into a werewolf, represents the type of colonialist Kipling always condemned—imported sahibs utterly ignorant about Indian society. Fleete's fate is thus the price of cultural ignorance. The story juxtaposes Fleete and Strickland, the policeman who judiciously uses Western rationality to gain knowledge and control over Indians. Strickland not only "knows as much of the natives of India as is good for any man" (MB 178); he also "hates being mystified by natives, because his business in life is to overmatch them with their own weapons." But even Strickland, the narrator informs us, "has not yet succeeded in doing this, but in fifteen or twenty years he will have made some small progress" (181). This is a variation of a familiar theme in Kipling's fiction—the fashioning of a cultural androgyne who would dominate by virtue of his intimacy with India but somehow without foregoing his fundamentally unified imperial identity. From this perspective Strickland may be regarded as a rudimentary version of an ideal that Kipling would embody more fully in Kim, the ultimate cultural androgyne.

Kim: Text and Context

The publication of Kim in 1901 came after a long period of personal and political turmoil for its author. Kipling's return to London, following his marriage to the American Caroline Balestier, his efforts to live in the United States, and the death of his daughter, was strained by an overwhelming sense of loss, by homesickness for his childhood India, by alienation from English men and women of all classes, and by a general hostility toward English literary society.[27] His dilemma was that he could not accept his bicultural identity, which he decried as an undefined sense of self. Since he wished to be either English or Indian, Kipling remained a hybridized sahib alienated from England and India alike. On the one hand, he was a loud champion of the values of Western civilization, an upholder of public school herd morality, a devotee of the Victorian cult of manliness. But, on the other hand, he was an Indianized Westerner who silently hated the West within him. Not unlike the Bengali babus he condemned, Kipling himself had been an effeminate, weak, individualistic, and rebellious soul unwilling to live by the manly codes of open aggression, sportsmanship, fair play, obedience, self-reliance, and disciplined work. Young Rudyard's corrosive encounter with a punishing evangelicalism at "The House of Desolation" and the torments he subsequently suffered at the hands of older boys and masters at United Service College or Westward Ho! (an experience that prompted him to imitate Dante and write an "Inferno" in which, under appropriate tortures, he put all his "friends" and most of the masters) had left Kipling with a strong aversion to the very qualities he nevertheless felt compelled to admire.

   Kipling's tragic condition must be understood not simply as an effect of individual psychobiography but, rather, as a historical effect of colonialism itself. In order to be efficient colonialism required white men who could interface cultures, infiltrate colonized society, and indoctrinate colonized peoples. Cultural androgynes like Kipling (and Kim) were therefore prized not only as mediators but also as instruments of imperial surveillance. At the same time, however, colonialism required every White Man to deny his cultural androgyny, to either go native or be sahib. The colonial machine took away the wholeness of every White Man and replaced it with a new self-definition that, while local or provincial in its cultural orientation, was global or universal in its geographical reach. To maintain his racial supremacy, cultural superiority, and political authority, the White Man had to constitute himself in opposition to the Oriental, just as he had to constitute the Oriental in opposition to himself. The tragedy of colonialism, as Ashis Nandy eloquently observes, was that it "expelled that other Orient which had once been a part of medieval European consciousness—an Orient which, even when regarded as an enemy was grudgingly respected. This Other Orient did not fit the needs of colonialism because it carried intimations of an alternative cosmopolitan multicultural living. So colonialism forced every bicultural westerner to make his choice."[28] Like the most memorable characters he created, Kipling was at once a hero who interfaced cultures and an antihero who despised cultural hybrids.

As Kipling struggled with his own effeminacy or cultural androgyny, the empire fought to survive against growing nationalistic movements within India (never to be mentioned in Kipling's fiction), an external threat from Russia, as well as a variety of small and large wars all over Asia and Africa. Matters came to a head in 1897, when, for the first time, the colonial conference recognized potential problems in lands as far flung as Australia, the Cape Colony, Natal, and India. Then, as Kipling puts it, "into the midst of it all came the Great Queen's Diamond Jubilee, and a certain optimism that scared me."[29] Kipling vociferously refused to celebrate Queen Victoria's Jubilee by publishing "Recessional," a dire warning against a land "drunk with sight of power." James Morris captures the shocking effect of such unexpected views from a writer like Kipling: "Like a slap in the face from an old roistering companion, Henry V turned princely, one morning that festive summer Kipling's poem *Recessional* appeared in *The Times*. It sounded a somber, almost frightened note, a warning against over confidence, 'frantic boast and foolish word.' Its sacramental solemnity jarred, and seemed to imply that the Jubilee celebrations were all tinsel and conceit."[30]

The year 1898 is regarded by historians as the turning point in Britain's imperial connections. It marks the start of England's self-perception as "the weary Titan" (a phrase used by Chamberlain and subsequently by historians), the beginning of ententes with France and Russia against Germany, and the end of the Anglo-Japanese alliance. February 1898 also saw the destruction of the U.S. battleship *Maine* and the beginnings of the Spanish-American War. Kipling's warning to the English now expanded to include the Americans (particularly their role in the Philippines). Germany's entry into a new phase of open rivalry with Britain and the czar's designs on British territory were also subjects of Kipling's satires. But, in spite of all the turmoil, Kipling's stories of the 1890s largely deal with subjects who empower themselves against great odds and eventually triumph over adversity. Some critics feel that distance gradually turned India into the picturesque and the pastoral, allowing Kipling to domesticate his anxiety about authority and to manage his nostalgia for India, while others have recognized that the stories of the 1890s represent Kipling's attempt to find solutions to the imperial problems he diagnosed during the 1880s.[31]

Kim, perhaps Kipling's most reified romance about India, has been praised as well as criticized for representing a magical, mythical place untouched by the forces of history. "Kipling's admirers and acolytes," Edward Said observes,

> have often spoken of his representations of India as if the India he wrote about was a timeless, unchanging, and "essential" locale, as a place almost as much poetical as actual. This, I think, is a radical misreading . . . If Kipling's India has qualities of the essential and unchanging, it was because . . . he deliberately chose to see India that way. [It must be interpreted] as a territory dominated by Britain for three hundred years, but beginning at that time to exhibit the increasing unrest which would culminate in decolonization and independence.[32]

Yet, it seems to me, this picaresque adventure tale is neither a sentimental expression of nostalgia nor simply a willful evasion of history. Rather, I suggest we see *Kim* as a symbolic resolution of a particular political controversy that raged in the mid-1880s: the native volunteer movement.

The Native Volunteer Movement, 1885–86

Sixteen years before the publication of Kim, in March 1885, in the wake of a Russian war scare, the viceroy Lord Dufferin called for an increase in the strength of the Volunteer Force in India by authorizing the creation of a Volunteer Reserve Force. Following the call to raise more volunteers, the Anglo-Indian recruiting officer in Madras accepted the offers of service from four "native gentlemen"; however, shortly afterward, the invitation to the Indian volunteers was rescinded in compliance with a telegram from the Military Department of the Government of India. The rebuff to the native volunteers in Madras was followed by demands all over India for the creation of separate native volunteer corps. Petitions poured in from Madras, Bengal, Oudh, Punjab, Assam, and Bombay. By June 1885 the Bengal government alone had received twenty-seven petitions with over eighteen hundred signatures. The call for native volunteering was led by the Indian press in urban centers such as Calcutta, Bombay, Madras, Poona, Allahabad, Meerut, Benares, Lahore, and in numerous *mofussil* centers, especially in Bengal. Throughout the year both the Indian and the Anglo-Indian press hotly debated the merits of native volunteering. In March 1886, almost a year after the government had received volunteer petitions from all over India, Dufferin formally rejected the demands for native volunteering at a public gathering in Madras.[33]

The native volunteer movement, as Mrinalini Sinha's lucid account reveals, brought the colonial ideology of martial traditions to a crisis. Colonial rule in India had long been partial to the martial traditions of select landowning, aristocratic native groups, giving them limited opportunities for advancement in the regular army. Volunteering, however, remained the exclusive racial privilege of Anglo-Indians and Eurasians. But, since the support of native elites in perpetuating the colonial order could not be overlooked, the Volunteer Act of 1857 was left deliberately vague about the possibility of non-Europeans contributing to the Volunteer Force, even though in practice natives were systematically discouraged from volunteering. While this expedient policy of official neutrality held together the colonial ideology of martial traditions for some time, it could not satisfactorily resolve the tension between the racial exclusivity of volunteering and the class interests of native elites for long. What is more, sections of the native elites that had hitherto been excluded from a military role in colonial society took up the demand for native volunteering. Foremost among those spearheading the demand was the elite group of Bengali babus—a fact that was eventually used to discredit the entire native volunteer movement.

The native volunteer movement was a powerful testimony to the continued investment of Indian elites, despite the criticism of specific colonial policies, in the colonial social structure. The show of loyalty, coming so soon after the bitterness of the Illbert Bill controversy and at a time when the threat of Russian hordes swarming across the northwest frontier was very much alive, was no doubt gratifying to the colonial authorities. "The nature of the volunteer movement," observes Mrinalini Sinha, made any outright defense of the racial exclusivity of volunteering in India by the colonial authorities unwise; instead, the logic of colonial masculinity was deployed to provide a more ingenious response to the native demands. It permitted the continued expression of special favour to Indian elites whose worthiness to volunteer could be recognized in terms of the rights of manly or martial races. At the same time, however, the dynamics of colonial masculinity could block actual and concrete demands for native volunteering by conjuring up the specter of the "effeminate babu."[34]

Sinha's account of the debate over native volunteering shows that it was the alleged effeminacy of educated native volunteers that attracted the most antipathy and provided the most popular defense against the extension of volunteering privileges to Indians. Anglo-Indian officials argued that native volunteers would consist primarily of effeminate babus who alone would have either the time or the motivation to serve as *mufli sepuis*, or unpaid soldiers. Expressing a fairly common Anglo-Indian opinion, the *Civil and Military Gazette* of Lahore declared that "none but fighting classes should be enrolled [in the Volunteer Corps]. The clerkly element should be as conspicuous by its absence, as it is in the regular army . . . the babu although a valiant wielder of the pen, is not so handy with the sword."[35] Colonial officials were at pains to distinguish between the "bonafide eagerness of the warlike races . . . to share in the burdens of the country and the risks of defensive war" and the "utter sham" of the "landless, comparatively poor, and socially inferior" who were merely using the question of volunteering "to strip away any apparent distinction which belongs to their fellow subject."[36] The *Englishman* was skeptical of the military value of volunteering from the educated community of Bengal: "should native loyalty ever be put to that crucial test, it is needless to ask where, during the fierce struggle that must ensue, will be found the race, who in the language of Macaulay 'would see his country over-run, his house laid to ashes, his children murdered or dishonoured without having the spirit to strike one blow.'"[37] An article in the *Asiatic Quarterly Review* confidently claimed that "not a single Bengali babu from Assam to the Sunderbunds would fire a shot for the English if they were engaged in a war *l'outrance* with Russia."[38] Anglo-Indian officials also raised the fear that the volunteer corps would be converted into political societies that would make native politicians formidable by giving them an armed body of men. Such an identification of the native volunteer movement with the new development in elite Indian politics, Mrinalini Sinha suggests, allowed the colonial authorities to dismiss the entire volunteer movement as a "Bengali agitation," "artificially stimulated by the press and wirepullers."[39]

Interestingly, the notion of effeminacy, Sinha points out, was used not only by those who opposed the native volunteer movement but also by those handful of Anglo-Indians who supported it.[40] These supporters suggested that the effeminacy of the educated community was, in fact, a compelling reason for extending the privilege of volunteering to and securing the gratitude of the educated community. Since the educated community posed no military threat to the colonial government, the supporters felt it was both militarily safe and politically expedient to gratify the desire of the educated community. Robert Knight, the liberal editor of the *Statesman,* argued that the "educated natives may not be warlike," but "the same reason makes them less of a menace."[41] Similarly, Henry Harrison, chairman of the Corporation of Calcutta, argued that because the educated community in India was "too unwarlike and too weak in numbers to be of much importance," its members did not "constitute any serious menace from the military point of view."[42] Both Knight and Harrison urged the colonial government to adhere to the ideals of the civilizing mission and allow the Indians to emulate the British in cultivating manly qualities.

If the specter of Bengali effeminacy provided colonial authorities with the rationale for finally rejecting the native volunteer demand, this rejection, Mrinalini Sinha notes, added a new dimension to the self-perception of effeminacy among elite Bengali men, allowing them now to hold the colonial government responsible for emasculating the Bengalis.[43] Since the demand for volunteering was part of a larger movement for the physical regeneration of the Bengalis, it was believed that the Bengalis had redeemed their manliness by their willingness to volunteer. Writing in the *Bengalee,* Banerjea, who had urged the educated community to recognize their special obligations to the colonial government and volunteer, declared that the enthusiasm for volunteering in Bengal had refuted "once [and] for all the imputation of unmanliness which our critics took a delight in bringing against us."[44] The official hostility toward native volunteering was seen as a deliberate plot to weaken Indians and crush out their manliness. The *Bengalee* hinted that the government might actually have an interest in keeping Indians emasculated: "are we to be debarred from cultivating the manlier qualities because, forsooth the possession of them by a subject race might be a source of embarrassment to the Government?"[45] The *Praja Bandhu* asked: "are the English afraid of Bengalis, or do they not trust them? Are Bengalis quite unable to bear arms, or is this the result of the one-sidedness so conspicuous in English character?"[46] The *Amrita Bazaar Patrika* similarly took comfort in the explanation that it was the fear of the Bengalis, rather than their weakness, that had led the colonial authorities to reject the native volunteer demand.[47]

Into this dense historical context I propose to insert Kipling's *Kim* as a symbolic solution to the question of native volunteering. It has been frequently noted that the novel does not so much challenge colonial stereotypes as find appropriate roles for them in the imperial service. Yet, it seems to me, Kipling's understanding of effeminacy is somewhat different from the standard Anglo-Indian perspective. Insofar as Indian elites shared the colonial ideology of masculinity, Mrinalini Sinha is correct to conclude that the native volunteer movement failed to mount a full-scale challenge to colonialism.[48] If, however, we view effeminacy neither as an insufficient platform for confrontation nor as an inadequate subject position but, rather, as an everyday practice of colonial androgyny or cultural hybridity, it becomes not only a subterraneous place of escape or refuge but also a potentially explosive site of subversion and resistance. Kipling, it would appear, saw effeminacy precisely in this light. That is why, even though he also believed the effeminate babu to be incapable of armed warfare, he does not dismiss the babu as weak and worthless. In fact, Kipling seems quite anxious to yoke the devious, cunning, conniving babu to the wheel of empire, to put his cultural dexterity to work for, instead of against, the British. To this end he offers a unique resolution to the Indian demand for volunteering by creating a different kind of volunteer corps—the colonial secret service—in which a martial Pathan, an Indianized Irish boy, and a consummately effeminate Bengali babu join hands to defend the British Empire against Russian threat. But, as my discussion of *Kim* will demonstrate, in placing the Westernized babu alongside the Indianized Westerner, Kipling inadvertently turns Indian effeminacy into a terrifying mirror that reflects the problematic status of cultural androgyny in colonial society.

The Frontier Secret Service

Kipling's deployment of the colonial secret service to defend the Indian border must also be seen in the context of certain sweeping changes that took place in the decades following the Sepoy Mutiny. Terrified by the ferocity of Indian insurgency in 1857 and disillusioned by demands of the Indian middle class, the colonial administrators resolutely turned their backs on the restive urban centers and focused their attention on the northwest frontier, in the province of Punjab. The Punjab had been annexed to British India in 1849 after the defeat of the Sikhs. It was a rich and fertile agricultural land with a predominantly peasant population. Here the British cultivated a rugged, paternalistic style of imperialism that was being increasingly challenged in the urban centers, especially in Bengal. Far from administrative controls and regulations, the frontier could still provide a refuge for romance, exoticism, and adventure. At the same time, the frontier was a place of real business—a place where the struggle to expand and maintain the empire took place.

The expansion of the Russian Empire into Central Asia made the Indian territory of Punjab strategically important. Trying to obtain the support of the Afghans against the Russians prompted the British to pursue an aggressive frontier policy that involved a rash of wars and continuous intrigue. Kipling could thus use the frontier as a repression of work as well as the absent workplace itself. The wall of civilization, the frontier, may be defended by men of all nationalities under the Pax: it is the very idea of empire. The wonderful mysterious abstraction called the "Great Game" is such a vast network that one sees but little of it at a time. Players follow orders but enjoy a great deal of autonomy, since the very secrecy of their work keeps them outside the direct supervision of the colonial government. But, by the same token, they are also to a considerable extent beyond control—a fact that clearly generates considerable narrative anxiety in *Kim*.

The frontier also served as a convenient space to siphon off the restless energies of lower-class Anglo-Indians. The increasingly visible presence of the English lower classes in the bustling cities of Calcutta, Madras, and Bombay made it difficult for the ruling race to maintain its prestige. Since there was little room for spacious civil stations or cantonments that would segregate white from brown, the inevitable proximity to Indians that resulted made poor Europeans a source of racial and cultural threat. Moreover, empire could not be maintained without exploiting the labor of natives on the one hand and poor whites like Kim (the orphaned son of an Irish man who lived and died "as poor white do in India") on the other. Imperial service on the frontier, offered as an attractive option to poor Anglo-Indians, helped to reduce official embarrassment and alleviate class tensions. The frontier secret service thus allows Kipling to romanticize Kim, to restore him to the imperial fold in ways that not only pose no threat to the upper classes of Anglo-Indian society but, in fact, appropriate the boy's threatening cultural androgyny to the service of empire.

Another aspect to the attraction of the frontier was the male-dominated life of fighting and espionage, in which women were altogether absent and in which men confronted one another in open warfare. The frontier setting in which Kim's adventures take place, along with the militaristic, jesuitic, sportslike espionage ethos of the novel, allow Kipling to largely bracket the entire question of women. The strong, vigorous, masculine lifestyle of the frontier not only allowed for unrestrained expression of aggression; it rationalized, reproduced, and reinforced the values and attitudes of the Victorian public school. Schooling itself was a crucial link in ruling-class male homosocial formation. The public school cult of friendship allowed homosexual relationships among boys (as childishness/boyishness), although one had to put it away as an adult male (assume homophobic, heterosexual attitudes). Kim's India (like Lawrence's Arabia) is thus a kind of remedial public school, a predominantly male place in which it is relatively safe for men to explore the crucial terrain of masculine desire.

Kim and the Imperatives of Desire

Kim is perhaps one of the richest cartographies of colonial male homosociality.[49] Combining the modes of a picaresque adventure tale, a quest romance, and a bildungsroman, Kipling tells the story of Kim, an Irish orphan reared by Indians who grows up to become a spy for the colonial government. Since Kim is too young for anyone to expect him to route his passionate attachments to older men through a desire for women, he is able to explore the terrain of interracial male homosociality with considerable freedom and pleasure. Through tropes of male bonding the narrative gropes for an alternative model of colonial subjectivity—one that would be more open, flexible, and capable of crossing the boundaries of race and culture. Categorically rejecting the ideology of the "imported sahibs" with the "dull fat eyes" who style all Indians "niggers," Kipling tries to manufacture a bicultural colonialist who would not have to suffer from ignorance, alienation, and fear.

During the course of his adventures Kim is claimed by various father figures of both races. In this "story of the prolonged and unnatural recovery of the paternal function," Abdul JanMohammed argues, the struggle over Kim's inheritance is a manifestation of the conflict over cultural allegiance."[50] The question of whether the English or the

Indian fathers command Kim's love and loyalty prompts a narrative struggle in which the boy's body literally figures as the overdetermined arena of male embattlement. The relentless unfolding of this homoerotic economy generates a narrative intransigence that forces Kim the wonderboy to give up his marvelous cultural androgyny before he is allowed to claim his imperial patrimony. Kim's position of apparent hybridity turns into a sham that, while pretending to share equally in the qualities of the two symmetrically opposite racial groups, really manipulates the asymmetry of their status for personal advancement and political domination. Why does Kim's cultural flexibility atrophy into the rigidity of imperial surveillance? Why, if the tropology of male bonding in *Kim* holds out a promise of racial and cultural liberation, does colonial desire dissipate into denial? I shall attempt to answer these questions by tracing two different trajectories of desire in the novel: the mimicry linking the cultural androgyny of Kim and Huree Babu; and the struggle between the lama and the narrator for Kim's allegiance.

The Problematic of Colonial Cultural Androgyny

From the very beginning Kim is constituted as an overdetermined object of promiscuous desire. The "Little Friend of all the World" is a dispossessed Anglo-Indian orphan eagerly sought by blacks and whites, men and women, alike (K 3). This most celebrated symbol of syncretism is the consummate cultural amphibian whose value is predicated precisely on the hybridity literalized upon his body. Literally without origins and therefore without constraints, the wonderboy delights in disguise. Constantly changing his appearance and with it his identity, he mingles freely with a dizzying variety of English and Indian characters, shifting from one tongue to another, from one set of values to another, with utmost ease. Such cultural dexterity lends Kim an attractive suppleness, enabling him to slide past the rigid dichotomies of colonial society.

Kim's ability to shift subjectivity and become Other at will opens up new grounds for interracial cross-cultural male solidarity. Thus, in the figure of this wondrous adolescent the novel emblematizes a kind of effeminacy or cultural androgyny as a potentially liberating principle. "Kim and his celebration of Indian cultures," observes Abdul JanMohammed, "seem like perfect embodiments of Kipling's syncretic desires. In fact, the structures of Kim's character and his situation reveal the imperative that is essential for the fulfillment of that desire. Because Kim's self is entirely decentered and malleable, he finds pleasure in becoming an Other . . . This ability to forgo a permanent fixed self, which is essential if one is going to understand and appreciate a racial or cultural alterity, is turned into a positive principle in Kim."[51]

It is precisely his magical cultural malleability that marks Kim out as an invaluable instrument for the Great Game. Kim's unclassifiability is indeed unique, given the carefully detailed catalog of differences Kipling presents in the novel. The hierarchical order of race, caste, religion, language, custom, and tradition that determines the world of *Kim* is recognized and respected by both British and Indians alike. In fact, it is precisely this excess of colonized culture that the novel attempts to catalog and consolidate upon the very body of Kim. With the exception of Kim (and, to a lesser extent, Creighton) the lines of demarcation cannot be easily crossed by any character. Indians are particularly incapable of traversing the boundaries of culture. The Hindu boy in Lurgan's shop has a mind "keen as an icicle" but is unable to imaginatively "enter another's soul" and play the game of disguise as deftly as Kim (K 159). This racial failing finds its most elaborate expression in the caricature of Huree Babu.

As the prototype of the effeminate Bengali, Huree Babu is a quintessential cultural hybrid, the mimic man produced by British colonialism in India. Designed to provoke laughter, his appearance and actions are repeated failures at becoming a true English man. The babu is described in the novel as a "whale-like," man, wearing a "fringed shawl" round his head and showing a "fat openwork-stockinged leg" (K 161). He speaks in the characteristic style and idiom of "babu English," which is rich in historical and literary allusions. He quotes indiscriminately from English philosophers and desires to become a member of the Royal Society. His scientific interest in ethnography is curiously mixed up with belief in magic and superstition. Unlike Creighton's panoptic gaze, which dispassionately codifies the multifariousness of colonized culture into a system that can be comprehended and therefore controlled, Huree Babu's anthropological observations are riddled with epistemological confusions.[52]

Ridiculous he may be, but the effeminate babu is also one of the most consummate practitioners of the Great Game. Kipling's recruitment of the babu for colonial service is at once an implicit recognition of the potential challenge educated Indians represented to colonial rule as well as a masterful co-optation of that challenge. During the final decades of the nineteenth century many middle-class Bengali Hindu men like Huree Babu were actually members of nationalist organizations like the Indian National Congress. Indeed, by the turn of the century such congressmen could be spotted even in the remote frontier regions, propagating nationalist ideology among the hill tribes. But instead of portraying the urban, Western-educated Bengali as the nationalist threat he actually was, Kipling cleverly recruits the babu to the very cause of empire. Indeed, in his professional capacity the effeminate Indian with an uncanny ability for survival is actually presented as a role model to Kim. Kipling brings out the best of Huree Babu during the encounter with the Russian agents in the final sections of the novel. Ingratiating himself with the Russians, Huree Babu deceives them in the very idiom that challenged British rule. He becomes thickly treasonous and speaks of the indecency of a government that had forced upon him a White Man's education and then neglected to supply him with a White Man's opportunities and a White Man's salary. Thus, the very rhetoric of Indian nationalism, as voiced by the Bengali middle class, is transformed into a weapon for the defense of empire.

In yoking the cultural hybridity of Huree Babu to the imperial cause, Kipling appropriates certain modes of defense Indians had evolved in response to colonialism. Like all "devious" Orientals, Indians, even when they seemed totally controlled, managed to retain some indeterminateness and freedom in the practice of everyday life. Thus, for instance, superstitions and magic offer Huree Babu a potential sphere of action that remains largely outside the influence of imperial modes of knowledge. Even his ridiculous "babu English" can be said to represent a resistance to imperial codes of grammar. The effeminate Indian thus escapes the panoptic control of empire by resorting to the little ruses and tricks Michel de Certeau calls *la perruque*.[53] Instead of engaging in aggressive face-to-face manly combat as the colonizers expected and countered, Indians frequently fought back through inadequate compliance, adaptation, shirking, avoidance, nonviolence, and noncooperation. Because of this strategic refusal to engage the White Man on his own terms, the Indian had been labeled unmanly and effeminate. Although Kipling also despised Indians for failing to be ideal victims, he shrewdly sensed that the indirect passive defensive measures they adopted were nonetheless expressions of aggression. Only it was the violence of weak and dominated groups used to facing threatening situations with overwhelming disadvantages. And, as Kipling was well aware, lacking the legitimacy and authority of manly, direct, open violence, effeminate aggression, with its untargeted rage, fatalism, desperation, and "cowardliness," could become a fantasy rather than an intervention in the material world. Thus, like Dina Nath in Kipling's short story "The Enlightenment of Pagett, M.P.," the effeminate Indian who appears so frequently in Anglo-Indian literature is full of empty bombast and bluster, entertaining illusions of grandiosity. Although in many of his short stories Kipling dismisses the hybridized babu as a physical and moral weakling without strong traditional roots, the figure of Huree Babu indicates a repressed recognition that the wily babus could be supremely skilled at using the weapons of the weak to manipulate the White Man to their own ends—only, in the magical world of *Kim*, the babu's weapons are safely directed against the Russians instead of the English.

The frontier secret service that places Huree Babu next to Kim, moreover, turns effeminacy into a merciless mirror of colonial cultural androgyny, forcing Kipling's text inadvertently, even unwillingly, to register the unspeakable similarities between the Anglicized Indian and the Indianized English man. Kim and Huree Babu, the colonizer and the colonized, become savage mirror images linked in an inexorable display of mimicry. Despite the narrator's insistence to the contrary, Kim, like Huree Babu, embodies a mixture of English and Indian cultures. And, as is the case with the babu, it is Kim's cultural androgyny, his ability to interface cultures, that makes him a valuable commodity in the espionage game. Yet Kipling will have us believe that Kim's cultural dexterity is an act of free will, while Huree Babu's cultural hybridity, useful only when yoked to imperial service, remains ontologically ridiculous and signifies a paralyzing lack of choice. Just as Flora Annie Steel uses the ideology of free will to separate the English woman from her Indian counterpart, Kipling's narrative resurrects the fiction of free will to delink the effeminate Indian from the culturally androgynous English man.

Kim determinedly casts the Westernized Indian as a pathologically ridiculous creature trapped within his cultural hybridity while portraying the Indianized Westerner as an essentially unified subject who freely chooses to enter the space of biculturality. This determination, however, makes visible the devastating irony with which colonial mimicry declares itself. Kim's "invisibility" does indeed give him the pleasure of seeing without being seen. The novel calls attention to the boy's powers of observation as he is positioned "in the middle" of India, "more awake and more excited than anyone" (K 73). The pleasures of "invisibility," however, imply a perilous corollary: the boy who exuberantly fuses the excess of Indian diversity upon his own body is perilously close to being so thoroughly absorbed into the heterogeneity of colonized society as to be turned into just another hybrid among hybrids. As the proliferation of difference becomes frighteningly coterminous with the erasure of difference, the novel finds itself repeating the question it can answer only through a tautology: "Who is Kim? I am Kim."

Kipling's acute awareness of the destabilizing potential of Kim's cultural androgyny compels him to make the boy, through Creighton's intervention, the recipient of an imperial education so that his decentered multicultural vision may be translated into a hegemonic mode of surveillance. Imperial education thus serves as an ideological conduit through which the pleasures of cultural promiscuity are legitimized as Kim's imperial inheritance. Through this process of legitimation the novel refigures the historical liability of Kim's cultural hybridity as colonial autonomy, constructing a subjectivity that, instead of being forced to choose between the lama and the Great Game, enjoys the luxury of willing its own instrumentality.

It is interesting to compare Kipling's treatment of colonial cultural hybridity with Rabindranath Tagore's, especially since it brings out both the conflicts as well as the complicities between colonialism and nationalism. Published five years after *Kim,* Tagore's *Gora* (literally *Whitey,* a word applied to the British tommy but used here as an acceptable diminutive for Gaurmohan) features a protagonist who, like Kim, is an Indianized Irish orphan of the Indian Mutiny.[54] Unlike Kim, Gora becomes an orthodox Brahmin and a nationalist Indian. Both his Brahminism and his nationalism are gendered as hard and masculine. At the end of the novel, he finds out he is not only not a Brahmin but not even Hindu or Indian by birth. It is precisely at this moment that he realizes he is most truly Indian because he chooses to be so. Gora's realization, as Gayatri Spivak points out, "is embedded in a discourse of woman. First his identification of India with his (foster) mother who, unlike his (foster) father, did not observe caste difference; then the summons to the hitherto spurned untouchable servant; and finally the Mother's request to him to acknowledge the love of the emancipated Brahmo heroine."[55] Cultural contradiction in Tagore's narrative thus becomes productive of a unified nationalist subject whose agency is derived from the colony as a nation. By contrast, true cultural hybridity in Kipling's tale remains profoundly unproductive, resulting only in paralysis. Despite this obvious difference, both novels rely on the theme of choice to affect ideological closure. If colonialism compelled every man to choose sides, so did nationalism. Autonomy and agency are granted only to those who can exercise choice and achieve self-conscious subjectivity. Gora is thus forced to choose between Britain and India, and his free choice to return to colonized culture becomes the basis of his nationalist subjectivity. Huree Babu remains trapped by his ontological inability to make such self-conscious choices; by contrast, Kim is granted the freedom to return to colonized culture at will. But Kim's return, unlike Gora's, is not indelibly marked by colonized culture because it is temporary, superficial, and exploitative.

The Love Triangle: Kim, the Lama, and the Narrator

I now turn to another expression of masculine desire in *Kim:* the triangulated relationship between Kim, the lama, and the narrator. The bond between Kim and the lama is posited on a paternal ascetic ideal that excludes sex, marriage, and domesticity. Traveling unencumbered over the length and breadth of India, the incongruous couple of questers become intertwined in a relationship of mutual dependence that at first appears to offer an enchanting possibility of racial and cultural symbiosis. But, as the novel unfolds, the narrator appears to become increasingly jealous of Kim's intimacy with the lama. While the earlier sections of the novel focus prominently on the reciprocal relationship between Kim and the lama, the latter sections are dominated by the narrator's emotional investment in Kim. Who loves Kim more, the lama or the narrator? This question prompts a narrative struggle for racial/cultural allegiance in which Kim's body literally figures as the overdetermined arena of male embattlement. The relentless unfolding of this homoerotic economy generates a narrative intransigence that, ironically, determines and delimits Kim's destiny as much as it does the lama's.

The erotic trajectory of *Kim* is controlled by the bewildering ambivalence with which desire declares itself. The initial rupture of desire is marked by an outburst of cultural astonishment. Kim, "who thought he knew all castes," is startled by the sight of a man whose kind he had never seen: "He was nearly six feet high, dressed in fold upon fold of dingy stuff like horse-blanketing, and not one fold of it could Kim refer to any known trade or profession" (K 4). The unexpected intrusion of an unreadable difference sows the seeds of desire in Kim: "This man was entirely new to all his experience, and he meant to investigate further, precisely as he would have investigated a new building or a strange festival in Lahore city. The lama was his trove, and he pur-

posed to take possession. Kim's mother had been Irish too" (12). Kim's
excitement at the lama's newness expresses itself in terms of territorial-
ity and possession. This epistemological slippage from novelty to possession initiates a series of critical misreadings about what cultural signs
may signify. Once the slip has been made, the bond between Kim and
the lama can hereafter be written and read only within the grim logic of
possession and dispossession.

Kim's determination to seize the lama for his adventure intersects
with the lama's wish to secure the boy as a guide for his spiritual quest.
If the lama's newness has surprised Kim into desire, the discovery of
Kim's racial identity astonishes the lama in turn:

> "A sahib and the son of a sahib—" The lama's voice was harsh with pain.
> "But no white man knows the land and the customs of the land as thou
> knowest. How comes it this is true?" . . . "As a boy in the dress of white
> men—when I first went to the Wonder House. And a second time thou
> wast a Hindu. What shall the third incarnation be?" He chuckled drearily.
> "Ah, chela, thou hast done a wrong to an old man because my heart went
> out to thee." (K 91)

Clearly, the monk who desires only to be desireless has been powerfully
distracted by the wonderboy.

The monk may be "simple," but he clearly grasps the commodification of merit and wisdom within the economy of colonialism. Apparently acting upon his code of "acquiring merit," the old man negotiates
shrewdly with the two English clergymen and arranges to buy the best
imperial education for his disciple. But, instead of liberating Kim from
ignorance, the lama's participation in this colonial transaction inadvertently ensures the boy's insertion into the imperial order. The implacable progress of colonial intimacy binds both lama and chela firmly to
the wheel of empire. Thus, Kim's entry into the Great Game literally
transforms the sheet of "strangely-scented yellow Chinese paper," on
which the lama had drawn his picture-parable of the Wheel of Life, into
a survey map and the holy man's rosary into an instrument for measuring distance.

Possession is the desired prize on which the narrative struggle
turns. But we cannot grasp its specificity until we sense the difference
between this object and all those other equally desirable goals, aims, or
ends around which the apparent content of the narrative is organized.
The manifest content of the story—the adventure of the Road for Kim
and the salvation of the River for the lama—leads us to believe that

"experience," or "knowledge," has intrinsic value and may therefore be legitimately sought as an end in itself. But, between Kim's determination to seize the lama's wisdom for his own adventure and the lama's complicity in procuring an imperial education for his beloved disciple, knowledge is commodified such that under the historical conditions of late-nineteenth-century colonialism it becomes available only as an overabundance of unintelligible "information." As the currency of colonial power, information acquires exchange value: it can be bought, sold, or stolen. Information thus emerges as the prize of a new kind of quest, a commodified quest in a commodified world that now produces the commodified hero—the spy or the secret agent.

The improbable intimacy into which the novel impels its participants raises questions about the historical necessity determining both Kim's role in the secret service as well as the lama's spiritual quest. Kim and the lama undertake two journeys together, each of which ends in an important discovery. The first journey leads to the discovery that Kim is a sahib; the second is concerned with discovering what it means to be a sahib. In typical Victorian fashion the discovery of a new identity implies a need to be reeducated into new social norms, and this is what the curiously truncated middle period between the two journeys indicates. The immediate consequence of the discovery that Kim is white is his separation from the lama.

The exchange of messages between the monk and the boy during the period of separation, Sara Suleri points out, supplies a dramatic illustration of the mediated and deferred nature of colonial desire.[56] The messages between Kim and the lama are conveyed through the figure of the "letter-writer." Described in the novel as "a bureau of general misinformation" (K 115), the letter-writer—who jauntily mixes oral and written, informal and official, vernacular and imperial, codes—symbolizes the potential for misinterpretation in all colonial cross-cultural communication. The intensity of mutual desire to communicate, however, overcomes and overflows the limits of cultural exegesis. Thus, the lama's letter from Benares carries to his "oppressors" a convoluted message that Kim alone unravels accurately. And, in turn, Kim's letter appeals to the lama with an urgency that cannot be easily misunderstood. Although the boy is unable to give the exact location of the school to which he is to be sent and has to pay the letter-writer to supply the information, his "come to me! come to me! come to me!" leaves the lama in no doubt.

The ensuing scene of reunion and re-separation, which takes place outside the "gates of learning," is sedimented with a profound and painful recognition of the emotional impoverishment colonial intimacy entails. The lama waits at the entrance of St. Xavier's school in response to the plea from his beloved disciple. Yet he disingenuously insists on segregating himself from the demands of colonial desire by appealing to the illusion of utilitarianism: "A day and a half have I waited—not because I was led by any affection towards thee—that is no part of the Way—but, as they said at the Tirthankars' Temple, because, money having been paid for learning, it was right that I should oversee the end of the matter. They resolved my doubts most clearly. I had a fear that, perhaps, I came because I wished to see thee—misguided by the Red Mist of affection." However much the lama may deny it, Kim has indeed diverted his mind from the River. Intuitively sensing the lama's anguish, Kim responds by refusing the matter-of-fact account: "'But surely, Holy One, thou hast not forgotten the Road and all that befell on it. Surely it was a little to see me that thou didst come?' . . . 'I am all alone in this land; I know not where I go nor what shall befall me. My heart was in that letter I sent thee . . . I have no friend save thee, Holy One. Do not altogether go away'" (K 1221–22). The bond between Kim and the lama is increasingly expressed in terms of urgent need rather than in terms of free choice.

As the narrative moves inexorably toward a crisis, the interdependence between the old man and the young boy increases in intensity, until it becomes more and more difficult to distinguish between the imperatives of their respective quests. Instead of diverging, the lama's quest for the River and Kim's quest for the Road are made to converge in a remarkable scene in which the monk, meditating upon the Wheel of Life, is assaulted by the Russian spies, and, in the very process of defending the old man, Kim skillfully manages to steal certain important documents from the foreigners. The convergence of Road and River proves devastating indeed. Bereft of health and serenity, the old monk and the young boy wander through the hills. The lama is overcome by his awareness of how much farther his spiritual goals have now receded. Kim, for his part, is not only filled with fear for the lama but is literally burdened by the weight of the stolen documents he carries close to his heart. Waiting to be relieved of the burden, the boy, who before his formal induction into the Great Game had been characterized by tremendous physical energy, succumbs to bodily illness. If Kim's ability to pass off for an Indian commodifies the Other and increases the colonialist's exchange value, the potentially liberating cultural androgyny incarnated in the wondrous boy becomes a paralyzing historical liability, commodifying his body into an efficient instrument of imperial surveillance.

What rituals must Kim and the lama undergo before being healed? And to what positions are they finally restored? These questions return the plot to the unresolved issue of who loves Kim more, the lama or the narrator. The moment of Kim's healing is consequently split into two. The first follows upon a profound sense of dislocation Kim experiences after being relieved of the incriminating documents:

> Then he looked upon the trees and the broad fields, with the thatched huts hidden among crops—looked with strange eyes unable to take up the size and proportion and use of things—stared for a still half-hour. All that while he felt, though he could not put it into words, that his soul was out of gear with its surroundings—a cog-wheel unconnected with any machinery, just like the idle cog-wheel of a cheap Beheea sugar-crusher laid by in a corner . . . "I am Kim. I am Kim. And what is Kim?" His soul repeated it again and again. He did not want to cry—had never felt less like crying in his life—but of a sudden easy, stupid tears trickled down his nose, and with an almost audible click he felt the wheels of his being lock up anew on the world without. Things that rode meaningless on the eyeball an instant before slid into proper proportion. Roads were meant to be walked upon, houses to be lived in, cattle to be driven, fields to be tilled, and men and women to be talked to. (K 282)

The mechanical metaphor suggesting Kim's reawakening to a sense of control over the world and the utilitarian code in which this control is conveyed semanticize Kim's rebirth in the very idiom of English imperialism. From a spontaneous participator in the life around him, Kim has become a cog in the wheel of empire. As the reader is forced to observe an unnaturally silent Kim through the eye of the narrator, the sense of immediacy that characterized the boy's experiences in the earlier sections of the novel is missing from this supreme moment of rebirth. Indeed, in the closing sections of the novel the boy, who had earlier functioned as the lama's eyes and ears, is refigured by the narrator into a sensuous aesthetic image for visual consumption: "The pallor of hunger suited Kim very well as he stood, tall and slim, in his sad-coloured, sweeping robes, one hand on his rosary and the other in the attitude of benediction, faithfully copied from the lama. An English observer might have said that he looked rather like the young saint of a stained-glass window, whereas he was but a growing lad faint with emptiness" (K 195).[57] For all the caressing solicitations of the text the narrator's desire to claim Kim's racial/cultural allegiance ends up objectifying rather than subjectifying the colonialist.

The second moment of Kim's healing comes from the lama. By choosing to return freely from Nirvana for the sake of his beloved disciple, the lama commits a supreme act of self-sacrifice characteristic of the Bodhisattva. But, in fact, the lama's final act of benediction becomes complicitous, providing spiritual cover for material exploitation. Contrasting with the mechanical metaphors employed by the narrator and invested with great emotional value, the monk's Orientalist rhetoric of mysticism defuses or represses the ideological tensions that nevertheless remain sedimented in the narrative. The lama enables Kim to acquire gratuitously the other-worldly values of spiritual contemplation without forsaking the material benefits he will reap in this world as a sahib.

There is, no doubt, a strong wish-fulfilling element in this novel that attempts to position the colonialist as both friend and master. But, unlike more degraded and commodifiable colonial romances, Kipling's texts entertain a far more implacable conception of the fully realized fantasy, one that is not to be satisfied by immediate gratification or easy omnipotence. Indeed, at certain privileged moments the ineluctable logic of Kipling's inexorable realism involves complex mechanisms that forge such inconceivable links between desire and history that the fantasy narrative registers its own illusoriness and fragility. The lama's last blessing is clearly one such moment. Through the ineluctable logic that binds the colonizer and the colonized, the lama's passionately inclusive vision of redemption, which restores Kim to the center of all things, also mercilessly reduces the boy into a silent recipient of salvation. Thus, Kim's voice is altogether absorbed by the lama, who is, significantly, given the last word in the novel: "He [the lama] crossed his hands on his lap and smiled, as a man may who has won salvation for himself and his beloved" (K 289). Between the narrator and the lama, Kim is finally reduced to a silent object of homoerotic adoration. Like the curator of the Lahore Museum, who is recalled at the very end, Kipling's text is indeed "the keeper of Images," framing colonizer and colonized in a mutually disempowering bond.

6

A Grammar of Colonial Desire:
E. M. Forster's *A Passage to India*

Codifying Colonial Erotics

A Passage to India (1924) has not only provided the West with its most durable image of India, but through its tropological use of rape the novel has, ironically, encouraged a continuing equation between (hetero)sexual violence and imperialism.[1] Adela Quested, a visiting English woman, accuses Dr. Aziz, an educated Muslim, of sexually assaulting her in one of the mysterious Marabar caves. Adela's accusation sparks off a predictable racial hysteria among the Anglo-Indian residents of Chandrapore, who set in motion a judicial juggernaut that condemns Aziz even before he is brought to trial. As the victim of an unjust colonial system, Aziz becomes a heroic cause for Indian nationalists to champion. Against the forces marshaling on either side of the racial divide, the novel pits the puny efforts of two men to connect on a personal level. In the wake of the rape charge and throughout the trial Fielding, the liberal-minded Anglo-Indian schoolteacher, tries to befriend Aziz against insurmountable odds. The plot takes a dramatic turn as Adela's testimony falls apart when, under interrogation, she breaks down and claims to have made a mistake. Through Adela's unexpected retraction Forster disrupts a normative racial narrative that reduces the Indian male to his pathological lust for white women. Strategically reversing the roles of assailant and victim, the novel exposes the real rape to be an abuse of power that can only hasten the end of colonial rule. Fielding's trust in the Indian is thus found to be eminently justified. But, despite this justification, the homoerotic intimacy between Fielding and Aziz, which Forster's narrative pursues so ardently even after the conclusion of the rape trial, is not consummated.

Authorial reticence about rape is critical to the indeterminacy of meaning by which Forster tries to convey the "mystery" and "muddle" of India. We are never clearly told whether Adela was really raped by someone/something or whether she had simply imagined the whole thing. At the end of the "Caves" section, when Fielding makes an ineffectual attempt to ascertain the "truth," he is met with Adela's indifferent response: "Let us call it the guide . . . It will never be known. It's as if I ran my finger along that polished wall in the dark, and cannot get further" (PI 261). This absence of resolution has left readers of *A Passage to India* obsessed with the question of what "really" transpired in the Marabar cave. Not only has the question attracted a great deal of critical commentary over the years, but it has divided readings along gender lines. Adela's hallucination appears to be the most preferred explanation for what happened in the caves. These explanations, even when they engage the problem of colonial representation, usually point to Adela's repressed sexuality as the source of rape fantasy.[2] Seeking to defend Adela from masculinist charges of hallucination, frigidity, and sexual hysteria, feminist critics such as Elaine Showalter and Brenda Silver have sought to situate the alleged rape within the larger frame of women's oppression.[3] But, as Jenny Sharpe points out, while these feminist readings illuminate Adela's gendered role as sex object, they fail to situate the rape within "a system of colonial relations."[4] In their anxiety to rescue the white woman they tend either to ignore or to collapse the different positions occupied by the Anglo-Indian woman and the Indian man. Thus, for instance, Silver equates Adela's status as sex object in white patriarchal society with Aziz's status as objectified native in colonial society, thereby enabling both Adela and Aziz to occupy, on different trajectories, the feminized space of the rape victim. By conflating the discontinuous histories of colonialism in India and sexual oppression in England, Silver reads Aziz as rapist when spoken of as male and as rape victim when spoken of as colonized Indian.[5] Similarly, Frances Restuccia also suggests that Aziz is "raped" by British imperialism.[6]

Questioning such promiscuous deployments of rape as a master metaphor for the exploitation of white women and colonized people alike, Jenny Sharpe usefully relocates colonial rape within a discourse of power that strategically codes anticolonial rebellion as the sexual assault of white women by brown men. Forster's manuscript revisions of *A Passage to India* indicate that he had originally used the rape motif in the most culturally determined way, imagining the dark Indian sexually attacking the white woman, who is unconventionally aggressive in fighting off her attacker. While feminist critics such as Restuccia and Silver had seen Forster's deletion of this scene as symptomatic of a more pervasive silencing of women in his novel, Sharpe correctly points out that the novel can replace white-woman-as-victim with white-woman-as-agent only at the risk of confirming the rape and thereby objectifying the Indian male as rapist.[7] Focusing on the ideological linkage of race, rape, and rebellion in the colonial context, Sharpe argues that the indeterminacy of sexual assault in *A Passage to India* drives a wedge of doubt between a colonial discourse of rape and its object, thus disrupting the causal connection established during the Sepoy Mutiny between Indian assault of English women and British suppression of anticolonial resistance.[8]

While my own approach to *A Passage to India* draws support from Sharpe's attempt to ground the rape motif within the historical context of the British Raj, my aim is to link the question of rape to what I consider to be the novel's real subject: masculinity and masculine desire. Such a linkage will, I believe, show Forster's use of the rape motif to be an effect of his exploration into male relations in colonial society. Clearly, Forster's interest in Adela is quite limited, for, instead of coming to an end at the conclusion of the rape trial, *A Passage to India* continues to chart the checkered course of interracial male friendship. Adela's rape becomes a narrative ploy for satirizing the imperial paternalism of the Turtons and Burtons, on the one hand, and, on the other, for advancing the plot toward its real concern with the latent homoerotic relationship between Fielding and Aziz. Indeed, what Forster disguises in his heterosexual figuration of colonial rape is a homosexual scene of exploitation—a scene he starkly depicted in the self-censored, "Kanaya" memoir of *The Hill of Devi*, in which the subaltern Indian male is violated by the lustful white man.

Being one of the most utopian quests for cross-cultural intimacy on the plane of English imperialism, *A Passage to India* derives its narrative energy by generating a transgressive homoerotic desire to overcome the barriers of race, caste, and class. Integral to this quest for interracial intimacy is a search for an alternative model of imperial masculinity, one that would be more open, fluid, flexible, almost androgynous in sensibility. Forster's use of androgyny as a narrative device to track the boundaries of masculinity is not very different from Virginia Woolf's use of androgyny to critique gender roles in *Orlando*. What *A Passage to India* proposes, however, is an entire grammar of colonial desire that not only codifies the rules governing colonial relations but also explores and expands the full spectrum of male relations in colonial society. Forster's grammar accomplishes two important things: one, it complicates the racialized opposition between English manliness and Indian effeminacy; and, two, it furtively draws the homosocial into the orbit of the erotic, allowing us to posit a potential continuity between the homosocial and the homoerotic, between the sanctioned and the tabooed, between the speakable and the unspeakable, in colonial culture.

The hypothesis of such a potential continuity should not be taken as a suggestion to locate homosexual desire at the root of all other forms of male patriarchal-homosocial relations but, instead, as a critical strategy or a methodological tool for reading the works of E. M. Forster, J. R. Ackerley, and others as explorations into the politics of race and gender constitution in colonial society rather than as the internal psychology of a few individual men with a "minority" sexual orientation.[9] As a critical strategy, hypothesizing a potential structural congruence between homosociality and homosexuality can help us trace the ways in which *A Passage to India* simultaneously intervenes and participates in the economy of colonialism, a contradiction that perhaps mirrors the ambiguous role of Anglo-Indian homosexuality as an oppositional underground culture that nevertheless operated within colonial hierarchies of race, caste, and class. My reading of *A Passage to India* will therefore be guided throughout by the novel's homoerotic desire.

The Pre-post-erous Sexuality of Hindu India

A Passage to India does not feminize Hindu India in a straightforward, stereotypical way. Instead, Forster's grammar of colonial erotics places Hindu India totally outside the purview of the sexual, within a paradoxical space of the pre-sexual and the post-sexual. The resolutely anti-exotic rhetoric of the novel constitutes colonized geography in terms of emptiness, absence, barrenness, failure, denial, and disappointment. Manifested most powerfully in the Hindu space of the Marabar cave, this profound primordial pre-sexual emptiness at once provokes and frustrates colonial naming. In his Italian novels, *Where Angels Fear to Tread* (1905) and *A Room With a View* (1908), Forster contrasts Italy to England. In each novel, the Italian landscape offers a passionate release to repressed English characters, some of whom ultimately achieve a delicate balance between spontaneity and restraint, even if this achievement is severely bounded by a sense of human limitation. India, especially Hindu India, however, is the ultimate negation of Italy: "To regard an Indian as if he were an Italian is not, for instance, a common error, nor perhaps a fatal one, and Fielding often attempted analogies between this peninsula and that other, smaller and more exquisitely shaped, that stretches into the classic waters of the Mediterranean" (PI 79). The comparison does not work; the experience of India only drives Fielding (as it drives Adela, Mrs. Moore, and the narrator) to retreat to the safety of the Mediterranean. The relief and pleasure known by both Fielding and Adela on their return voyages is confirmed by the narrator, and the paean to Venice is eloquent evidence of the text's ambivalence toward India.

When the unofficial bridge party at Fielding's house fails and everyone leaves feeling cross, the narrator observes, "It was as if irritation exuded from the very soil. Could one have been so petty on a Scotch moor or an Italian alp? Fielding wondered afterwards. There seemed no reserve of tranquility to draw upon in India. Either none, or else tranquility swallowed up everything, as it appeared to do for Professor Godbole" (PI 95). This invocation of Godbole is no accident for the Hindu is the human counterpart of the mysterious Marabar cave. Unlike Aziz's Muslim hybridity, which is rendered comparatively simple even in its confusions and contradictions, Godbole's cultural androgyny remains a textual enigma, caught in a cusp between the comical and the sublime. He is introduced to us as "elderly and wizen with a gray moustache and gray-blue eyes, and his complexion was as fair as a European's. He wore a turban that looked like pale purple macaroni, coat, waistcoat, dhoti, socks with clocks. The clocks matched the turban, and his whole appearance suggested harmony—as if he had reconciled the products of the East and West, mental as well as physical, and could never be discomposed" (PI 89). One might say that, like the Gokul Ashtami festival, Godbole manages to include East and West mainly by abandoning good taste. If this indiscriminate inclusiveness of Hinduism suggests an alluring possibility of bridging all social divisions, the attendant dissolution of all boundaries and demarcations generates an intractable anxiety that is most eloquently articulated in the philosophical speculations of Mr. Sorley, the liberal missionary, who is left wondering about the scope and limits of all invitations (PI 58).

As for Godbole, he betrays no sense of conflict between his colonial role as Fielding's assistant and his orthodox Hinduism. In fact, as evident in his professed desire to start his own school in the English model (and to name it after an English sovereign), Godbole not only uses English education to advance himself but is quite enthusiastic about extending English education to all of India. Yet this orthodox Brahmin's inner life seems to lie largely beyond colonial influence. One of the most significant actions performed by Godbole in the novel is the singing of the song during Fielding's unofficial bridge party. After he sings, he explains the song to the equally uncomprehending audience of Muslim and British listeners:

> It was a religious song. I place myself in the position of a milkmaiden. I say to Shri Krishna, "Come! come to me only." The god refuses to come. I grow humble and say: "Do not come to me only. Multiply yourself into a hundred Krishnas, and let one go to each of my hundred companions, but one, O Lord of the Universe, come to me." He refuses to come. . . . I say to Him, Come, come, come, come, come, come. He neglects to come. (PI 96)

Here the male Hindu performs the traditional transvestite act of playing the yearning female to the inaccessible male deity. Such a fluidity of sexual identity coupled with Godbole's age intimates a potential transcendence of gender and sexuality. Despite the erotic elements of the Radha-Krishna mythology that Godbole's song represents, his performance is singularly without erotic appeal to his audience. Indeed to the Western ear, the song, like the Gokul Ashtami ceremony, seems to lack form and climax. Significantly, the song evokes a sensuous response only from the low-caste Hindu servants on the margins. In one of many moments in the text when the colonized nude male body rents critical scenes of cross-cultural interpretation, the water-chestnut gatherer rises naked out of the tank, his lips parted in pleasure and disclosing a wet tongue. The song is thus only indirectly accessible to colonial desire through the visual erotics of the low-caste Hindu male body. Godbole's song brings together the pre-sexual barrenness of colonized geography and the post-sexual fluidity of Hindu male subjectivity. There are, of course, no Hindu women in *A Passage to India*.

English Paternalism and Its Discontents

A Passage to India plots colonial masculinity on a continuum that stretches from the rigid patriarchal ideal of English manliness embodied by the "Turtons and Burtons" of Chandrapore to the fluid "un-English"

A GRAMMAR OF COLONIAL DESIRE

androgyny suggestively sketched in the "horizon figure" of Ralph Moore. Fielding represents a symbolic midpoint on this continuum.

The Turtons and Burtons, mercilessly satirized by Forster, embody the colonial ideal of English manliness grounded in a paternal code of chivalry, duty, and honor. They are the celebrated "heroes" of nineteenth-century colonial literature: civil servants deeply committed to the goals of the civilizing mission, toiling without expectation of gratitude or reward, protecting the defenseless and the weak, keeping a stiff upper lip amid crises, confusions, and conflicts. In Forster's anti-imperial allegory these heroes become villains. They are revealed to be no more than a bunch of petty bureaucrats whose bloated sense of racial superiority makes them strut around in India "posing as gods," believing, as Ronny Heaslop does, that the English are in India not to be "pleasant" but to do "something more important": "do justice and keep the peace" (PI 69). In keeping with Anglo-India's official policy of aloofness, the Turtons and Burtons refuse to mix with the Indians, whom they treat with authoritarian contempt and whose lives they micromanage through various technologies of power. Turton, the district collector of Chandrapore and a prototype of the sahib, authoritatively asserts that he has "never known anything but disaster result when English people and Indians attempt to be intimate socially. Intercourse—yes. Courtesy—by all means. Intimacy—never, never" (PI 173–74). This fear of intimacy, as discussed earlier, took on a distinct sexual tone during and after the Sepoy Mutiny, congealing in the Orientalist belief that "the darker races are physically attracted by the fairer, not vice versa" (PI 222). The crisis in Forster's novel is precipitated precisely when Adela, Mrs. Moore, and Fielding try to cross the racial line and become intimate with Aziz. The disastrous attempts at intimacy that *A Passage to India* chronicles bear Turton out but in ways that vastly amplify and complicate the meaning of his statement.

Fielding is the figure through whom Forster expresses his discontent with the paternalism of the Turtons and Burtons. As a type of the liberal English gentleman, Fielding "had been caught by India late" and, as such, has managed to avoid becoming a pukka sahib. He is described in the novel as follows: "Outwardly of the large shaggy type, with sprawling limbs and blue eyes, he appeared to inspire confidence until he spoke. Then something in his manner puzzled people and failed to allay the distrust which his profession naturally inspired." What Fielding's manly physique conceals is a sympathetic heart: "The world, he believed, is a globe of men who are trying to reach one another and can best do so by the help of good will plus culture and intelligence—a creed ill suited to Chandrapore, but he had come out too late to lose it." His "liberal" ideological role as an "educator" clashes with the "conservative" bureaucratic function of the Turtons and Burtons. The Anglo-Indian community of Chandrapore regards Fielding as a disruptive force for increasing "the evil of brains in India" (PI 79–80). Fielding is an alienated intellectual—alienated in a special way, namely by that form of treason that is sympathy toward those on the other side of the racial divide.

"Still," the narrator informs us "the men tolerated him [Fielding] for the sake of his good heart and strong body; it was their wives who decided that he was not a sahib really." Colonialism, Forster shows, has arrested the growth of feminism in Anglo-Indian society and fossilized gender roles. Therefore, Fielding's failure to conform to an anachronistic code of chivalry that "would have passed without comment in feminist England" causes him a great deal of harm in "a community where the male is expected to be lively and helpful." He discovers early on that it is possible to associate with English men and with Indians but that he who would associate with English women must drop the Indians: "The two wouldn't combine. Useless to blame either party, useless to blame them for blaming one another. It was just so, and one had to choose. Most Englishmen preferred their own kinswomen, who, coming out in increasing numbers, made life on the home pattern yearly more possible. He had found it convenient and pleasant to associate with Indians and he must pay the price" (PI 80). It is this opposition between English women and Indians that is forced to a crisis by Adela's accusation of Aziz.

Although he is more open and forthright about it, Fielding is not alone in viewing the English woman as the chief hurdle to colonial relations. This opinion is, in fact, shared to a lesser or greater degree by all the male characters (English and Indian) in the novel and soundly endorsed by the narrator/author as well—a fact that makes visible the homosocial foundations of colonial culture. Far more than their male counterparts, the women are shown to be thoroughly insensitive to and ignorant about Indians. The Anglo-Indian women repeatedly disregard Indians to the point of rendering them invisible. Mrs. Turton addresses the Indian women at the Bridge Party in the third person as if they do not exist, and she is totally surprised when one of the women actually replies in English. Mrs. Callender stares right through Aziz when she takes his carriage. Aziz, on his part, gives the English woman barely six months in India (to the English man's two years) to metamorphose into a full-fledged memsahib.[10]

Even those English men who rally behind Adela secretly blame the women for the racial tensions in colonial society. Turton, we are told, "retained a contemptuous affection for the pawns he had moved about for so many years, they must be worth his pains. 'After all, it's our women who make everything more difficult out here,' was his inmost thought . . . and beneath his chivalry to Miss Quested resentment lurked, waiting its day—perhaps there is a grain of resentment in all chivalry" (PI 217). Forster, however, draws a distinction between this and Fielding's attitude toward Anglo-Indian women. He endorses Fielding's position as one entirely justified by the abominable behavior of the women but condemns the Turtons and Burtons for hypocritically venerating the institution of womanhood while misogynistically using the women as pawns to control Indian men. The most sensational narrative device Forster uses to separate Fielding's liberal masculinity from the conservative paternalism of the Turtons and Burtons is, of course, rape.

Rape as an Instrument of Homosocial Colonialism

A Passage to India at once codifies and questions colonial homosociality through the figure of rape. The year 1919 was a critical year in colonial Indian history, and it provides the most immediate context for Forster's decision to use the rape motif to expose the hypocrisies of colonial paternalism. It was the year in which agitation against the proposed Rowlatt Acts culminated in the disastrous massacre of Indians at Amritsar. The Rowlatt Acts of 1918 would have given the government permanent powers to crush suspected seditionists by allowing judges to try political cases without juries, by admitting in evidence statements made by the dead or the absent, which thus could not be subject to cross-examination, and by granting internment without trial. Gandhi, who had returned from South Africa in 1915, after having led civil disobedience protests in support of Indians in that country, launched a series of stayagraha campaigns in 1919 against the Rowlatt Acts. On April 9 that year, the day Gandhi was arrested, the lieutenant-governor of Punjab ordered the arrest and deportation of two political prisoners from Amritsar. The next day, amid riots that broke out when an Indian crowd was prevented from entering the European cantonment, an English missionary, Miss Marcella Sherwood, was dragged off her bicycle, badly beaten, and left for dead. Although public meetings were prohibited following the riot, a large crowd gathered at the Jallianwalla Bagh in Amritsar on April 13. The Bagh was an enclosed space, and, when

British troops under General Dyer opened fire, the demonstrators, who had no means of escape, became easy targets. According to the official report, the troops fired 1,650 rounds, killing 379 and wounding 1,200.[11] These figures were much higher by Indian estimates. On April 15 martial law was declared for the first time since the Sepoy Mutiny of 1857. Four days later, under the sanction of martial law, General Dyer issued his infamous "crawling orders," which required all Indians entering the road where Marcella Sherwood had been attacked to crawl on all fours.

The Amritsar massacre, at which British troops had killed defenseless Indians, including large numbers of women and children, unmasked the image of the colonizer as civilized, restrained, and chivalrous. The gap between the professed ideals of the civilizing mission and the practiced brutality of colonialism that Amritsar exposed was predictably papered over by British historians by isolating Dyer's order as a sinister and singular act rather than as an officially authorized one.[12] Although the government officially condemned Dyer's actions, investigations were initiated only after a gap of eight months and then only in response to mounting Indian protest. But for many civil servants, for the military, for large portions of the British press, as well as for a significant number of English women, Dyer was a hero, for whom they raised twenty-six thousand pounds as a testimonial.[13] A committee of 13 Anglo-Indian women was formed to raise money for the Dyer Appreciation Fund. In Bengal 6,250 women signed a petition protesting the inquiry and claiming that the general's actions had prevented them from being subjected to "unspeakable horrors."[14]

But what of Marcella Sherwood herself? Luckily, she survived the attack. What is more, Sherwood refused to accept government compensation and publicly wrote to the *Times* to point out that she had actually been saved by the parents of her Indian students.[15] But by then Sherwood, like Adela in *A Passage to India*, had been emptied into a symbol in the homosocial politics of colonial rule and anticolonial resistance. The Amritsar massacre revived all the predictable fears and responses of the mutiny. The sexual threat to English womanhood was once again used to rationalize and justify the brutalities inflicted upon Indians. As a retaliatory gesture, Indian nationalists issued the "Ravishment Proclamations," calling for the "dishonor" of English "ladies." These incendiary posters are cited in the memoirs of Michael O'Dwyer, then lieutenant-governor of Punjab. In his book O'Dwyer repeatedly returns to the sexual threat the rioters posed to English women as a reference point for reconstructing the Punjab disturbances.[16] Similarly, in *The Other Side*

of the Medal (1925) the historian and novelist Edward Thompson rationalizes the Amritsar massacre as a momentary lapse brought on by
memories of "helpless women and children" killed by Indians during
the mutiny.[17] By extending the (ideo)logic of the 1857 mutiny narratives
to explain the 1919 massacre at Amritsar, these explanations, Jenny
Sharpe points out, renew the value of English womanhood as currency
in colonial transactions.[18]

Forster clearly refuses the seductions of such ideological closures.
Through several interventionary allusions Forster demonstrates how
the racial memory of the mutiny, crystallized in the Anglo-Indian imagination as the originary crime of sexual assault, resurfaced at moments
of crisis to provide legitimacy for colonial repression.[19] The Anglo-Indians of Chandrapore thus think of Aziz's "crime" as "the unspeakable
limit of cynicism untouched since 1857," while the district superintendent of police, Mr. McBryde, advises Fielding to "read any of the Mutiny
records" for evidence of criminality in the Indian mind. Instead of
invoking the "protection of women and children" as an emotionally
potent justification for police and military action, *A Passage to India* par-
odically portrays how the powerful catchphrase invokes an antiquated
code of chivalry, honor, and duty that conveniently excuses English
men from any wrongdoing and effectively legitimizes violence toward
Indian men.

Although *A Passage to India* does not directly allude to the historical
events, the drama surrounding the rape charges and the trial in the fic-
titious town of Chandrapore ironically restages many of the events that
unfolded in Amritsar. Major Callander's outburst to "call in the troops
and clear the bazaars" recalls General Dyer's orders to shoot to kill. Mrs.
Turton's advocacy of "a show of force," and her suggestion that every
native who dared to look at an English woman should be made to crawl
from Chandrapore to the Marabar caves echoes the infamous crawling
order (PI 220). At the trial itself there is an implicit reference to the
Rowlatt Acts (which the massacred Indians at Amritsar had gathered to
protest) in the discussion over whether Mrs. Moore's "evidence" is
admissible, the witness herself being absent.

Besides such references to the immediate political context, there are
allusions to other historical moments that are constitutive of events in
Chandrapore. The fact that an Indian judge is appointed to try Adela's
case recalls the Illbert Bill controversy of 1883–84, another critical historical moment in which the image of the white-woman-as-rape-victim-of-
brown-male had been deployed by the Anglo-Indian community to

deny political power to Indian men. As I discussed in chapter 4, the Illbert Bill, which sought to allow Indian judges to try cases involving
Europeans, had been vehemently opposed, especially by Anglo-Indian
women, on the grounds that it would give Indian men legal power over
European women. The vociferous opposition forced Lord Ripon, then
viceroy, to retreat and revise the offending clauses of the bill, thus killing
any impetus for political reform. It was not until 1923 that Indian judges
were finally granted jurisdiction over English subjects through an
amendment of the Indian Criminal Procedure. Thus, in *A Passage to India*
(1924) an Indian could be appointed to preside over the rape trials, even
though Mr. Das's appointment is mainly calculated to give an impression of fairness, while in reality he is expected to be a "puppet judge"
and condemn Aziz. Even so, Mr. Das's appointment, as Forster shows, is
not without controversy: many of the Anglo-Indian residents of Chandrapore are "convulsed" by "wrath" at the idea of an Indian man having legal hold over an English woman.

As the court case draws near, the nervous Anglo-Indian residents
of Chandrapore gather in the club to strategize ways for managing the
Indian mobs demanding the release of Aziz. Their discussion, which
revolves around defending the women and children, is punctuated by
emotional calls for revenge. A young woman whose husband is away is
afraid to go home "in case the niggers attacked." With her "abundant
figure and masses of corn-gold hair" she is transformed into a symbol
"of all that is worth fighting and dying for." Through such satirical por-
traits Forster reveals how English womanhood was invested with the
value of colonialism even as the women themselves were reduced to
empty tokens in a deadly game of racial politics. The rape allegation
immediately diminishes Adela, evacuating her into a symbolic site of
male embattlement. At the same time, the defense of womanhood
serves as a rallying cry for the Anglo-Indian community. Forster tells us
that "Miss Quested was only a victim, but young Heaslop was a mar-
tyr; he was the recipient of all the evil intended against them by the
country they had tried to serve; he was bearing the sahib's cross."
Through the phrase *sahib's cross*, which shuts out the Anglo-Indian
woman from a share in the glories of colonial martyrdom, Forster par-
odies the homosocial understanding of the rape of a woman as an indirect challenge to the man/men to whom she supposedly belongs.[20] In
this manner *A Passage to India* simultaneously figures and deconstructs
Anglo-India's normative rape narrative to expose the hypocrisies
underlying British patriarchal codes of chivalry, honor, and duty,

allowing us to see race, gender, and sexuality as ideological counters deployed in the game of colonial politics.

Adela's accusation forces racial tensions between English and Indian to a crisis. Breaking loyalty with the Turtons and Burtons who jingoistically rally behind the symbol of violated English womanhood, Fielding decides to stand by Aziz. That it is, after all, an English woman who makes Fielding's overture to Aziz possible is one of the ironies through which colonial desire declares itself in *A Passage to India*.

Many Ways of Being a Man: Fielding and Aziz

Can Fielding succeed where the Turtons and Burtons fail? Is he more capable of developing interpersonal relations in the colonial situation? Forster explores this alluring possibility through Fielding's friendship with Aziz. But, instead of untroubled (ad)ventures into homoerotic intimacy, *A Passage to India* turns out to be a tale of tremulous meetings and anguished partings that inevitably empty homoerotic desire into deferral and disappointment. Why does the promise of sexual, racial, and cultural liberation invested in the tropology of male friendship ultimately atrophy into denial and disempowerment? To answer this question is to understand the historical limits of colonial desire.

By the time Forster came to unravel the mystery muddle of India, the stereotype of Indian effeminacy had already been public property in the British imagination for over a century. The accounts by and of Forster, Ackerley, and others further suggest that early-twentieth-century middle-class English male homosexuality was being organized to a striking degree around the differential objectification of proletarian men at home and colonized men abroad.

Forster's very first encounter with an Indian in the person of Syed Ross Masood, the man to whom *A Passage to India* was originally dedicated, involved him a rather atypical, confused, and unrequited homoerotic relationship. As P. N. Furbank's biography suggests, Forster's love for Masood reveals a profound turmoil not only because the Indian did not reciprocate his love but also because their friendship itself was based on different conceptions of love, enigmatic and unexplained.[21] Masood's appeal may have been his exotic difference: he was handsome in appearance, regal in style, histrionic in manner; he could be emotional and recite Urdu poetry. But, at the same time, he did not altogether conform to the stereotype of the passionate, passive, effeminate Oriental. Brash, bold, athletic, and dominating, "manliness" was, as

Rustom Bharucha notes, second nature to him.[22] In this, too, Masood presented a dramatic contrast to Forster, who with his frail physique, his abhorrence of athletics and aggression, his "effeminate" image,[23] did not meet the criteria of English manliness. These conflicting notions of gender and sexuality, Englishness and Orientalness, clearly have a bearing on Forster's quest for alternative models of masculinity in *A Passage to India*.

Aziz is the touchstone against which three distinct models of English masculinity—embodied by the Turtons-Burtons, Fielding, and Ralph Moore—are tested and judged in the novel. Forster's characterization of Aziz must be squarely placed within the ideologeme of effeminism. The Indian, as Lionel Trilling has observed, is recognizably un-English: he is handsome, volatile, tender, sensitive, sensuous, with a hint of cruelty, much warmth, a love of pathos, and a desire to please even at the cost of insincerity. He, like his friends, is not prompt, not efficient, not neat, not really convinced of Western ideas, even in science (when he finally retires to a native state he slips back to mix a little magic with his medicine), and he, like them, is acutely self-conscious about his faults. He is hypersensitive, imagining slights even when there are none, full of humility, and full of contempt. He desperately wants to be liked.[24] Indeed, when placed alongside Aziz, the liberal Fielding is quite English: rational, reasonable, and restrained. Even their physical appearance presents a contrast. Unlike the large, sprawling English man, the Indian is described in diminutive terms as "an athletic little man, daintily put together, but really very strong" (PI 40). The process of miniaturization and fragmentation deflects attention from the disturbing beauty of Aziz's body, which the novel will not directly embody—a fact that must be placed alongside the full-blown embodiment of the untouchable punkah-wallah. In keeping with colonial notions of Mughal decadence that sanctioned British colonization of India, this Mughal descendant is sexually licentious, visiting prostitutes in Calcutta and offering to arrange for Fielding "a lady with breasts like mangoes." And, like the men identified as the most savage mutineers in 1857, the man who stands accused of Adela's rape is a Muslim who indulges in wild fantasies about the return of Mughal rule to India.

Despite his un-English qualities, Aziz, however, is a quintessential cultural hybrid and a product of English colonialism. Trapped in imperialist definitions, Aziz's own sense of manliness is quite confused. Even when he becomes aggressively "anti-British" and "an Indian at last," all he has is rhetoric and emotion. Aziz is unable to free his idea of manhood from aggression and domination. Ronny Heaslop ridicules the Indians' often humiliating attempts to emulate tough English ways: "They used to cringe, but the younger generation believe in a show of manly independence . . . Whether the native swaggers or cringes, there's always something behind every remark he makes, and if nothing else, he's trying to increase his izzat—in plain Anglo-Saxon, to score" (PI 54). Even at the end of the novel, when Aziz finally leaves British India for the native kingdom of Mau, he writes confused nationalistic poems about oriental womanhood that call for abolishing purdah. His espousal of the women's cause signifies a feeble attempt to assert his manliness by imitating the colonial codes of masculinity he has internalized.[25] Forster's characterization of Aziz does not break with the stereotype of the effeminate Asiatic. Instead, it re-presents the stereotype sympathetically, with a veiled acknowledgment of its erotic potential.

In the very first meeting that transpires between Aziz and Fielding, the two men tentatively grope for an opening into intimacy. The setting for the encounter is an alternate yet ambiguous space situated between the intimacy of the bedroom and the formality of the living room. When Aziz arrives, Fielding is naked and hidden in the bedroom, exposed yet concealed from Aziz's curious gaze. Compelled to wait, Aziz satisfies his longing to "know everything about the splendid fellow—his salary, preferences, antecedents, how best one might please him" by surveying Fielding's personal possessions (PI 78). This erotically charged scene explores various ways in which colonizing and colonized men may be revealed or concealed, made visible or invisible, see or be seen in each other's eyes

Muddying the boundary between conventionality and unconventionality, the exchange between Fielding and Aziz explores the tragic failures of communication between colonizing and colonized men. The English man, half-concealed in the bathroom, spontaneously invites the Indian to "make himself at home." To Aziz this casual remark "had a very definite meaning. 'May I really, Mr. Fielding? It's very good of you,' he called back; 'I like unconventional behavior so extremely'" (PI 81). Fielding's remark about the obscurity of postimpressionism offends the Indian, who finds meanings in them that the speaker had not intended. These gaps are repeated and amplified in the notoriously erotic dressing scene through metaphors of clothing. Aziz wrenches off his own stud to replace the one Fielding has accidentally broken. This object of exchange creates a temporary feeling of closeness between the men.

The next meeting between the Fielding and Aziz, which takes

place in the private space of the Indian's home, also involves an object of exchange that subscribes a compact between the two men: the photograph of Aziz's dead wife. Forster's portrayal of Indian women in *A Passage to India* would lead us to believe they were existing under unchanging condition of oppression, waiting for Indian men to liberate them. Thus, it is Aziz who "unveils" his wife's photograph, allowing her to come out of the purdah, and it is he who writes nationalistic poems about the liberation of Indian womanhood. But, in fact, the 1920s saw the rise of an Indian women's movement that fought its battle for emancipation on two fronts: sexual equality and national liberation. Even those women who were not active in feminist organizations, which spoke more directly to the concerns of urban, middle-class women, participated in anticolonial demonstrations and acts of civil disobedience. Forster's novel is largely silent about these struggles, except for one reference to Muslim women who are on hunger strike in protest of Aziz's arrest: "And a number of Mohammedan ladies had sworn to take not food until the prisoner was acquitted; their death would make little difference, indeed, being invisible, they seemed dead already, nevertheless it was disquieting" (PI 218). Despite Forster's muted criticism of the Anglo-Indian mentality, his words end up containing Indian women's noisy resistance within the figure of the silent and hidden purdah woman.[26] A similar gesture of containment is evident in some contemporary feminist readings of *A Passage to India*. In Brenda Silver's essay, for instance, Adela is the agent who voices not only the subjugation of Indians in general but also the sexual oppression of Indian women in particular: "Being English, she [Adela] has the power to speak the position of otherness denied to the Indian in general and doubly denied to the invisible and silent Indian woman, whose resistance resides in absence and negativity, and she uses this power to unsettle the dominant discourse."[27] Understanding colonial structures of power as a doubling of the white female sexual oppression that Adela alone has the power to speak, Silver produces a category of Other that once again keeps the colonized, particularly the sexed and colonized subject, hidden from history.[28]

What the unveiling of Aziz's dead wife's photograph shows is that, in the presence of a woman who can be seen as innocent, ignorant, or pitiable, men are able to exchange power and to confirm one another's value even in the context of remaining inequalities in their power. But once again the feeling of intimacy is fragile and temporary. Since the pervasive violence of colonialism makes the personal political and the political personal, even the smallest gesture of goodwill becomes an act of violation. When the Indian tries to reach out by unveiling the photograph of his wife, he not only moves the reserved English man but also makes him feel uneasily obligated in a barter of confidences. As a result, Fielding begins phantasmatically to imagine India demanding from him an "occasional intoxication of the blood" (PI 128) and promptly retreats to the safety of "equilibrium": "'I shall not really be intimate with this fellow' Fielding thought, and then 'nor with anyone'" (129). Both men are left feeling diminished by an emotional encounter that unsteadily oscillates between excess and restraint.

The verbal exchange that takes place between Aziz and Fielding after the victory banquet comes deliciously close to declaring the narrative's submerged homoerotic intent. The narrating eye appreciatively notes that Aziz was "full of civilization this evening, complete, digni fied, rather hard" (PI 251). Fielding and Aziz seem poised on the brink of a beautiful intimacy. This beautiful hope, however, is rudely disrupted by Aziz's obscene wish to extract monetary compensation from Adela. The look of consternation and anxiety on the English man's face, makes Aziz remark cynically, "I know what you are going to say next: Let Miss Quested off paying, so that the English may say, 'Here is a native who has actually behaved like a gentleman; if it was not for his black face we would almost allow him to join our Club.' This approval of your compatriots no longer interests me, I have become anti-British, and ought to have done so sooner, it would have saved me numerous misfortunes" (PI 250). At the moment of his transformation into an anticolonial nationalist, Aziz aggressively rejects colonial masculinity by refusing to live up to its code of chivalry. But in the absence of an alternative notion of masculinity to give him integrity and dignity, Aziz's refusal takes the form of a crude sexism that only ends up confirming colonial stereotypes about Indian men. Thus when an annoyed Fielding suggests that he be merciful like the Mughal emperors and accept a written apology, instead, Aziz sarcastically dictates an imaginary apology note: "Dear Dr. Aziz, I wish you had come into the cave; I am an awful old hag, and it is my last chance" (252). Fielding is predictably put off by the Indian's sexual snobbery. He is unable to come to terms with Aziz's refusal (or failure) to adopt what he considers to be the proper and fair code of conduct toward women. "It is the one thing in you I can't put up with," Fielding tells Aziz. Forster's narrative appears to fall back on a stale Orientalist explanation here, implying that the incompatibility between Fielding and Aziz is ultimately due to their incom-

patible attitudes toward women. Forster does indeed savage the antiquated Victorian code of chivalry adopted by the sahibs and memsahibs and powerfully refigures the trope of rape, but he does not altogether refrain from using the status of women as a sign of the racial
and cultural differences between England and India. Like most Western-educated Indian male nationalists, Aziz oscillates uncertainly
between rejecting the chivalric code of colonial masculinity and asserting his own manliness by espousing the cause of Indian women's liberation. But he remains outside, enviously looking in on the companionate comradery English men and women enjoy. During the
Fieldings's final visit to Mau, Aziz, in stereotypical Oriental style,
inquisitively rifles through the English man's private letters in his
absence and reads one written by Adela to Mrs. Fielding: "It was all
'Stella and Ralph,' even 'Cyril' and 'Ronny'—all so friendly and sensi-
ble, and written in a spirit he could not command." The narrator
informs us, *He envied the easy intercourse that is only possible in a nation
whose women are free* (PI 303; emph. added). So this, after all, is the
final reason why Fielding and Aziz are unable to consummate their
friendship? Perhaps, Forster equivocates.

At the victory banquet following the trial, when a "friendly and
domineering" Aziz cajoles Fielding to "give in to the East" and live "in
a condition of affectionate dependence upon it," Fielding demurs at giving up his independence and becoming subservient like Mohammed
Latif: "When they argued about it, something racial intruded—not bit-
terly, but inevitably, like the colour of their skins: coffee colour versus
pinko-grey" (PI 259). Not "black" and "white" maybe, but it is still the
immutability of skin color that calls a halt to the flight of homoerotic
desire. Forster is finally forced to register the disturbing fact that colonial friendship cannot be abstracted from the obdurate presence of the
racial body.

At the Margins of Homoerotic Desire:
The Punkah-Wallah

The most elaborate embodiment of homoerotic desire in *A Passage to
India* is not the central Indian character Aziz but the marginal yet unfor-
gettable punkah-wallah, who, like a god, presides over Aziz's trial and
precipitates the dramatic reversal of Adela's charge. If Adela's rape
charge puts into operation all the Orientalist stereotypes of colonial ideology, her recantation calls the veracity of these stereotypes into ques-

tion by deconstructing the homosocial-heterosexual racism instituted in the myth that "the darker races are physically attracted by the fairer, not vice versa" (PI 222). The moment of reversal is contingent upon the eruption of a transgressive homoerotic desire made visible through the iconic figure of the punkah-wallah. The punkah-wallah is a peripheral yet pivotal figure, symbolizing the silence of the subaltern.[29]

The punkah-wallah who attracts Adela's attention in the crowded courtroom is an untouchable. As such, he marks the margins of a caste-ridden society that shuns him as a source of pollution. Contrary to popular belief, neither colonialism nor nationalism destroyed the caste system, which, albeit in an altered form, remains a powerful organizing principle in Indian society to this day. Colonialism did not so much erode the Hindu caste system as reinvent it by inscribing an emergent class hierarchy within the older form of occupational status to produce an amalgamated caste-class hierarchy. Indian nationalism, despite its success in mobilizing many marginal segments of society for the struggle against colonial rule, ultimately only rearticulated traditional caste hierarchies in terms of class. Even Gandhi himself, despite his efforts to end untouchability and include untouchables in the nationalist fold, did not unequivocally oppose untouchability as a fixed occupational status, which he justified in terms of moral duty.[30]

In *A Passage to India* the punkah-wallah is at once marginal and central to the climax of the courtroom drama. The nameless punkah-wallah, who has "no bearing officially on the trial," is nevertheless strategically positioned on a raised platform placed diametrically opposite to another platform on which Mr. Das, the assistant magistrate emblematizing colonial authority, is also seated. These two colonized figures represent the opposite ends of colonized society: the Western-educated, "cultivated, self-conscious, and conscientious" assistant magistrate is the preeminent product of colonialism and (like Aziz) the potential subject of nationalism; the uneducated untouchable mechanically operating the hand-pulled fan, barely cognizant of his surroundings, is tangential to the histories of colonialism as well as nationalism. Yet it is the untouchable rather than the assistant magistrate who elicits the truth. Significantly, it is also the menial laborer (and others like him—e.g., the water chestnut gatherer), rather than the educated Indian who provides the novel with its most overt and full-blown embodiment of homoerotic desire.

If the disruption produced by the punkah-wallah is an effect of a homoerotic desire that detonates the homosocial economy of colonialism, the tender gaze that conjures up the punkah-wallah is itself an effect of colonialism. The vast distance between the European and the lowly untouchable ensures that the latter can only be the erotic object of a Western gaze. Sara Suleri has suggested that the passage describing the punkah-wallah evokes caste in such a way that untouchability no longer refers to caste alone but is, instead, extended to include an embodiment of homosexual desire itself.[31] Although homosexuality was an oppositional underground culture in Anglo-Indian society, it was not outside the social hierarchies of race, caste, and class. Indeed, as we read in the accounts by Forster and Ackerley, Anglo-Indian homosexuality was contingent upon the commodification of subaltern Indian men.

Forster's own relationships with low-caste Indian men were directly and explicitly sexual. While traveling in India, Forster (like his friend Ackerley) came into contact mainly with the indigenous royalty and their low-caste servants from whom the royalty extracted, among other things, sexual value. Although it is not clear whether there was a distinct homosexual subculture in existence for Indian men of various castes/classes or whether they largely operated in a cognitive vacuum, we know that most of the spectrum of male bodily contacts had not yet been legally codified or criminalized, as it had been in England with the Labouchere amendment of 1885. In general, the king as well as his young male menials enjoyed the benefits of a legitimizing heterosexual marriage while maintaining considerable latitude to engage in promiscuous homoerotic relationships. Besides, in a society that strictly segregated the sexes and encouraged strong same-sex relationships, friendships could easily leak into the domain of the erotic. If this seems similar to the homosexuality prevalent among boys in English public schools, the imperial rulers did not recognize it. The homosexuality of the English schoolboy was seen as an aspect of his childishness, something he would put aside when, as an adult male, he assumed homosocial-patriarchal attitudes. By contrast, the Indian male's proclivity for homosexual activity was considered a racial failing.

The accounts by Forster and Ackerley indicate that part of the unspoken privileges European men visiting the royal courts of India enjoyed was sexual access to the king's menials. At this juncture I wish to call attention to a self-censored segment in *The Hill of Devi* (1953): the unpublished "Kanaya" memoir subsequently included in Elizabeth Heine's edition, which Forster had felt "couldn't go in because it couldn't."[32] In the memoir Forster records his covert sexual experiences with the Rajah's servants at the Dewas court and his attendant confusion and guilt. He describes himself as "disintegrated and inert" at the end of a game of sexual politics in which the object of desire was "a slave, without rights, and I a despot whom no one could call to account."[33] By altogether eliminating the woman as mediator of male relations, this narrative not only recodes the trope of rape in an explicitly homosexual register, but it also reverses the colonial myth of the lascivious Oriental and replaces it with the colonial reality of the lascivious European. The concurrence of sexual and political domination inscribed in the image of the white male as rapist is offset by the abject figure of the subaltern Indian male, serially victimized by Indian feudalism and English colonialism. The "Kanaya" episode represents a scene of exploitation that is usually hidden to and hidden by Western representation. It is also the scene that is at once concealed and revealed through Forster's use of heterosexual rape and the romanticized figure of the punkah-wallah in *A Passage to India*.

Just as the "slave, without rights" in the "Kanaya" memoir compels Forster to uneasily characterize himself as "a despot whom no one could call to account," the lowly fan puller in *A Passage to India* provokes Adela to question the superiority of her race and to recognize the provincial nature of what the English arrogantly assume to be "civilization":

> Almost naked, and splendidly formed, he sat on a raised platform near the back, in the middle of the central gangway, and he caught her attention as she came in, and he seemed to control the proceedings. He had the strength and beauty that sometimes come to flower in Indians of low birth. When that strange race nears the dust and is condemned as untouchable, then nature remembers the physical perfection that she accomplished elsewhere, and throws out a god—not many, but one here and there, to prove to society how little its categories impress her. This man would have been notable anywhere; among the thin-hammed, flat-chested mediocrities of Chandrapore he stood out as divine, yet he was of the city, its garbage had nourished him, and he would end on its rubbish-heaps. Pulling the rope towards him, relaxing it rhythmically, sending swirls of air over others, receiving none himself, he seemed apart from human destinies, a male Fate, a winnower of souls. Opposite him, also on a platform, sat the little Assistant Magistrate, cultivated, self-conscious and conscientious. The punkah-wallah was none of these things; he scarcely knew that he existed and did not understand why the court was fuller than usual, indeed he did not even know he worked a fan, though he thought he pulled a rope. Something in his aloofness impressed the girl from middle-class England, and rebuked the narrowness of her sufferings. In virtue of what had she collected this roomful of people together? Her particular brand of opinions, and the suburban Jehovah who sanctified them—by what right did they claim so much importance in the world, and assume the title of civilization? (PI 220–21)

Instead of seeing the untouchable as an incarnation of filth and pollution, Adela sees him as a vision of beauty and perfection. He appears to
her as a mythological creature removed from time and place. The
mythic force of the punkah-wallah breaks the historical opposition
between the English woman and the Indian man, prompting Adela to
revoke her charges against Aziz. This is also the moment of Aziz's transformation from a "good" colonial subject to an anti-British nationalist,
from a Muslim to "an Indian at last." But, while the Western-educated
Indian becomes the subject of nationalism, the uneducated subaltern
remains silent, marginal to the events in the courtroom, and unaware of
what is transpiring around him.

At the same time there is a certain Orientalist romanticism in
Forster's eroticized description that objectifies the nameless untouchable as a possible gateway to the "real India" (a phrase that Forster's
narrative both mocks and exemplifies). The opposition between the
mongrelized urbanite and the authentic peasant is one of the most
enduring and pernicious ones to persist in Anglo-Indian writing.
Michael O'Dwyer, the lieutenant-governor of the Punjab and the man
responsible for the Amritsar massacre, wrote in his memoir the year
after Forster published *A Passage to India:* "[colonial reformers] went
astray because they did not understand the *real India.* They legislated for
the English-educated India, a minority of less than one percent . . .
Meantime the *real India* is drifting away from the justice and authority to
which it was so securely moored."[34] Forster also romanticizes the
untouchable, but unlike most colonial writers, he does not take it upon
himself to speak for the subaltern who cannot speak for himself.[35] Sedimented in his portrait of the punkah-wallah, therefore, is an implicit
recognition of the limits of colonial representation. The punkah-wallah
becomes available to the Western homoerotic gaze only as an object of
visual consumption, not as a consciousness for cognitive consumption.
In fact, we might say that the colonial imagination can grasp his consciousness only as an absence. As the most elaborate embodiment of
homoerotic desire in the novel, the punkah-wallah provides a measure
for the conflict as well as the complicity between English/Anglo-Indian
homosexuality and homosocial colonialism.

Colonial Androgyny: Ralph Moore

Throughout, *A Passage to India* maintains the proprieties of heterosexuality, routinely redirecting homoerotic desire through sanctioned chan-

nels of homosocial male bonding (marriage, prostitution, rape). Yet the narrative is deeply infused with a utopian longing to eliminate the woman as the middle term in interracial relations. Although Fielding refuses to manipulate white women to dominate brown men, as the Turtons and Burtons do, he too does not succeed in eliminating the Anglo-Indian woman as the middle term who at once links and divides English and Indian men. Till the very end Fielding's relationship with Aziz is haunted by Adela's ghost. And, finally, his marriage to Stella not only widens the gap between him and Aziz but also contributes to his retreat into Europe. For a more successful attempt to eliminate female mediation, we must await the arrival of Ralph Moore.

Ralph Moore, far more than Fielding, represents the boldest alternative to the paternalism of the Turtons and Burtons. Unlike Fielding, Ralph does not even outwardly fulfill the colonialist's concept of manliness. He is described as a "strange-looking youth, tall, prematurely aged, the big blue eyes faded with anxiety, the hair impoverished and tousled! *Not a type that is often exported imperially*" (PI 203, emph. added). However, to Aziz's poetic sensibility, Ralph seems quite beautiful. As the biological and spiritual son of Mrs. Moore, Ralph is a man with a decidedly feminine sensibility. He, like his mother, is intuitive and intense. Through him, as through Fielding and Aziz, Forster shows us that "there are many ways of being a man" (267). Ralph Moore embodies a kind of androgyny that promises to undo the opposition between English manliness and Indian effeminacy. This promise is tested in the final sections of the novel, where Ralph and Aziz are brought together.

Aziz's meeting with Ralph, which takes place against the background of the ecstatic Gokul Ashtami festival, is not only erotic and intimate but echoes his earlier encounters with Fielding (and even Mrs. Moore and Adela), whose failures may be seen as emblematic sacrifices pointing to the syncretic possibility suggested in Ralph Moore. The scene, in which Ralph suddenly appears spiritlike, reenacts Aziz's first meeting with Mrs. Moore in the mosque. The young man is described as "extraordinary," a word used by Forster to designate the Marabar caves. And, in a startling replay of the erotic dressing scene between Aziz and Fielding, the doctor solicitously applies ointment to heal the Englishman's bee stings. The revelation that Ralph's trip to India has been paid for by Adela as a repayment of a debt she felt she owed the country allows us to read Ralph as the compensation Aziz had wanted from Adela.

The potential for friendship between Aziz and Ralph represents a "rumour of salvation," or an answer to the question of whether it is possible for Indians and Englishmen to be friends. Racial, sexual, and national differences between English and Indian are reversed, and even temporarily erased, in Aziz's acceptance of Ralph as an Oriental (PI 308). At their very first meeting, when the Indian stumbles upon the unexportable English man getting stung by bees and sternly admonishes him to pull himself together and "be a man," Aziz takes on a rather aggressive and patronizing attitude, especially as Ralph seems so timid and submissive (PI 295). When later he calls on Ralph to treat the bee stings, he feels he can treat the patient just as the English doctor of Chandrapore had treated his Indian patients. He speaks "threateningly" as he roughly applies a salve to the wounds (PI 304). The unkindness and cruelty hidden behind the Indian doctor's solicitousness are immediately sensed by the intuitive English man. As they converse, Aziz realizes that Ralph, "though frightened, was not weak" (PI 305). Gradually, Aziz softens and opens up his heart to the English man. He even goes to the extent of taking Ralph out for a boat ride to show him the Gokul Ashtami procession as a final "act of homage to Mrs. Moore's son" (PI 307). During the boat ride, when Ralph directs them to the very spot where the dead body of the Rajah has been secretly hidden away so as not to disturb the religious festivities, Aziz is overcome with an uncanny sense that "his companion was not so much a visitor as a guide" (PI 308). Thus, the un-English English man appears, at least to Aziz, more Indian than the Indian himself.

Ralph's arrival in India is too late, however, and the fond hope that he will fulfill the desires of cultural syncretism is marked off by the narrative as a merely "ideal," unrealizable one. As Aziz says to Fielding, "we wanted to know you ten years back—now it's too late" (314). Ralph is a kind of "horizon figure" who cannot be assimilated into the historical trajectory of Forster's narrative. The nostalgic hope that Ralph Moore will somehow combine English/masculine values with Indian/feminine sensibility and make the empire a kinder, gentler institution can be envisioned in the text only as a lost opportunity or as a utopian possibility.[36] This, then, is the ultimate sense in which the novel's comic yet rueful ending—the ultimate fate of Aziz and Fielding, kissing and separating all at once—figures homoerotic desire both as a tantalizing possibility and as an unattainable opportunity in colonial society.

Conclusion

The subject of desire is an especially overdetermined site for the exchange of meanings between race, gender, class, and caste, the sets of categories by which we have generally sought to describe relations of power and divisions of human labor. Theorizing desire therefore calls for a fundamental reconfiguration of the conventionally conceived relationship between the political and the psychological, or the public and the private. It also calls for a radical change in the widespread use of gender, race, class, or caste as analytical categories in various contemporary critical discourses. Yet the inflated rhetoric, claims, counterclaims, and dismissals we hear in the charged atmosphere of (post)colonial cultural studies suggest that we have all too often resorted to allegorical mystifications in our scramble to construct what Alok Bhalla has aptly called "revenge histories."[1] It is against this background that *Effeminism* strongly reiterates the need for discrimination before judgment, for careful contextualization before hasty generalization.

My study has attempted to fulfill this need in certain specifiable ways. First, I have attempted to reiterate the assertion that the historical/political and the sexual are zones sharing contiguous, arbitrary, unreliable boundaries that are subject to continual alteration.[2] At the same time, in order to escape the unproductive mystifications of allegorical reading, this project has maintained, in critical practice, a productive tension between the political and the sexual, *interrupting* one with the other rather than *interpreting* one in terms of the other. Second, I have sought to break with the practice of promiscuously deploying subalternity as a trope for all kinds of exploitation and victimization, since such a practice not only ignores the different historical and material contexts of oppression but also erases crucial differences within subaltern groups that modify their exercise and experience of power. Therefore, following recent feminist scholarship that has extended the use of gender as an analytical category to the study of issues beyond women and sexuality,[3] I have used masculinity to investigate the multiple axes along which power was constituted and contested in colonial society.

Effeminism has sought to further our understanding of colonialism by making two fundamental arguments about colonial desire and colonial stereotypes. The first argument is that the production of a stereotype, like the production of desire, is not a smooth, unified operation but, rather, an uneven, contradictory process that defines and delimits the colonizer as well as the colonized, albeit in very different ways. As such, we need to recognize that deviant, unacceptable, unassimilable, contradictory modes of desire did indeed shatter imperial unity, estrange colonial identity, fracture colonial ideology, and limit colonial hegemony in ways that not only impeded total conquest of particular colonized groups but also opened up subterraneous spaces of refuge and escape with potential for intervention, subversion, and resistance, especially by certain elite colonized groups. In other words, we need to understand that colonialist hegemony was constantly under seige both from without and from within. To assert the internal fissures in colonialism is not to minimize the role of Indian resistance (militant or otherwise) but, rather, to harness the "family quarrels" of Orientalism and imperialism for the politics of decolonization. If we fail to recognize that deferral and denial, division and dissension, fracture and failure, are integral to the efficient operation of the colonial machine, we only end up reifying the omnipotence of empire and reinforcing neocolonial conditions of reading. Therefore, instead of making desire and sexuality entirely sublimatable and amenable to political or economic service, I have tried to emphasize the resistant and unassimilable modes of masculine desire sedimented in Raj fiction. The colonial production of the stereotype of Bengali/Indian effeminacy, I have sought to show, was not so much an unimpeded expression of English hegemony as a contradictory and contested attempt to establish total hegemony.

The second central argument of *Effeminism* has been that the colonial construct of Indian effeminacy is not simply a false or untrue stereotype, a mere illusory projection of the self onto the Other, but, rather, a misvalued and distorted recognition of an alternative and resistant cultural reality. I have suggested that androgyny represented a credible spiritual ideal and cultural hybridity a viable way of life for most Hindu men until late-nineteenth-century Hindu revivalist nationalism bought into the Manichean legacy of Macaulay and internalized the colonial devaluation of androgyny and hybridity as effeminacy. Attempting to move beyond critiques that focus on the complicity inscribed in Indian self-perceptions of effeminacy and on the tragic inadequacy of Indian effeminacy as a site of anticolonial nationalistic confrontation, I have tried to understand colonized effeminacy as an everyday practice of cultural androgyny that not only created unsuspected subterranean spaces of refuge but also opened up potential sites of subversion for the weak and wily. I have argued that, unlike most militant forms of nationalism, which, as Ashis Nandy points out, were indeed limited by their complicity with the colonial ideology of masculinity, Gandhian nationalism did manage to wrest effeminacy out of the colonial script and give it a different reading that proved emancipatory not so much for Indian women but for elite Indian men. Burdening Indian womanhood with the weight of tradition and spirituality, Gandhian nationalism empowered elite Indian men precisely by legitimizing effeminacy as a morally superior model of masculinity. Did this model take root in independent India, or was it supplanted by a Nehruvian ideal that accommodated to neocolonial conditions, paving the way, first, for crony socialism and, more recently, crony capitalism? What impact does the current resurgence of Hindu fundamentalism have on performances of gender in India? What characterizes postcolonial masculinity? What is the relationship between postcolonial and postmodern masculinity? What are the implications for postcolonial feminist politics and practices? These are important questions that need to be addressed in future studies.

Notes

Chapter 1

1. Edward Said, *Orientalism* (New York: Vintage Books, 1978), 6.

2. Although ignored by early male theorists of colonialism, subsequent scholarship has established gender as a constitutive category. For a comprehensive overview, see Ann Laura Stoler, "Carnal Knowledge and Imperial Power: Gender, Race, and Morality in Colonial Asia," in *Gender and the Crossroads of Knowledge: Feminist Anthropology in the Postmodern Era*, ed. Micaela di Leonardo (Berkeley: University of California Press, 1991): 51–100.

3. Said, *Orientalism*, 222.

4. Ashis Nandy, *The Intimate Enemy: Loss and Recovery of Self under Colonialism* (Delhi: Oxford University Press, 1983), 4.

5. A representative as well as influential study in this category is Gauri Viswanathan's, *Masks of Conquest: Literary Study and British Rule in India* (New York: Columbia University Press, 1989).

6. Rashmi Bhatnagar, "Uses and Limits of Foucault: A Study of the Theme of Origins in Said's 'Orientalism,'" *Social Scientist* 16, no. 7 (1986): 15.

7. Studies in this category generally take their lead from O. Mannoni's pioneering work, *Prospero and Caliban: The Psychology of Colonization,* trans. Pamela Powesland (Ann Arbor: University of Michigan Press, 1990). Despite powerful criticisms of Mannoni articulated by Franz Fanon, in *Black Skin, White Masks,* and by Aimé Césaire, in *Discourse on Colonialism,* his influence is evident in recent studies such as Patrick Brantlinger's *Rule of Darkness: British Literature and Imperialism, 1830–1914* (Ithaca: Cornell University Press, 1988).

8. Homi Bhabha has developed his theory by appropriating Lacanian psychoanalysis as routed through Frantz Fanon. See essays in Bhabha's *The Location of Culture* (London/New York: Routledge, 1994).

9. The term *Manichean* is used by Abdul R. JanMohammed to denote the flexible but unchanging oppositions that structure the discursive/ideologi-

cal field Said has designated as "Orientalism." Interestingly, both JanMohammed and Homi Bhabha use Lacan routed via Fanon, but in very different
ways. See JanMohammed, *Manichean Aesthetics* (Amherst: University of Mass-
achussets Press, 1983); also "The Economy of Manichean Allegory: The Function of Racial Difference in Colonialist Literature," in *Race, Writing and Difference*, ed. Heny Louis Gates (Chicago: University of Chicago Press, 1986):
78–106.

10. In this, I have followed the lead of Giles Deleuze and Félix Guattari,
Anti-Oedipus: Capitalism and Schizophrenia, trans. Robert Hurley et al. (Minneapolis: University of Minnesota Press, 1983); and Fredric Jameson, *The Political Unconscious: Narrative as a Socially Symbolic Act* (Ithaca: Cornell University
Press, 1981). Following Deleuze and Guattari, who appropriate Franz Fanon's
insights, Jameson formulated the notion of the "political unconscious" in an
attempt to reassert the specificity of the political content of everyday life and of
individual fantasy-experience and to reclaim it from that reduction to the
merely subjective and to the status of psychological projections.

11. Fredric Jameson, *The Political Unconscious*, 79.

12. "The ideologeme," Jameson explains, "is an amphibious formation
whose essential structural characteristic may be described as its possibility to
manifest itself either as a pseudo idea—a conceptual or belief system, an
abstract value, an opinion or prejudice—or as a protonarrative, a kind of ultimate class fantasy about the 'collective characters' that are the classes in opposition"; ibid., 87.

13. Ranajit Guha, "Dominance without Hegemony and its Historiography," in *Subaltern Studies*. My point here bears comparison with Guha's argument that British rule in India was ultimately based on "dominance without
hegemony." See vol. 6, *Writings on South Asian History and Society*, ed. R. Guha
(Delhi: Oxford University Press, 1989), 210–309.

14. Gayatri Chakravorty Spivak, "Three Women's Texts and a Critique of
Imperialism," *Critical Inquiry* 12, no. 1 (fall 1985): 243–61. For typical defenses
against Spivak's charge, see May Ellis Gibson, "The Seraglio or Suttee: Brontë's
Jane Eyre," *Postscript* 4 (1987): 5; Laura E. Donaldson, "The Miranda Complex:
Colonialism and the Question of Feminist Reading," *Diacritics* 18, no. 3 (fall
1988): 75. Pointing to Charlotte Brontë's references to harem women and sati,
pashas, and sultans as metaphors for sexual relations in England, Gibson
argues that "metaphorically Jane is on the side of Heathen women," while Donaldson contends that "the trope of 'race' . . . evokes Jane's subjection in, yet
resistance to, patriarchy."

15. Brenda Silver, "Periphrasis, Power and Rape in *A Passage to India*,"
Novel 22 (fall 1988): 86–105.

16. Sara Suleri, *The Rhetoric of English India* (Chicago: University of
Chicago Press, 1992), 16.

17. In taking such an approach, I follow the suggestion made by Stuart
Hall in "Culture, Media and the 'Ideological Effect,'" in *Mass Communication
and Society*, ed. James Curran et al. (Beverley Hills, Calif.: Sage, 1979), 327.

18. For example, see George Mosse, *Nationalism and Sexuality: Respectability and Abnormal Sexuality in Modern Europe* (New York: H. Fertig, 1985); Cather-

ine Hall and Leonore Davidoff, *Family Fortunes: Men and Women of the English Middle Class, 1780–1850* (Chicago: University of Chicago Press, 1987); M. Roper and J. Tosh, eds., *Manful Assertions: Masculinities in Britain since 1800* (London: Routledge, 1991); Jeffrey Weeks, *Sex, Politics, and Society: The Regulation of Sexuality since 1800* (New York: Longman, 1981); and Brian Harrison, *Separate Spheres: The Opposition to Women's Suffrage in Britain* (London: Croom Helm, 1978).

19. An exception is Kenneth Ballhatchet's *Race, Sex and Class under the Raj: Imperial Attitudes and Policies and their Critics, 1793–1905* (New York: St. Martin's Press, 1980). Although this book does not focus exclusively on men or masculinity, its historically grounded account of how race, sex, and class were deployed in colonial politics throws much light on the way colonial masculinity was constructed.

20. For example, Joseph Bristow, *Empire Boys: Adventures in a Man's World* (London: HarperCollins, 1991), offers an account of imperial relations and masculine desire in adolescent and children's fiction. Joseph Boone, "Mapping of Male Desire in Durrell's Alexandria Quartet," in *Displacing Homophobia: Gay Male Perspectives in Literature and Culture,* ed. Ronald R. Butters et al. (Durham: Duke University Press, 1989), 73–106; also Boone, "Vacation Cruises; or the Homoerotics of Orientalism," *PMLA* 110, no. 1 (1995): 89 107; and Christopher Lane, *The Ruling Passion* (1995), offer interpretations of both European male homosexuality and colonialism. Sara Suleri, *The Rhetoric of English India* (Chicago: University of Chicago Press, 1992), includes a rather tangential and decidedly ahistorical account of colonial masculinity.

21. Mrinalini Sinha, *Colonial Masculinity: The Manly Englishman and the Effeminate Bengali in the Late Nineteenth Century* (Manchester: Manchester University Press, 1995), 10.

22. James Scott, *Weapons of the Weak: Everyday Forms of Peasant Resistance* (New Yaven: Yale University Press, 1985).

23. Pierre Macherey, *A Theory of Literary Production,* trans. Geoffrey Wall (London: Routledge, 1978), 87.

Chapter 2

1. Rudyard Kipling, "The Ballad of East and West." In *Rudyard Kipling's Verse,* Inclusive Edition (Garden City: Doubleday, Page and Co., 1922), 272.

2. George L. Mosse, *The Image of Man: The Creation of Modern Masculinity* (New York: Oxford University Press, 1996), 26–27.

3. My discussion of nervousness draws on George Mosse's (ibid., 60–62).

4. See Norman Vance, "The Ideal of Manliness," in B. Simon and I. Bradley, eds., *The Victorian Public School: Studies in the Development of an Educational Institution* (Dublin: Gill and Macmillan, 1975), 115–28; also Vance's *The Sinews of the Spirit: The Ideal of Christian Manliness in Victorian Literature and Religious Thought* (Cambridge: Cambridge University Press, 1985); David Newsome, *Godliness and Goodlearning: Four Studies on a Victorian Ideal* (London: John

Murray, 1961); and J. A. Mangan, *Athleticism in the Victorian and Edwardian Public Schools* (Cambridge: Cambridge University Press, 1981).

5. Michael Rosenthal, *The Character Factory: Baden Powell's Boy Scouts and the Imperatives of Empire* (New York: Pantheon, 1984).

6. Rajeswari Sunder Rajan, *Real and Imagined Women: Gender, Culture and Postcolonialism* (London: Routledge, 1993), 42.

7. I take the term *homosocial* from Eve Kosofsky Sedgwick to designate desire between men that is channeled through women, who are used as exchange objects in transactions that primarily promote the interests of male rivalry and/or male solidarity. And, because homosocial desire operates through enforced heterosexuality, it is generally (though not always) homophobically proscribed (Eve Kosofsky Sedgwick, *Between Men: English Literature and Male Homosocial Desire* [New York: Columbia University Press, 1985]).

8. Ashis Nandy, *The Intimate Enemy*, 8.

9. For a fascinating account of a remarkably similar shift that took place in Jewish self-image in fin-de-siècle Europe, see Daniel Boyarin, *Unheroic Conduct: The Rise of Heterosexuality and the Invention of the Jewish Man* (Berkeley: University of California Press, 1997).

10. *Mimicry* and *hybridization* are terms used by Homi Bhabha to describe the terrifying ambivalence produced when colonial authority is split by the exorbitant object of discrimination. See Homi Bhabha, "Signs Taken for Wonders: Questions of Ambivalence and Authority under a Tree Outside Delhi, May 1817," *Critical Inquiry* 12, no. 1 (Autumn 1985): 144–65.

11. Robert Orme, *Historical Fragments of the Mogol Empire: Of the Morattoes, and the English Concerns, in Indostan, from the Year M,DC,LIX* (London: Printed for C. Nourse, 1782), 472.

12. Mosse, *Image of Man*, 9.

13. Ketaki Dyson, *A Various Universe: A Study of Journals and Memoirs of British Men and Women in the Indian Subcontinent, 1765–1856* (New Delhi: Oxford University Press, 1978), 93.

14. William Hodges, *Travels in India* (London, n.p., 1793), 1–2; quoted in Dyson, *Various Universe*, 134.

15. Christine Bolt, "Race and the Victorians," in *British Imperialism in the Nineteenth Century*, ed. C. C. Eldridge (New York: Macmillan, 1984), 129.

16. Flora Annie Steel, *The Garden of Fidelity* (London: Macmillan, 1929), 28.

17. E. M. Forster, *The Hill of Devi and Other Indian Writings*, ed. Elizabeth Heine (London: Edward Arnold, 1983), 125.

18. William Jones, *Translations from Oriental Languages* (New Delhi: Pravesh Publications, n.d.), 1:348.

19. Ibid., 1:358.

20. E. Guest, *A History of English Rhythms* (London: George Bell & Sons, 1828/1882), 703.

21. Rev. J. George, *The Mission of Great Britain to the World or some of the Lessons which She is Now Teaching* (Toronto: Dudley & Burns, 1867), 6.

22. Ibid., 4.

23. Otto Jespersen, *Growth and Structure of the English Language* (Toronto: Collier-MacMillan, 1938/1968), 2.

24. Ibid., 16.

25. Otto Jespersen, *Language, its Nature, Development and Origin* (London: George Allen & Unwin, 1922/1969), 430.

26. Thomas Babington Macaulay, "Clive," in *Historical Essays of Thomas Babington Macaulay,* ed. Ernest Rhys (London: J. M. Dent and Sons, 1907), 1:503.

27. Thomas Babington Macaulay, "Hastings," in Rhys, *Historical Essays of Thomas Babington Macaulay,* 1:562.

28. James Mill, *History of British India* (1817; reprint, New Delhi: Associated Publishing House, 1972), 1:486.

29. Ibid., 1:287.

30. Sinha, *Colonial Masculinity,* 17.

31. Ibid., 18.

32. *Civil and Military Gazette* 15 (September 1888): 3.

33. F. Nietzsche, *On the Genealogy of Morals* (New York: Random House, 1969), 1:10.

34. Fredric Jameson, *The Political Unconscious,* 201–2.

35. Sigmund Freud, *Moses and Monotheism: Three Essays,* vol. 23: *The Standard Edition of the Complete Psychological Works of Sigmund Freud,* ed. and trans. James Strachey and Anna Freud (1939; reprint, London: Hogarth, 1955), 112–13.

36. Ibid., 116–17.

37. Ibid., 112.

38. Gayatri Spivak, "Psychoanalysis in Left Field and Fieldworking: Examples to Fit the Title," in *Speculations after Freud: Psychoanalysis, Philosophy and Culture,* ed. Sonu Shamdasani and Michael Munchow (London: Routledge, 1994), 60.

39. Christiane Hartnack, "Vishnu on Freud's Desk," *Social Research* 57 (1990): 921–49; also "British Psychoanalysts in Colonial India," in *Psychology in Twentieth Century Thought and Society,* ed. Mitchell G. Ash and William Woodward (New York: Cambridge University Press, 1987), 233–57.

40. Homi Bhabha, *The Location of Culture* (London: Routledge, 1994), 89.

41. Sigmund Freud, *Totem and Taboo,* vol. 13: *The Standard Edition of the Complete Psychological Works of Sigmund Freud,* ed. and trans. James Strachey and Anna Freud (1913; reprint, London: Hogarth, 1955), 3–149.

42. *Group Psychology and the Analysis of the Ego,* vol. 18: *The Standard Edition of the Complete Psychological Works of Sigmund Freud,* ed. and trans. James Strachey and Anna Freud (1913; reprint, London: Hogarth, 1955), 67–143.

43. Sander L. Gilman, *The Jew's Body* (London: Routledge, 1991); see also *Freud, Race, and Gender* (Princeton: Princeton University Press, 1993).

44. Daniel Boyarin, *Unheroic Conduct,* 262.

45. Ibid., esp. 187–270.

46. Sheldon Pollock, "Deep Orientalism? Notes on Sanskrit and Power

beyond the Raj," in *Orientalism and the Postcolonial Predicament*, ed. Carol A. Breckenridge and Peter van der Veer (Philadelphia: University of Pennsylvania Press, 1993), 76–133.

47. Richard F. Burton, "Terminal Essay," in *A Plain and Literal Translation of the Arabian Nights' Entertainments, Now Entitled The Book of the Thousand Nights and a Night, With Introduction Explanatory Notes on the Manners and Customs of Moslem Men and a Terminal Essay upon the History of the Nights*, Medina Edition (London: Burton Club, 1886), 10:63–302.

48. *The Complete Letters of Sigmund Freud to Wilhelm Fleiss, 1887–1904*, ed. and trans. Jeffrey Moussaieff Masson (Cambridge, Mass.: Harvard University Press, Belknap Press, 1985), 246; quoted in Boyarin, *Unheroic Conduct*, 195.

49. Louis Crompton, "Gay Genocide: From Leviticus to Hitler," in *The Gay Academic*, ed. Louie Crew (Palm Springs, Calif.: ETC Publications, 1978), 67; quoted in Sedgwick, *Between Men*, 94.

50. For a discussion of the sexual opportunities empire made available to the white male, see Richard Hyam, *Sexuality and Empire: The British Experience* (Manchester: Manchester University Press, 1990); for a critique of Hyam, see Mark T. Berger, "Imperialism and Sexual Exploitation," *Journal of Imperial and Commonwealth History* 17, no. 1 (1988): 83–89.

51. Burton, *Thousand Nights*, 206–7.

52. Sedgwick, *Between Men*, 183.

53. George MacMunn, *The Underworld of India* (London: Jarrolds, 1933), 202; quoted in Benita Parry, *Delusions and Discoveries: Studies on India in the British Imagination, 1880–1930* (Berkeley: University of California Press, 1972), 62–63.

54. Sedgwick, *Between Men*, 93.

55. See MacMunn, *Underworld of India*, 201; among recent works that call attention to this aspect of colonial thinking are the following: Wurgaft, *Imperial Imagination*, 50; and Sinha, *Colonial Masculinity*, 19.

56. Burton, *Thousand Nights*, 235; quoted in Sedgwick, *Between Men*, 190.

57. Sedgwick, *Between Men*, 193.

58. Said, *Orientalism*, 24–43.

59. T. E. Lawrence, *Seven Pillars of Wisdom: A Triumph* (Garden City, N.Y.: Doubleday, Doran, 1935), 444–45; quoted in Sedgwick, *Between Men*, 194–95.

60. Sedgwick, *Between Men*, 196–97.

61. E. M. Forster, *The Hill of Devi and Other Indian Writings*.

62. Patrick Brantlinger, *Rule of Darkness*.

63. This point is made by Sedgwick (*Between Men*, 191).

64. Mrinalini Sinha, "Colonial Policy and the Ideology of Moral Imperialism in Late Nineteenth-Century Bengal," in *Changing Men: New Directions in Research on Men and Masculinity*, ed. Michael S. Kimmel (London: Sage Publications, 1987), 230.

65. Bhabha, "Signs Taken for Wonders," 154–55; Sinha, "Colonial Policy," 229–30.

66. Homi K. Bhabha, "Of Mimicry and Man: The Ambivalence of Colonial Discourse," *October* 28 (spring 1984): 127.

67. Homi K. Bhabha, "Difference, Discrimination, and the Discourse of Colonialism," in *The Politics of Theory*, ed. Francis Barker et al. (Colchester: University of Essex, 1983): 205.

68. Bhabha, "Signs Taken for Wonders," 162.

69. Bhabha, "Signs Taken for Wonders," 154.

70. Luce Irigaray, *This Sex Which Is Not One*, trans. Catherine Porter (Ithaca: Cornell University Press, 1985). Irigaray here develops Joan Riviere's idea of femininity as masquerade. See Riviere, "Womanliness as Masquerade," in *Formations of Fantasy*, ed. Victor Burgin, James Donald, and Cora Kaplan (London: Methuen, 1986), 35–44.

71. Irigaray, *This Sex Which Is Not One*, 76.

72. Anne McClintock, *Imperial Leather: Race, Gender and Sexuality in the Colonial Contest* (London/New York: Routledge, 1995), 64–65.

73. Diana Fuss, "Interior Colonies: Framtz Fanon and the Politics of Identification," *Diacritics* 24, nos. 2–3 (summer–fall, 1994): 24.

74. Ibid., 25. Fuss refers to the following studies on whites in black masks: Kaja Silverman, "White Skin, Brown Masks: The Double Mimesis or With Lawrence in Arabia," *differences* 1, no. 3 (fall 1989): 3–54; Kobena Mercer, "Black Hair/Style Politics," *New Formations* 3 (winter 1987): 33–54; and also Mercer, "Skin Head Sex Thing: Racial Difference and the Homoerotic Imaginary," *New Formations* 16 (spring 1992): 1–23.

75. Jenny Sharpe, "Figures of Colonial Resistance," *Modern Fiction Studies* 35, no. 1 (spring 1989): 137–55.

76. McClintock, *Imperial Leather*, 63.

77. Nandy, *Intimate Enemy*, 48.

78. Ibid., 75–76, 108.

79. James C. Scott, *Weapons of the Weak: Everyday Forms of Peasant Resistance* (New Haven: Yale University Press, 1985); see also James C. Scott and Benedict J. Tria Kerkvliet eds., *Everyday Forms of Peasant Resistance in South-east Asia*, Special Issue of the *Journal Peasant Studies* 13 (1986): 1–150.

80. Scott, *Weapons of the Weak*, 68.

81. Michel de Certeau, *The Practice of Everyday Life*, trans. Steven F. Rendall (Berkeley: The University of California Press, 1984), 25–28.

82. Douglas Haynes and Gyan Prakash eds., *Contesting Power: Resistance and Everyday Social Relations in South Asia* (Berkeley: University of California Press, 1991): 3.

83. It may be useful to consider the extent to which such a privileging of consciousness may resurrect a Cartesian subject as the preeminent locus of colonized resistance or agency. For careful critiques of these theorists, especially on the question of intention/reception, see Diana Fuss, "Interior Colonies"; Carole-Anne Tyler, "Female Impersonators" forthcoming; and Judith Butler, *The Psychic Life of Power* (Stanford: Stanford University Press, 1997).

84. Wendy Doniger O'Flaherty, *Women, Androgynes, and Other Mythical Beasts* (Chicago: University of Chicago Press, 1980), 88–90.

85. Ibid.

86. Quoted in Kalpana Seshadri-Crooks, "The Primitive as Analyst: Post-colonial Feminism's Access to Psychoanalysis," *Cultural Critique* 28 (1994): 198. Seshadri-Crooks is most illuminating on Bose in general.

87. Ibid., 198.

88. It is in this light that the semen itself is sometimes spoken of as female, as shakti. See O'Flaherty, *Women, Androgynes, and Other Mythical Beasts,* 317–18.

89. For a discussion of women in the Bhakti movement, see Revathi Krishnaswamy, "Subversive Spirituality: Woman as Saint-Poet in Medieval India," *Women's Studies International Forum* 16, no. 3 (1993): 139–47.

90. James C. Scott, *Weapons of the Weak,* 82.

91. For a Freudian reading of Vivekananda, see Sudhir Kakar, *The Inner World: A Psychoanalytic Reading of Childhood and Society in India* (New Delhi: Oxford University Press, 1981), 160–81. For a more thorough analysis of Ramakrishna and Vivekananda in the context of religion, gender, and colonialism, see Parama Roy, *Indian Traffic: Subjects in Motion in British India* (Berkeley: University of California Press, 1998); esp. the chapter entitled "As the Master Saw Her: Religious Discipleship and Gender Traffic in Nineteenth Century India."

92. Vivekananda, *The Yogas and Other Works,* ed. Nikhilananda (New York: Ramakrishna-Vivekananda Center, 1953), 151.

93. Ibid., 128.

94. Vivekananda, *Collected Works of Swami Vivekananda,* vol. 3 (Calcutta: Advaita Ashrama, 1970), 224.

95. Vivekananda, *The Yogas,* 151.

96. Vivekananda, *Collected Works,* 4:143.

97. Tanika Sarkar, "The Hindu Wife and the Hindu Nation: Domesticity and Nationalism in Nineteenth-Century Bengal," *Studies in History* 8, no. 2 (1992): 213–35.

98. Nandy, *Intimate Enemy,* 8–9.

99. Benita Parry, "Problems in Current Theories of Colonial Discourse," *Oxford Literary Review* 9, nos. 1–2 (1987): 42.

100. Nandy, *Intimate Enemy,* 54.

101. For feminist readings of Gandhian nationalism, see Tanika Sarkar, "Politics and Women in Bengal—the Conditions and Meaning of Participation," in *Women in Colonial India: Essays on Survival, Work and the State,* ed. J. Krishnamurthy (Delhi: Oxford University Press, 1989), 231–41; Devaki Jain, "Gandhian Contributions towards a Theory of 'Feminist Ethic,'" in *Speaking of Faith: Cross-Cultural Perspectives in Women, Religion and Social Change,* ed. Devaki Jain and Diana Eck (Delhi: Kali for Women, 1986), 255–70; Madhu Kishwar, "Women in Gandhi," *Economic and Political Weekly* 20, nos. 40–41 (1985): 1691–1702, 1753–58; Sujata Patel, "The Construction and Reconstruction of Women in Gandhi," *Economic and Political Weekly* 23, no. 8 (1988): 377–87.

102. Gayatri Spivak, "Subaltern Studies: Deconstructing Historiography," in *In Other Worlds: Essays in Cultural Politics* (New York: Routledge, 1988), 197–221.

103. James Mill, *History of British India,* vol. 1 (1817; reprint, New Delhi: Associated Publishing House, 1972).

104. Gayatri Chakravorty Spivak, "Can the Subaltern Speak? Specula-tions on Widow-Sacrifice," *Wedge* 7–8 (winter–spring, 1985): 121.

105. For a discussion of how the ideology of chivalry underwrites repre-sentations of sati in the novels of Jules Verne and M. M. Kaye, see Rajeswari Sunder Rajan, *Real and Imagined Women*, 42–44.

106. Lata Mani, "Contentious Traditions: The Debate on Sati in Colonial India," in *Recasting Women: Essays in Colonial Indian History*, ed. Kumkum San-gari and Sudesh Vaid (New Brunswick: Rutgers University Press, 1990), 88–126; Sinha, "Colonial Policy," 221–25; also Sinha, *Colonial Masculinity*; 138–80; see also Sangari and Vaid, *Recasting Women*.

107. Rosalind O'Hanlon, "Issues of Widowhood in Colonial Western India," in *Contesting Power: Resistance and Everyday Social Relations in South Asia*, ed. Douglas Haynes and Gyan Prakash (Berkeley: University of California Press, 1991), 76–79.

108. Barbara Ramusack, "Cultural Missionaries, Maternal Imperialists, Feminist Allies: British Women Activists in India, 1865–1945," *Women's Studies International Forum* 13, no. 4 (1990): 309–21.

109. Jenny Sharpe, *Allegories of Empire* (Minneapolis: University of Min-nesota Press, 1993), 8, 4.

110. These posters are cited in the report of the Hunter Committee, which conducted an official inquiry into the events at Amritsar, and in the memoirs of Michael O'Dwyer's, then lieutenant-governor of the Punjab. See *Report of the Committee Appointed by the Government of India to Investigate the Disturbances in the Punjab, etc.* (London: n.p., 1920), 53; and O'Dwyer, *India as I Knew It, 1885–1925* (London: Constable, 1925), 291–92.

111. Rudyard Kipling, *Kim*, ed. Alan Sandison (Oxford: Oxford University Press, 1987), 257.

112. E. M. Forster, *A Passage to India*, ed. Oliver Stallybrass (Har-mondsworth: Penguin, 1980), 217.

113. Such views can be found in all the following books: Percival Spear, *The Nabobs* (London: Oxford University Press, 1963), 140; Mark Nadis, "Evolu-tion of the Sahib," *Historian*, 19, no. 4 (August 1957): 430; Charles Allen ed., *Plain Tales from the Raj: Images of British India in the Twentieth Century* (New York: St. Martin's Press, 1976). For a recent expression of the same view, see David Lean, quoted in "Sayings of the Week," *Observer*, February 24, 1985; cited in Helen Callaway, *Gender, Culture, and Empire: European Women in Colonial Nigeria* (Urbana: University of Illinois Press, 1987), 3.

114. John McBratney "Images of Indian Women in Rudyard Kipling: A Case of Doubling Discourse" in *Inscriptions*, nos. 3–4 (1988): 53–54.

115. Nandy, *Intimate Enemy*, 10.

Chapter 3

1. Sara Suleri, *The Rhetoric of English India* (Chicago: University of Chicago Press, 1992), 53–61.

2. Leonore Davidoff and Catherine Hall, *Family Fortunes: Men and Women of the English Middle Class, 1780–1850* (Chicago: University of Chicago Press, 1987), 111–12.

3. Hilary Callan and Shirley Ardener, eds., *The Incorporated Wife* (London: Croom Helm, 1984).

4. I have discussed the nexus between evangelicalism, imperialism, and feminism in "Evangels of Empire," *Race and Class* 34, no. 4 (April–June 1993): 47–62.

5. For a discussion of this point, especially in the works of Mary Martha Sherwood, see ibid.

6. R. C. Majumdar, *History of the Freedom Movement in India* (Calcutta: Firma K. L. Mukhopadhyay, 1962), 161.

7. Jenny Sharpe, *Allegories of Empire*, 61–68.

8. Pat Barr, *The Memsahibs: The Women of Victorian India* (London: Secker and Warburg, 1976), 113.

9. Jenny Sharpe, *Allegories of Empire*, 4.

10. S. N. Mukherjee, "Class, Caste and Politics in Calcutta, 1815–38," in *Elites in South Asia*, ed. Edmund Leach and S. N. Mukherjee (Cambridge: Cambridge University Press, 1970), 33–78.

11. For a discussion of the rebellion in terms of the leadership of various landed classes, see S. B. Chaudhuri, *Theories of the Indian Mutiny (1857–59)* (Calcutta: World Press, 1965); for a description of the rebellion in terms of the participation of various subaltern classes, see Gautam Bhadra, "Four Rebels of Eighteen-Fifty-Seven," in *Selected Subaltern Studies*, ed. Ranajit Guha and Gayatri Chakravorty Spivak (New York: Oxford University Press, 1988), 129–75.

12. K. K. Sengupta, *Recent Writings on the Revolt of 1857: A Survey* (New Delhi: n.p., 1975); Eric Stokes, *The Peasant Armed: The Indian Revolt of 1857* (Oxford: Oxford University Press, 1986); and *The Peasant and the Raj: Studies in Agrarian Society and Peasant Rebellion in Colonial India* (Cambridge: Cambridge University Press, 1978); Ranajit Guha, *Elementary Aspects of Peasant Insurgency in Colonial India* (New Delhi: Oxford University Press, 1983).

13. Alexander Duff, *The Indian Rebellion: Its Causes and Results* (London: James Nisbet, 1858), 54–55.

14. *News of the World*, 30 June 1857; quoted in Sharpe *Allegories of Empire*, 65.

15. Ascott Hope, *Story of the Indian Mutiny* (London: n.p., 1896), 49.

16. John William Kaye, *A History of the Sepoy War in India, 1857–58* (London: n.p., 1867), 2:208.

17. Christopher Hibbert, *The Great Mutiny, India 1857* (London: Penguin, 1980), 79, 82, 85.

18. Guha, *Elementary Aspects of Peasant Insurgency in Colonial India*, 259.

19. Ibid., 106.

20. Ibid., 16–17.

21. Sharpe, *Allegories of Empire*, 69–73.

22. Ibid., 70.

23. Ibid., 74.

24. *Times*, 16 October 1885; cited by an Indian student, *India before and after the Mutiny* (Edinburgh: Livingstone, 1886), 60; quoted in Sharpe, *Allegories of Empire*, 75.

25. Sharpe, *Allegories of Empire*, 75.

26. Ibid., 67.

27. Hibbert, *Great Mutiny*, 209–10.

28. Sharpe, *Allegories of Empire*, 69.

29. Francis Hutchins, *The Illusion of Permanance* (Princeton: Princeton University Press, 1967), xi.

30. Colin Campbell, *Narrative of the Indian Revolt from Its Outbreak to the Capture of Lucknow* (London: George Victers, 1858), 20; quoted and discussed in Sharpe, *Allegories of Empire*, 69.

31. Louis D. Wurgaft, *The Imperial Imagination: Magic and Myth in Kipling's India* (Middletown, Conn.: Wesleyan University Press, 1983), 5.

32. Such colonial strategies of counterinsurgency, Sharpe observes, are attributes of that "great spectacle of physical punishment" that, according to Foucault in his study of prison reform, ended in the nineteenth century. Although *Discipline and Punish* acknowledges the "trace of 'torture' in the modern mechanisms of criminal justice," physical punishment drops out of Foucault's discussion once spectacular forms of punishment such as public execution is replaced by the less spectacular corrective technology of the penal system. Because Foucault's theory of disciplinary power is Eurocentric, Sharpe points out, "it cannot be used to address the colonial situation, in which technologies of discipline are overdetermined by imperial structures of power" (see Sharpe, *Allegories of Empire*, 79).

33. Bosworth Smith, *Life of Lord Lawrence* (London: n.p., 1885), 2:227.

34. Kaye, *History of the Sepoy War in India*, 2:208.

35. John Kaye, *Lives of Indian Officers* (London: n.p., 1867), 2:448.

36. Michael Edwardes, *Bound to Exile: The Victorians in India* (London: Sidgwick and Jackson, 1969), 100; quoted in Benita Parry, *Delusions and Discoveries: Studies on India in the British Imagination 1880–1930* (Berkeley: University of California Press, 1972), 128.

37. Kaye, *History of the Sepoy War*, 2:399.

38. Wurgaft, *Imperial Imagination*, 83–89.

39. Eric Stokes, *The English Utilitarians in India* (Oxford: Oxford University Press, 1959), 308–10.

40. Kenneth Ballhatchet, *Race, Sex and Class under the Raj*, 20.

41. Even a sympathetic character like Fielding in *A Passage to India* becomes acutely uncomfortable in the face of what he considers to be Aziz's emotional/sexual intemperance. And paralleling Fielding's discomfort in the novel is the narrator's own ambivalence toward the geographic "excess" of India and the spiritual excess of Hinduism.

42. Sinha, "Colonial Policy," 225–26.

43. Quoted in ibid., 226.

44. Kumkum Sanghari, "Relating Histories: Definitions of Literacy, Literature, Gender in Early Nineteenth-Century Calcutta and England," in *Rethinking English: Essays in Literature, Language, History,* ed. Svati Joshi (New Delhi: Trianka, 1991), 36.

45. For a discussion of the colonial transformation of caste, see Rashmi Pant, "The Cognitive Status of Caste in Colonial Ethnography," *Indian Eco-*

nomic and Social History Review 24 (1987): 145–62; Arjun Appadurai, "Putting Hierarchy in Its Place," *Current Anthropology* 3, no. 1 (February 1988): 36–49; Nicholas Dirks, "Castes of Mind," *Representations* 37 (winter 1992): 56–78. For the colonial invention of "martial" and "nonmartial" races and its application in British recruitment policies in the colonial army, see David Omissi, " 'Martial Race': Ethnicity and Security in Colonial India, 1858–1939," *War and Society* 9, no. 1 (1991): 1–27. For a discussion of how the martial-nonmartial distinction conditioned colonial response to the native volunteer movement of the 1880s, see Sinha, *Colonial Masculinity*, chap. 2, 69–99. For the preference of the martial races in colonial employment more generally, see David Arnold, "Bureaucratic Recruitment and Subordination in Colonial India: The Madras Constabulary, 1859–1947," in *Subaltern Studies*, vol. 4: *Writing on South Asian History and Society*, ed. Ranajit Guha (Delhi: Oxford University Press, 1985), 1–53.

46. Wurgaft, *Imperial Imagination*, 48.

47. Rudyard Kipling, "The Enlightenment of Pagett, M.P.," *Contemporary Review* 58 (1890): 352, 353.

48. Wurgaft, *Imperial Imagination*, 48.

49. In "To Be Filed for Reference" Jellaludin pays with his life for the forbidden knowledge he has acquired by "going native"; in "Without Benefit of Clergy" Holden's idyllic romance is brought to a tragic end by the death of Ameera; in "Beyond the Pale" Trejago is wounded in the groin for having an illicit affair with a young Indian widow; in "False Dawn" and "On the City Wall" the narrators are made to feel ashamed for losing control over their emotions and acting with abandon.

Chapter 4

1. Flora Annie Steel, *The Garden of Fidelity* (London: Macmillan, 1929), 15–16.

2. Flora Annie Steel, *On the Face of the Waters: A Tale of the Mutiny* (London: Heinemann, 1896; rev. ed., 1897). All further references to this work, abbreviated as OFW, will be included in the text. Page numbers refer to the 1897 edition.

3. Steel, *Garden of Fidelity*, 226.

4. Ibid., 203–12.

5. Ibid., 228.

6. Jenny Sharpe, *Allegories of Empire*, 88.

7. Fanny Parks, *Wanderings of a Pilgrim, in Search of the Picturesque, during Four-and-Twenty Years in the East; with Revelations of Life in the Zenana* (London: n.p., 1850), 2:420–21.

8. Maud Diver, *The Englishwoman in India* (London: W. Blackwood, 1909), 168–69.

9. "The Indian Mutiny in Fiction," *Blackwood's Edinburgh Magazine* 161 (February 1897): 229.

10. Mrinalini Sinha, " 'Chathams, Pitts and Gladstones in Petticoats': The

Politics of Gender and Race in the Illbert Bill Controversy, 1883–84," in *Western Women and Imperialism: Complicity and Resistance,* ed. Nupur Chaudhuri and Margaret Strobel (Bloomington: Indiana University Press, 1992), 98. My own discussion of the Illbert Bill controversy relies greatly on Sinha's insightful account.

11. Ronald Hyam, *Britain's Imperial Century, 1815–1914: A Study of Empire and Expansion* (London: B. T. Batsford, 1976), 233.

12. *Legislative Department Papers of Act 1–111 of 1884,* paper no. 55; quoted in Sinha, "'Chathams, Pitts and Gladstones in Petticoats,'" 100.

13. Quoted in ibid.

14. *Englishman,* April 26, 1883, 2; quoted in ibid.

15. Ibid.

16. Quoted in *Reis and Reyyet,* April 21, 1883, 182; cited in Sinha, "'Chathams, Pitts and Gladstones in Petticoats,'" 100–101.

17. Margaret MacMillan, *Women of the Raj* (London: Thames and Hudson, 1988), 221–22.

18. *Englishman,* March 13, 1883, 2; quoted in Sinha, "'Chathams, Pitts and Gladstones in Petticoats,'" 101.

19. *Englishman,* April 3, 1883, 2; quoted in ibid., 110.

20. *Englishman,* March 6, 1883, 2.

21. Quoted in Sinha, "'Chathams, Pitts and Gladstones in Petticoats,'" 101.

22. *Pioneer,* March 3, 1883.

23. Gibbs to Ripon, *Ripon Papers: India Miscellaneous Public Documents* BP 7/6 (November 18, 1883); quoted in Sinha, "'Chathams, Pitts and Gladstones in Petticoats,'" 99.

24. Ripon to Kimberley, *Ripon Papers: India Miscellaneous Public Documents* BP 7/6; quoted in ibid., 99.

25. Dacca Prakash, June 24, 1883, Report on Native Newspapers of Bengal Presidency, no. 26 (1883): 353; quoted in ibid.

26. *Reis and Reyyet,* April 28, 1883, 196; quoted in ibid.

27. Sharpe, *Allegories of Empire,* 91.

28. Wilfred Scawen Blunt, *Ideas about India* (London: Kegan Paul, Trench, 1885), 47; quoted in ibid.

29. Ballhatchet, *Race, Sex and Class under the Raj,* 5.

30. *Observer,* "Saying of the Week," February 24, 1985; quoted in Helen Callaway, *Gender, Culture, and Empire: European Women in Colonial Nigeria* (Urbana: University of Illinois Press, 1987), 3; also in Margaret Strobel, *European Women and the Second British Empire* (Bloomington: Indiana University Press, 1991), 1.

31. V. S. Naipaul, *Area of Darkness* (London: Andre Duetch, 1964), 222.

32. Margaret Strobel, *European Women and the Second British Empire* (Bloomington: Indiana University Press, 1991), 1.

33. Flora Annie Steel and Grace Gardner, *The Complete Indian Housekeeper and Cook: Giving the Duties of Mistress and Servants, the General Management of the House, and Practical Recipes for Cooking in all its Branches* (1888; rev. ed., London: Hienemann, 1921), 9.

34. Ibid., 21.

35. Ibid., 8.

36. Beverley Bartrell, "Colonial Wives: Villains or Victims?" in Callan and Ardner, *Incorporated Wife*, 165–85; Janice Brownfoot, "Memsahibs in Colonial Malaya: A Study of European Wives in a British Colony and Protectorate, 1900–1940, in Callan and Ardner, *Incorporated Wife*, 186–210; Callaway, *Gender, Culture and Empire*; Mary Ann Lind, *The Compassionate Memsahibs: Welfare Activities of British Women in India, 1900–1947* (New York: Greenwood Press, 1988); Nupur Choudhuri, "Memsahibs and Motherhood in Nineteenth-Century Colonial India," *Victorian Studies* 31, no. 4 (summer 1988): 517–35.

37. For a discussion of the role domesticity played in imperialism, see Mary Poovy's chapter on Florence Nightingale in *Uneven Developments: The Ideological Work of Gender in Mid-Victorian England* (Chicago: University of Chicago Press, 1988), 164–98.

38. For a discussion of the intersection between evangelicalism, feminism, and colonialism, see my essay "Evangels of Empire," in *Race and Class* 34, no. 4 (April–June 1993).

39. Even the "domestic" feminist individualist Jane Eyre empowers herself by positioning herself as a missionary. An invocation of the racial superiority implicit in the ideology of the civilizing mission thus helps rhetorically to resolve Jane's class and gender inferiority in patriarchal England.

40. The option to go along was not available to Jane Eyre, who refuses to go to Calcutta as the missionary wife of St. John but expresses a desire to go by herself and work with Indian women.

41. Rosemary Mangoly George, "Homes in the Empire, Empires in the Home," *Cultural Critique* (winter 1993–94): 107.

42. Ballhatchet, *Race, Sex and Class under the Raj*, 112–16.

43. Quoted in ibid., 115.

44. Lady Wilson (Anne Campbell Macleod), *Letters from India* (London: William Blackwood and Sons, 1911), 33.

45. J. E. Dawson, "Woman in India: Her Influence and Position" and "The Englishwoman in India: Her Influence and Responsibilities," *Calcutta Review* 83, no. 167 (October 1886): 347–70. Discussed in Sharpe, *Allegories of Empire*, 95–96.

46. Sharpe, *Allegories of Empire*, 96–97.

47. Antoinette M. Burton, "The White Woman's Burden: British Feminists and the Indian Woman, 1865–1915," *Women's Studies International Forum* 13, no. 4 (1990): 295; see also Burton, "The Feminist Quest for Identity: British Imperial Suffragism and 'Global Sisterhood,' 1900–1915," *Journal of Women's History* 2, no. 1 (spring 1990): 8–34.

48. Due to the exclusively metropolitan frame of reference, even such a fine study as Nancy Armstrong's *Desire and Domestic Fiction* (Oxford: Oxford University Press, 1987) fails to recognize how colonial ideologies of womanhood feed into domestic discourses on gender. Two feminist scholars who have, in recent years, drawn attention to the way in which sati feeds into Victorian constructions of femininity are Nancy Paxton and Rajeswari Sunder Rajan. See

Nancy Paxton, "Unma(s)king the Colonial Subject: Subjectivity and the Female Body in the Novels of Flora Annie Steel and Anita Desai," paper presented at the MLA Convention, 1988; Rajeswari Sunder Rajan, *Real and Imagined Women: Gender, Culture and Postcolonialism* (London and New York: Routledge, 1993), chaps. 2 and 3.

49. Quoted in Arvind Sharma, "Suttee: A Study in Western Reactions." *Journal of Indian History* 54, no. 3 (1976): 598.

50. Such as Edward Thompson's, *Suttee* (London: Allen and Unwin, 1928), 25.

51. Dorothy Figueira, "Die Flamberte Frau: Reflections on Sati in European Culture" (paper presented at "New Light on Sati/Suttee" conference, Southern Asia Institute, Columbia University, October 21, 1988), 5–6.

52. Sharma, "Suttee," 592.

53. Gayatri Spivak, "Can the Subaltern Speak? Speculations on Widow Sacrifice," *Wedge* 7–8 (winter–spring 1985): 125.

54. Lata Mani, "The Production of an Official Discourse on *Sati* in Early Nineteenth Century Bengal," in *Europe and Its Others*, ed. Francis Barker et al., 2 vols., Essex Conference on the Sociology of Literature (Colchester: University of Essex Press, 1985), 1:111.

55. Sharma, "Suttee," 604.

56. Suvendrini Perera, *Reaches of Empire: The English Novel from Edgeworth to Dickens* (New York: Columbia University Press, 1991), 92.

57. Paul B. Courtright, "The Iconographies of Sati" (paper presented at "New Light on Sati/Suttee" conference, Southern Asia Institute, Columbia University, October 21, 1988).

58. Rajeswari Sunder Rajan, "The Subject of Sati: Pain and Death in Contemporary Discourse on Sati," *Yale Journal of Criticism* 3, no. 1 (1990): 1–27. Reprinted in Sunder Rajan, *Real and Imagined Women: Gender, Culture and Postcolonialism* (London and New York: Routledge, 1993), 15–39.

59. Ibid.; also Sunder Rajan, "Representing Sati: Continuities and Discontinuities," *Real and Imagined Women*, 45–46.

60. Parks, *Wanderings of a Pilgrim*, 2:420–21.

61. Dorothy K. Stein, "Women to Burn: Suttee as a Normative Institution," *Signs* 4, no. 2 (1978): 266.

62. Sunder Rajan, "Representing Sati," 46.

63. Ibid.

64. Sunder Rajan, "Subject of Sati," 34.

65. Here I am paraphrasing Teresa de Lauretis's position in *Alice Doesn't: Feminism, Semiotics, Cinema* (Bloomington: Indiana University Press, 1982), 103–57.

66. Sharpe, *Allegories of Empire*, 99.

67. Spivak, "Three Women's Texts and a Critique of Imperialism," 244–45.

68. Flora Annie Steel, *The Law of the Threshold* (New York: Macmillan, 1924), 117.

69. Ibid., 99.

70. Ibid., 199.

71. Sharpe, *Allegories of Empire*. Sharpe's analysis follows Gayatri Spivak's argument in "Three Women's Texts and a Critique of Imperialism," 259.

Chapter 5

1. Robert Buchanan, "The Voice of the Hooligan," in *Kipling and the Critics*, ed. Elliot L. Gilbert (New York: New York University Press, 1965), 20–32.

2. Lionel Trilling, "Kipling," in *Kipling and the Critics*, 95.

3. J. M. S. Tompkins, *The Art of Rudyard Kipling* (London: Methuen, 1959).

4. Edward Said, *Orientalism*, 226–28.

5. Ibid., 228.

6. Ibid., 227.

7. The phrase is Fredric Jameson's; see *The Political Unconscious: Narrative as a Socially Symbolic Act* (Ithaca: Cornell University Press, 1981), 180.

8. Angus Wilson, *The Strange Ride of Rudyard Kipling: His Life and Work* (New York: Penguin, 1979).

9. Lisa Lowe, *Critical Terrains: French and British Orientalisms* (Ithaca: Cornell University Press, 1991); Ali Behdad, *Belated Travellers: Orientalism in the Age of Colonial Dissolution* (Durham: Duke University Press, 1994).

10. Noel Annan, "Kipling's Place in the History of Ideas," in *Kipling's Mind and Art*, ed. Andrew Rutherford (Stanford: Stanford University Press, 1964), 102.

11. Briton Martin Jr., *New India, 1885: British Official Policy and the Emergence of the Indian National Congress* (Berkeley: University of California Press, 1969), 321.

12. Eve Kosofsky Sedgwick, *Between Men*, 91.

13. Ibid.

14. Rudyard Kipling, "The Strange Ride of Morrowbie Jukes," in *The Man Who Would Be King and Other Stories*, ed. Louis Cornell (Oxford: Oxford University Press, 1987), 3–25. All further references to this work, abbreviated as SRMB, are indicated in the text.

15. Lewis Wurgaft has pointed out the similarity in black and white "magic" or in the rituals of control practiced by the colonizer and the colonized; see *The Imperial Imagination*.

16. Rudyard Kipling, "To Be Filed for Reference," in *Plain Tales from the Hills*, ed. Andrew Rutherford (Oxford: Oxford University Press), 234–41. All further references to this work, abbreviated as TBFR, are included in the text.

17. Pierre Macherey, *A Theory of Literary Production*, trans. G.Wall (London: Routledge, 1978), 238.

18. Homi Bhabha, "The Other Question: Difference, Discrimination and the Discourse of Colonialism," in *Literature, Politics and Theory: Papers from the Essex Conference, 1976–1984*, ed. Francis Barker et al. (London: Methuen, 1986), 148–72.

19. Rudyard Kipling, "On the City Wall," in *The Man Who Would Be King and Other Stories*, 221–43. All further references to this work, abbreviated as OCW, are included in the text.

20. Rudyard Kipling, "In The House of Sudhoo," *Plain Tales from the Hills*, 108–15. All further references to this work, abbreviated as IHS, are included in the text.

21. Rudyard Kipling, "Beyond the Pale," ibid., 127–32. All further references to this work, abbreviated as BP, are included in the text.

22. Lucy Carroll, "Law, Custom and Statutory Social Reform: The Hindu Widow's Remarriage Act of 1856," *Economic and Social History Review* 20, no. 4 (1983): 363.

23. Rosalind O'Hanlon, "Issues of Widowhood in Colonial Western India," in *Contesting Power*, ed. Douglas Haynes and Gyan Prakash, 62–108.

24. Rudyard Kipling, "The Phantom Rickshaw," in *The Man Who Would Be King and Other Stories*, 26–48. All further references to this work, abbreviated as PR, are included in the text.

25. Rudyard Kipling, "The Mark of the Beast," in *Life's Handicap*, ed. A. O. J. Cockshut (Oxford: Oxford University Press, 1987), 178–91. All further references to this work, abbreviated as MB, are included in the text.

26. David Bromwich, "Kipling's Jest," *Grand Street* (winter 1985): 175.

27. Wilson, *Strange Ride of Rudyard Kipling*, 148–50.

28. Nandy, *Intimate Enemy*.

29. Rudyard Kipling, *Something of Myself* (Garden City, N.Y.: Doubleday, Doran, 1937), 141.

30. James Morris, *Pax Britannica: The Climax of an Empire* (Middlesex: Penguin, 1968), 347.

31. The former position can be seen in Zoreh T. Sullivan, *Narratives of Empire: The Fictions of Rudyard Kipling* (Cambridge: Cambridge University Press, 1993); the latter can be seen in John McClure, *Kipling and Conrad: The Colonial Fiction* (Cambridge: Harvard University Press, 1981).

32. Edward Said, "Kim: The Pleasures of Imperialism," *Raritan* 2 (fall 1987): 29.

33. I have relied mainly on two sources for information about the native volunteer movement: Sinha, *Colonial Masculinity*, chap. 2; and Martin, *New India*, chap. 5.

34. Sinha, *Colonial Masculinity*, 79.

35. Quoted in ibid., 80.

36. Quoted in ibid., 87.

37. Quoted in ibid., 80.

38. Quoted in ibid.

39. Ibid., 87.

40. Ibid., 81.

41. Quoted in ibid.

42. Quoted in ibid.

43. Ibid., 93.

44. Quoted in ibid.

45. Quoted in ibid.

46. Quoted in ibid.

47. Quoted in ibid.

48. Ibid.

49. Rudyard Kipling, *Kim,* ed. Alan Sandison (Oxford: Oxford University Press, 1987). All further references to this work, abbreviated as K, are included in the text.

50. Abdul R. JanMohammed, "The Economy of Manichean Allegory," 79.

51. Ibid., 78.

52. Edward Said has drawn attention to the fluent interchange between anthropology and colonial work emblematized in Creighton; see "Kim: The Pleasures of Imperialism," 51–53.

53. Michel de Certeau, *The Practice of Everyday Life,* 25–28.

54. Rabindranath Tagore, *Gora* (Bengali: n.p., 1910); trans. W. W. Pearson (London: Macmillan, 1924).

55. Gayatri Chakravorty Spivak, "The Burden of English," in *Orientalism and the Postcolonial Predicament,* ed. Carol A. Breckenridge and Peter van der Veer, 143.

56. Suleri, *Rhetoric of English India,* 123–24.

57. In such visual figurations, Sara Suleri observes, Kim has become "the image of the colonizer, but one that is elegiacally mourned as passing in its prematurity . . . After having established Kim as the inevitable victim of imperial education . . . Kipling seems drawn to an anthropologist's farewell to the emblem that finally reveals the classifiability of cultural dexterity" (ibid., 129–30).

Chapter 6

1. E. M. Forster, *A Passage to India,* ed. Oliver Stallybrass (Harmondsworth: Penguin, 1980). All further references to this work, abbreviated as PI, will be included in the text.

2. The following critiques are among those that attribute Adela's rape charge to a sexually repressed woman's imagination: Louise Dauner, "What Happened in the Cave? Reflections on *A Passage to India,*" in *Perspectives on E. M. Forster's "A Passage to India,"* ed. V. A. Shahane (New York: Barnes, 1968), 51–64; Benita Parry, *Delusions and Discoveries: Studies on India in the British Imagination* (Berkeley: University of California Press, 1972), 294–95; Barbara Rosencrance, *Forster's Narrative Vision* (Ithaca: Cornell University Press, 1982), 207; Abdul R. JanMohammed, "The Economy of Manichean Allegory: The Function of Racial Difference in Colonial Literature," 78–106; David Rubin, *After the British Raj: British Novels of India since 1947* (Hanover: University Press of New England, 1986), 66; Sara Suleri, "The Geography of A Passage to India," in *E. M.*

Forster's "A Passage to India," ed. Harold Bloom (New York: Chelsea House, 1987), 109–10.

3. Elaine Showalter, "A Passage to India as 'Marriage Fiction': Forster's Sexual Politics," *Women and Literature* 5, no. 2 (1977): 3–16; Silver, "Periphrasis, Power and Rape in *A Passage to India.*"

4. Sharpe, *Allegories of Empire,* 120.

5. Silver, "Periphrasis, Power and Rape in *A Passage to India,*" 97.

6. Frances Restuccia, "'A Cave of My Own': The Sexual Politics of Indeterminacy," *Raritan* 9, no. 2 (fall 1989): 114.

7. Ibid., 117; Silver, "Periphrasis, Power, and Rape in *A Passage to India,*" 86; Sharpe, *Allegories of Empire,* 126.

8. Sharpe, *Allegories of Empire,* 124–25.

9. In positing such a potential continuum between the homosocial and the homosexual, I'm following Eve Kosofsky Sedgwick, who finds it methodologically useful, as "a strategy for making generalizations about, and marking historical differences in the *structure* of men's relations with other men" (*Between Men,* 2).

10. Ironically, Adela's project not to become a pukka memsahib results only in the confirmation of her colonial identity, sentimentally acclaimed by her fellow Anglo-Indians and savagely asserted by Forster.

11. *Report of the Committee Appointed by the Government of India to Investigate the Disturbances in the Punjab, etc.* (London: n.p., 1920), 112.

12. Derek Sayer, "British Reaction to the Amritsar Massacre, 1919–1920," *Past and Present* 131 (May 1991): 132.

13. Judith Scherer Herz, *A Passage to India: Nation and Narration* (New York: Twayne Publishers, 1993), 19.

14. Sayer, "British Reaction to the Amritsar Massacre," 158; Margaret MacMillan, *Women of the Raj* (London: Thames and Hudson, 1988), 226.

15. M. M. Mahood, "Amritsar to Chandrapore: E. M. Forster and the Massacre," *Encounter* 41 (September 1973): 27; G. K. Das, "A Passage to India: A Socio-historical Study," in *A Passage to India: Essays in Interpretation,* ed. J. Beer (London: Macmillan Press, 1985).

16. Michael O'Dwyer, *India as I Knew It, 1885–1925* (London: Constable, 1925), 263–317.

17. Edward Thompson, *The Other Side of the Medal* (London: Hogarth Press, 1925), 109.

18. Sharpe, *Allegories of Empire,* 115–17.

19. Ibid., 123–24.

20. Ibid.

21. P. N. Furbank, *E. M. Forster: A Life,* vol. 1 (New York: Harcourt Brace Jovanovich, 1977).

22. Rustom Bharucha, "Forster's Friends," in Bloom, *E. M. Forster's "A Passage to India,"* 92.

23. Furbank notes how Forster's mother had wanted her young son to "be more manly" and "not cry so easily" (*E. M. Forster: A Life,* 1:23).

24. Lionel Trilling, *E. M. Forster* (New York: Harcourt Brace Jovanovich, 1980), 115.

25. Bharucha, "Forster's Friends," 97.

26. Jenny Sharpe, *Allegories of Empire,* 131.

27. Silver, "Periphrasis, Power and Rape in *A Passage to India,*" 104–5.

28. The point is made by Jenny Sharpe, *Allegories of Empire,* 129.

29. In the Spivakean sense of the subaltern, signifying those who cannot speak; see Gayatri Chakravorty Spivak, "Can the Subaltern Speak?"

30. Militant untouchables who prefer the name *dalits* to the name *hari-jans,* given by Gandhi, have spearheaded several liberation movements to advance their cause in independent India.

31. Sara Suleri, *The Rhetoric of English India* (Chicago: University of Chicago Press, 1992), 135.

32. E. M. Forster, *The Hill of Devi and Other Indian Writings,* ix.

33. Ibid., 324.

34. O'Dwyer, *India as I Knew It,* 451.

35. For this provocative and powerful theorization of speech and subalternity, see Spivak, "Can the Subaltern Speak," 120–30.

36. At some fantasy level Forster probably had himself in mind. Furbank has pointed out that Forster's young self probably provided the model for Ralph Moore *(E. M. Forster: A Life,* 262).

Conclusion

1. Alok Bhalla, "A Plea Against Revenge Histories: Some Reflections on Orientalism and the Age of Empire," in *Indian Responses to Colonialism in the Nineteenth Century,* ed. Alok Bhalla and Sudhir Chandra (New Delhi: Sterling Publishers, 1993), 1–13.

2. Giles Deleuze and Felix Guattari, *Anti-Oedipus;* Fredric Jameson, *The Political Unconscious;* Eve Sedgwick, *Between Men;* Nancy Armstrong, *Desire and Domestic Fiction;* Rajeswari Sunder Rajan, *Real and Imagined Women;* Gayatri Chakravorty Spivak, *In Other Worlds: Essays in Cultural Politics* (New York and London: Routledge, 1988).

3. Joan Scott, "Gender: A Useful Category of Historical Analysis," *American Historical Review* 91 (December 1986): 1053–75; Kumkum Sangari and Sudesh Vaid, "Recasting Women: An Introduction," in *Recasting Women: Essays in Indian Colonial History,* ed. Sangari and Vaid (New Brunswick: Rutgers University Press, 1990), 1–26.

Index